Financing Your Small Business

Robert W. Walter, J.D.
Holland & Hart LLP

BARRON'S

All inquiries should be addressed to:
Barron's Educational Series, Inc.
250 Wireless Boulevard
Hauppauge, NY 11788
www.barronseduc.com

International Standard Book No. 0-7641-2489-7

Library of Congress Catalog Card No. 2002038594

Library of Congress Cataloging-in-Publication Data
Walter, Robert (Robert William)
   Financing your small business / Robert W. Walter.
      p. cm.—(Barron's business library)
   Includes index.
   ISBN 0-7641-2489-7
   1. Small business—Finance.
I. Title. II. Series.
HG4027.7 .W357 2003
658.15′224—dc21   2002038594

Printed in the United States of America

9 8 7 6 5 4 3 2 1

Contents

Preface

Building a successful business requires capital. This book is written for entrepreneurs and small businesspeople who want to understand what funding sources are best for their business, how to find these sources, and what it takes to get financed. As anyone who has been through a financing knows, you can waste lots of time and money pursuing different financing options, especially if your business is relatively new. We've written this book to help you target financing sources that fund small businesses like yours, depending on its stage of development, size, product or service, and industry. Since getting capital when you need it can spell the difference between a growing business or liquidation, the goal of this book is to help you plan ahead for your financing needs. This means learning about the steps you'll go through in a financing, how long it takes to get financed, and what you can do now to lay the groundwork for your next financing. As your business matures, you'll want to understand how you can reduce your capital costs and generate liquidity for your stockholders. Our goal is to help you get the most from the time and resources you invest in the financing process and to give you the tools necessary to

▬ Evaluate the financing options realistically open to your business at various stages of its development

▬ Use Internet and other resources to target financing sources with investment or loan criteria that match your business

▬ Learn how investors and investment bankers calculate the value of your business

▬ Understand tradeoffs between valuation, cost, and timing issues

▬ Know what to expect when negotiating term sheets or letters of intent and what has to be done to close your financing

▬ Anticipate tough issues that come up after you've signed a term sheet or letter of intent and develop strategies on how to address them

■ Understand what agreements are used in different financings and how schedules and exhibits are important to your financing

■ Know some common legal and accounting issues that come up in financings

■ Appreciate your obligations to lenders and investors after the closing and help you create a cost-effective investor relations program

■ Maximize stockholder value when there is a liquidity event

ABOUT THIS BOOK

This book is organized to take you through the financing process as you'll experience it in the business world. The first few chapters deal with what financing sources are available to your business, how to find the right sources, and why some sources are better than others. The next several chapters discuss how to approach the financing sources you've chosen, what you need to focus on when negotiating a term sheet or letter of intent, and how to get from the preliminary commitment to a definitive agreement. These chapters are written to help you become familiar with financing paperwork and anticipate what business, legal, and accounting issues will come up as you proceed. Since your next financing might depend on how your existing investors or lenders feel about you, the next chapter covers the post-closing issues that you should keep in mind. The last chapter discusses liquidity options and the ways that you can maximize stockholder value once you've grown your business to the point that you or your investors want liquidity. We'll also discuss ways to

- Deal with unique financing issues that come up in your business's development
- Reduce your business's capital costs
- Raise the bottom line

As your business grows, its financing needs will change and you'll find yourself choosing among many financing options, each one with its own pluses and minuses. For example, if your business has $1 million in sales and a $75,000 bottom line, it will have fewer financing choices than a business that's doing $35 million in sales with a $2.5 million bottom line. Put another way, the mature business will have different financing needs and more sources available to it than an early-stage business.

THE CORPORATE LIFE CYCLE

To help you understand what financing options are open to your business, we've divided what we call the "corporate life cycle" into four stages:

- Development
- Operating
- Mature
- Liquidity

Table P-1 provides an overview of the corporate life cycle, including

- The most common types of financing you can expect to get in each stage
- Which investors or lenders provide this financing
- The documents used in each financing
- The advantages and disadvantages of each financing

While reading this book, you may occasionally want to refer to Table P-1 to help you take in the "big picture" view because it's easy to feel overwhelmed by details in the financing process.

Special note. Alternative financings in each stage of development are those *usually* available to the business. A business with a high growth rate and great margins can often get funding from sources that would normally offer financing only to later stage businesses. A small business with slow growth and narrow margins can find it hard to get financing that is usually available at its stage of development. Remember that as your business matures, it will increasingly rely on debt financing that carries a lower cost of capital and doesn't dilute your ownership. This will hold true unless you are considering ways to get liquidity for your stockholders, when you might choose to do an equity financing even though you'll experience some ownership dilution.

As you read this book, keep in mind the following points:

━ Securing financing for the small business is a process, not an event. The steps in the process are surprisingly similar whether you're raising debt or equity. We've focused on these similarities whenever possible to help you better understand the process. This will help increase your confidence even when talking with a possible lender or investor about a type of financing you haven't done before.

TABLE P-1
Funding of the Corporate Life Cycle

Stage	Funding Needs and Goals	Equity Financing Sources/Equity Instruments Used	Debt Financing Sources	Debt Financing Instruments
Development	Raise sufficient capital to finish research and development; set infrastructure; limit dilution to founders; limit "out-of-pocket" costs of financing to maximize available resources	Founders, friends and family, angel investors, venture capital firms, and private equity groups Common stock and principally convertible preferred stock, options, warrants and Payment in Kind (PIK) securities	Founders, friends, and family Small Business Administration (SBA)-guaranteed loans Equipment vendors Hard money lenders	Promissory notes SBA-guaranteed revolver or term note Leases Promissory notes with high interest and collateralized by personal assets
Operating	Sustain growth and fund strategic plans for expansion; expand infrastructure; cash flow	All development sources, plus retail private placements, institutional investors, public offerings	Banks Institutional investors and private equity groups	Revolvers Mezzanine facility, convertible debentures or securitizations

Mature	Lower growth rates and available cash flows reduce need for outside capital; mergers and acquisitions may add complementary business lines; capital structure may be simplified as convertible instruments are converted and warrants are exercised; founders' interest diluted by previous convertible financings; professional management may be brought in	and strategic partners	Equipment vendors and leasing firms	Leases
	increases may allow financing with higher out-of-pocket costs and lesser dilution; greater access to institutional capital sources	Common stock, preferred stock, and warrants		
		Public offerings, retail private placements, institutional investors, and strategic partners	Banks Institutional investors	Revolvers, term notes Mezzanine facility, securitizations, high-yield debt
		Common stock	Equipment vendors and leasing firms	Lease lines of credit

TABLE P-1
Continued

Stage	Funding Needs and Goals	Equity Financing Sources/Equity Instruments Used	Debt Financing Sources	Debt Financing Instruments
Liquidity	Founders, management, and important investors consider options for liquidity, including public offering, sale of business, mergers, stock redemptions, leveraged recapitalizations; capital requirements often related to liquidity needs rather than operating needs	Public offerings, private equity groups and strategic partners Common stock	Banks Institutional investors	Revolvers, term notes Rated debt, high-yield debt, securitizations

■■ **Investors and lenders often use different terminology, procedures, or documents in financing transactions, but the transactions' substance is nearly identical.** This book is written to help you sort through finance industry jargon and documents so that you'll understand the financing's substance and related issues. For example, some banks will give you a preliminary commitment for a revolving line of credit, while others will give you a term sheet. Is there a difference between these instruments? If so, what is it? Should you be concerned about a difference? Armed with answers to questions like this, you'll be able to evaluate competing offers critically, understand where different terminology might be important, and focus your energies on the major issues that need attention.

■■ **A glossary is included in the back of this book to define and explain key terms that are** commonly used by investors, lenders, and businesses in the financing process. For example, terms in Table P-1 that you aren't familiar with are defined in the glossary as well as in the chapters dealing with related issues. You may want to refer to the glossary when you come across a new term or need a quick refresher.

■■ **Whenever possible, we've included real life examples of small business financing successes and failures so you can learn from other entrepreneurs' experiences.** For client confidentiality, financing sources and amounts have been changed, but not in a way that changes the key issue. If experience is indeed the best teacher, these examples should be helpful to you. We've also included real world advice where appropriate to give you guidance on how to respond to issues that often come up in financings.

The financing process involves many agreements that are discussed throughout this book. We've also included some sample agreements in the appendix. The samples and related discussion are not legal advice but are only guides to the issues you'll run into during a financing. Federal securities laws apply to the sale of equity and debt securities and the disclosure you have to give investors and lenders. State laws concerning securities, business opportunities, franchises, and disclosure also apply to financings. You should consult a lawyer about these laws and your disclosure obligations before preparing or signing financing documents.

I want to thank my wife Anne and my children Lindsey, Stephanie, and Robby for their support and encouragement while I wrote this book. In addition, I want to acknowledge Wayne Barr and Robert O'Sullivan, my editors at Barron's, who gave generously of their time, talent, and patience to help complete this book.

Robert W. Walter, J.D.

Equity Financing Options for Your Small Business

INTRODUCTION AND MAIN POINTS

This chapter provides an overview of different types of equity financing available to a small business. Depending on the size of your business, you'll find there are various ways to get equity financing.

After studying this chapter, you will

▬ Understand what equity is, who buys it, and how it differs from debt

▬ Learn the basic features of different types of equity and how these features can impact your ownership position

▬ Know which types of equity financing are available to your business based on its stage of development

A note about taxes and choosing the right entity. When outlining financing options open to your business, our discussion will assume that your business operates as an "S" corporation until it no longer qualifies, or as a "C" corporation. An "S" corporation does not pay income taxes at the corporate level but passes its earnings or losses through to its stockholders. A "C" corporation pays taxes at the corporate level and is the type of entity used by public companies and most larger private companies to do business. We haven't discussed other entities like limited liability companies, limited partnerships, and general partnerships in this book because these entities are usually used by professional service companies and real estate firms. The vast majority of small businesses are first organized, or later reorganized, as "C" corporations, which is why we've assumed the use of a corporate entity. Because choosing the right entity involves complex business, legal, accounting, and tax issues, you should make that choice only in consultation with professionals experienced in these areas.

WHAT IS EQUITY?

Simply put, equity is ownership in your business. Equity represents ownership and the right to participate in earnings, while debt represents the right to be repaid with a set rate of return (interest). Equity is typically

* Common stock; or
* Preferred stock

When you form your business, you or your attorney file articles of incorporation with the secretary of state's office. The articles of incorporation are usually filed in the state where you live or want to conduct business. Among other things, the articles of incorporation

* Say who will be on the board of directors or allow the person forming the business to appoint directors
* Set aside a specific number of shares of common stock or preferred stock that the company can sell, or "issue"

The shares of stock described in the articles of incorporation are known as your company's "authorized" capital. It's up to the board of directors to decide when the company will sell stock, how much the stock will sell for, and who will be permitted to buy shares. When the board adopts a resolution that says the company will sell 100 shares of common stock to you for $100, the stock that you buy is now referred to as "issued and outstanding." If your company has issued 100 shares of common stock out of 500 shares that are authorized, the company can sell up to 400 more shares of common stock to you or other investors. If the articles of incorporation say your company has 500 shares of preferred stock authorized, the board can decide whether the company will sell those shares instead of common stock. After you pay for common or preferred stock and the company gives you your stock certificate, the stock certificate represents your ownership in the business.

Common Stock

Startups usually get their first financing by selling common stock to their founders. Often, this stock is sold to the founders for services rendered to the business. The services are valued by the board, typically at a token amount because the value of the stock is taxable income to the founder who receives it. Common stock can also be sold to founders and other investors for cash or assets like real estate or equipment.

An investment in common stock usually gains or loses more than all other forms of equity or debt. The reason for this is simple: common stock represents the right to share in the earnings of the business after payment of operating costs, interest, expense and dividends on preferred stock. Because earnings left over after payment of these items can be distributed to the common stockholders as dividends, common stock has an almost unlimited upside. There is no maturity date on common stock either, meaning that common stockholders have the right to share in earnings until the business liquidates or is sold. But, with reward comes risk: if the business has only enough earnings to pay interest on its debt and preferred stock dividends, common stockholders get nothing. Banks typically get first claim on assets because security for loans and preferred stock usually comes before common stock when dividends are paid. This is why common stockholders want greater rewards for risking their investment dollars.

A Word About Value and Valuation

Let's focus for a moment on how common stock is valued when it's sold to an investor. If your business is private and has higher earnings this year than last, it makes sense that the business is worth more today than it was a year ago. So if the board of directors decides that the business should raise more capital this year, it will set a price per share that reflects the higher value of the business today. While setting a share value is often more art than science, we'll see in later chapters that there are some well-known benchmarks used to value private companies. For a public company, its value is simply the trading price of the stock multiplied by the number of issued and outstanding shares. The trading price of the stock reflects several factors, including

- Market conditions
- Price-to-earnings multiples in the industry
- Demand and supply for the business's stock

The process of determining a business's value is called valuation. Your business will go through this process several times if you need multiple "rounds" of financing or if your business goes public. Whether you sell common stock or preferred stock, you'll find that investors and investment bankers will always focus on the same basic question: what is the business worth?

Preferred Stock

Preferred stock is called preferred because it has some rights or privileges that common stock doesn't have. Most often, these include rights to

- Get dividends before the common stockholders
- Make claims against the business's assets in a bankruptcy or liquidation that come before claims of common stockholders, known as a liquidation preference

Preferred stock is almost always issued in *series* or *classes*. For example, a company might have issued a Series B Preferred Stock that has a 10% dividend and a liquidation preference, as well as a Series C Preferred Stock that has a 12% dividend and no liquidation preference. Each series of preferred stock and its rights are described in the articles of incorporation or a designation of rights and preferences that's filed with the secretary of state. Preferred stock can come with a wide variety of rights for voting, board membership, conversion into common stock or debt, approval for capital expenditures or major purchases, dividends, and use of funds from the financing. This variety lets companies and investors custom design a class of preferred stock that has rights specifically tailored to a particular financing. For this reason, venture capital firms usually invest in a company by buying preferred stock. The venture capital firm will negotiate for a particular dividend and a liquidation preference that will give the venture firm first claim on assets after creditors are satisfied. If the venture firm is willing to take more risk, the rights of the preferred stock can be limited so that the preferred stock looks more like common stock. If the venture firm wants to take less risk, the rights can be adjusted so that the preferred stock looks more like debt.

UNDERSTANDING RIGHTS AND PREFERENCES OF PREFERRED STOCK

To know what to look for when negotiating a preferred stock investment with an outside investor, you must first come to grips with the terminology surrounding rights and preferences. Let's look at some of the more common preferred stock rights that are negotiated with a venture investor. As you review this terminology, keep in mind that it's also used by subordinated debt lenders and institutions that do mezzanine financings that combine features of equity and debt.

Antidilution rights. These rights are highly valued by venture investors. This fact alone tells you to be careful when negotiating them. These rights come in three forms.

━━ **Standard.** The most common and least offensive to businesses, standard antidilution rights keep the investor's ownership in the business constant if it has a common stock split or stock dividend. For example, if a business has a 2-for-1 common stock split, the venture investor holding preferred stock with antidilution rights can convert the preferred stock into twice as much common stock. In other words, the venture investor will still own the same percentage of the business whether it converts before or after the stock split.

━━ **Ownership maintenance.** Similar to a right of first refusal, ownership maintenance rights let investors *buy* into later financing rounds to keep their percentage ownership unchanged. These rights might not apply to all types of financings, but they are usually triggered if the business sells convertible debt or equity in later rounds.

━━ **Price antidilution.** This protection is more common in venture financings and is dangerous to you and the other stockholders who don't have it. Here's why: if the business sells convertible debt or equity in a later round, these rights entitle the venture firm to more stock that is priced below the conversion price of the investor's preferred stock. Here's the catch (and the difference between this and ownership maintenance antidilution): the investor *gets more stock for free* until the average price of all of its stock equals whatever the new round's investor paid. These rights can result in a venture firm getting large amounts of free stock if a business is forced to raise money in two or three *down rounds*, as later financing rounds at lower prices are known. Because venture investors won't allow you and the other managers to have price antidilution protection (they view that as rewarding nonperformance), you can see why these rights are valued by venture investors.

Board representation/board observer. Buyers of preferred stock typically get the right to appoint one or more directors of the company. Venture investors often have the right to increase their board representation if the business doesn't meet financial goals or if the management team changes. In some instances, the investor negotiates for rights to send an observer to board meetings so the investor isn't responsible for board decision making.

Convertibility. A conversion right lets the investor convert preferred stock into common stock. Most conversion rights are triggered only after the company is public and when the market price of the common stock is above the conversion price. Some investors ask for conversion at their election and also have automatic conversion rights that are triggered if the business is sold or taken public.

Cumulative versus noncumulative dividends.

When dividends are cumulative, they continue to accumulate from year to year *whether the business has the funds to pay the dividend or not*. When the funds are available, the business must pay the dividends that have accumulated. Preferred stock with a noncumulative dividend is just the opposite; that is, if the business doesn't have the funds to pay the dividend or a debt covenant prevents the payment, *the dividend does not accumulate and is never paid*. No matter what forms dividends take, venture firms look to dividends paid in cash or stock as one of their most important rights because

Dividends + Increased equity value = Total rate of return

Since the total rate of return is the most important factor in a venture firm's ability to attract new investors for their next fund, dividends are key to venture firms.

Equity "claw-backs" and "rachet" clauses.

Equity claw-backs are used to "bridge the gap" if the management team and a venture investor can't agree on the business's value. Here's how a claw-back works: if your business successfully meets revenue, EBITDA (earnings before interest, taxes, depreciation, and amortization), net income, or other targets, then you and the other managers get more stock or options. The claw-back usually says that the venture firm gets no antidilution protection if the performance criteria are met. The claw-back lets you increase your ownership in the business back up to an acceptable level and is attractive to the venture firm because its ownership is diluted only if you perform. There are two negative aspects to claw-backs. First, once you get stock, you may owe Uncle Sam more taxes; second, the business may have to record "compensation expense" on its financial statements when you get the stock. It is for these reasons that claw-backs sometimes don't use stock but instead use incentive stock options that vest on performance. The recent trend toward expensing stock options has eliminated much of the benefit that claw-backs using incentive stock options used to give businesses. A manager's individual tax consequences are usually more favorable if the claw-back uses incentive options rather than stock, but careful planning can reduce the tax impact of receiving stock.

A *rachet clause* works like an equity claw-back but reduces your ownership instead of increasing it. If the business doesn't meet its financial targets, the venture firm's preferred stock conversion price is reduced. In the end, the venture investor gets more common stock when it converts and increases its percentage ownership of the business, without putting in more money. If you use overly aggressive projections when you're negotiating a financing, venture firms might propose a rachet clause to make you accountable for your numbers. By tying your ownership percentage of the business to the financial results you've projected, nonperformance will reward the venture investor at your expense. If you're presented with such a clause, carefully consider why the venture firm is proposing it. Just as a claw-back works in your favor, a rachet clause works against you—and how it works out depends on the financial targets and the time you have to hit them.

Financial and other covenants. Sometimes the venture firm wants to structure its financing as more of a loan instead of an investment. In these situations, the purchase agreement will include financial ratios that must be met while the preferred stock is outstanding. These covenants might include debt service coverage, debt to EBITDA, and minimum tangible net worth ratios, to name a few. If the covenants aren't met, then the conversion price might be reduced or the venture investor might get more board seats. Preferred stock rights also include covenants covering

- The business's operations
- Historic financial reports the investor gets
- Budgets and projections the investor must approve
- Management and board composition
- Compensation and options
- Maintenance of insurance
- Regulatory compliance
- Related party transaction approvals by independent directors
- Mergers, asset sales, or other "extraordinary" transactions that the investor must approve
- Payment of dividends
- Making of investments or loans
- Approval of capital improvements

Covenants like this can really hamper your management and need to be carefully reviewed. Covenants don't usually go away until the business is sold, goes public, or some minimum time has passed. When negotiating covenants of preferred stock or debt, remember you have to live with them for awhile and plan accordingly.

Liquidation preferences. With the exception of dividends, liquidation preferences are the most important rights that preferred stockholders want when making their investment. If the business is liquidated and creditors are paid, the preference gives the preferred stockholders distributions of cash or other assets before the common stock gets anything. Figure 1-1 shows how a liquidation preference can impact common stockholders when a business is liquidated.

- **Result:** Bank gets $1 million credit line repaid in full as a secured creditor; unsecured creditors' $500,000 repaid in full; preferred stockholder gets entire remaining $1.5 million from asset auction because of liquidation preference; common stockholders get $0.
- If there were no liquidation preference, then $1.5 million remaining after debt repayment would be split among stockholders based on ownership. Since preferred stock would have converted into 30% ownership, the other common stockholders would have received just over $1 million of the $1.5 million remaining after debt repayment.

Sometimes the liquidation preference can be used by the venture firm to "guarantee" itself a certain minimum return if the business is sold. In these situations, the preference gives the investor a "preferred return" of, for example, two times its initial investment before the common stockholders get to share in the sale proceeds. If the venture firm is entitled to cumulative dividends and it hasn't been paid yet, the liquidation preference also gives the venture firm its unpaid dividends before the common stockholders get a dime. Liquidation preferences and cumulative dividends can make an enormous difference to returns for common stockholders. The sale of the business or its liquidation seem like the last things to think about when your business is first getting funded, but don't let that happen!

FIG. 1-1 *Impact of preferred stock liquidation preference on common stockholders*

| Business Formation Founders Own 100% | Common Stockholders Invest $500,000 for 22% | Bank Line of Credit for $1 million | Preferred Stockholders Invest $3.5 million with Right to Convert into 30% Ownership and a $3.5 million Liquidation Preference | Operational Difficulties Force Business Closing; Accounts Payable Equal $500,000 | Assets Are Auctioned Off for $3 million |

Real World Example

A management team that built an outstanding restaurant business went to a venture firm for expansion financing. Recognizing the business's potential, the venture firm invested $12 million in preferred stock with a 14% cumulative dividend. The purchase agreement said if the dividends weren't paid annually, they would accumulate and be paid out as a liquidation preference when the business was sold. Five years later, the business was sold for $35 million, but no dividends had been paid. When the managers figured out that the venture investor was to get over $20 million ($12 million invested plus $8.4 million in dividends) out of the $35 million price, they were furious. However, they had agreed to these terms and had no choice but to pay out the $20.4 million. Keep this example in mind when you're negotiating dividends and liquidation preferences with a venture investor.

Participating versus nonparticipating. Preferred stock is typically nonparticipating. This means dividends, like interest on debt, are paid at a fixed rate regardless of what earnings are or what dividends are paid on common stock. Participating preferred stock is allowed to share in the earnings of the business in the same way that common stock does. Most venture firms don't ask for participating preferred but get the same result by negotiating for preferred stock that shares in dividends on an *as-if-converted basis*. This means that the preferred stock gets dividends as if it had already been converted to common stock. This as-if-converted right is usually not one the venture firm will negotiate.

Rank. In its simplest form, rank refers to the right of the preferred stockholder to get dividends and liquidating distributions before common stockholders. If a business has more than one series or class of preferred stock, rank refers to the *relative rights* of the holders of each preferred stock class. For example, assume a business issued Series A 10% Convertible Preferred Stock and later issued a Series B 11% Nonconvertible, Cumulative Preferred Stock. Because the Series A is the first series issued, its rights will usually say that the

Series A gets dividends and liquidating distributions before any other classes of preferred stock. That language would include the Series B preferred stock unless the Series A holders consented to the Series B having the same rights to dividends and liquidating distributions. In this example, the Series A preferred ranks ahead of the Series B preferred.

Registration rights. These rights come into existence when the venture firm has converted its preferred stock to common stock; they require the business to register this common stock. Registration makes the common stock "freely tradable," meaning that the venture firm can sell the common stock in the public market. For that reason, most registration rights aren't triggered until after the business has gotten its Initial Public Offering, or IPO, done and has a public market for its common stock. There are two types of registration rights:

- **Piggyback.** The venture firm gets to "piggyback" its common stock onto a filing being made with the Securities and Exchange Commission (SEC) by the business. The business often makes this filing to register stock for sale by it for a follow-on offering, which is a public offering done by an already-public company.
- **Demand.** The venture firm can force the business to register the venture firm's stock in a separate filing with the SEC.

Both demand and piggyback rights are typically *exercisable by the venture firm at the company's expense*. This means that the business pays *all expenses* of registering the common stock held by the venture firm, including legal, accounting, and filing fees; printing expenses; and exchange listing fees. Usually, the only expense paid by the venture firm is the brokerage commission charged when the shares are sold. The cost of registering stock can add up quickly, and the cost of a demand registration is usually much more than a piggyback registration. This is because the business must do a new SEC filing just to get the venture firm's stock free trading.

Rights of first refusal. These rights vary but usually give the venture firm rights to buy their pro rata share of any stock sold after the preferred stock round. These rights also let preferred stockholders buy another preferred stockholder's share of the next round if one preferred stockholder decides not to use his or her rights. These rights extend for a period of time or up to a specific dollar amount raised in later financings. Keep in mind that every time a venture firm uses these rights, it will be maintaining or increasing its ownership percentage of the business, while your interest probably is being diluted. If the business gets multiple financings, the venture firm's interest will grow compared to yours unless you have the personal net worth to keep investing in later rounds.

Tag-along/drag-along rights.

These rights are aptly named. *"Tag-along" rights* let the venture firm tag along in a private sale of stock by the management or other large stockholders. Sometimes tag-along rights are exercisable only after the preferred stock converts into common stock; in others the tag-along rights are exercisable by the venture firm on an as-if-converted basis. Tag-along rights usually don't apply to sales of small amounts of stock or sales made for estate planning purposes. Tag-along rights are important to most venture firms, especially if management is interested in an early exit. *"Drag-along" rights* are the reverse of tag-along rights. They typically let the business drag along the venture firm in a sale or partial sale of stock by the business, its management team, or other large stockholders. You will want to negotiate for drag-along rights whenever you can, mostly to keep the ownership of the venture firm from growing too large if your management team sells some stock.

Voting.

Venture firms usually have the right to vote their preferred stock on an as-if-converted basis at stockholder meetings. This means that the venture firm will attend and vote at meetings of the common stockholders as if it had already converted its preferred stock into common. Most venture firms also have the right to vote the preferred stock as a separate class when stockholders vote on dividends, acquisitions, future issuances of stock, and changes in the board of directors. If state law says that all classes of stock must approve transactions like this, you can see that the venture firm holds veto power over these major events. Most classes of preferred stock also say that 75 or 80% of the preferred stockholders must approve extraordinary events like the sale of the company or changes in preferred stock rights. You can see that these rights give considerable power to venture investors and deserve attention when financing terms are being negotiated.

EQUITY "HYBRIDS"

Three types of equity "hybrids" are used in equity financings—warrants, options, and payment-in-kind (PIK) securities. We've excluded debt hybrids like convertible debt and leases from this discussion; these are reviewed in Chapter 2.

Warrants and Options

A warrant, like an option, lets an investor buy shares of common or preferred stock for a set price during a specific period of time. When an investor exercises a warrant, the number of shares of stock outstanding increases, and the business gets the cash exercise price. Most warrants have an exercise period of three to five years. During that time, the warrant holder can exercise the warrant at his or her discretion. Practically speaking, most investors won't exercise a warrant unless they can sell the stock in a public market at a price above the warrant exercise price. For this reason, warrants are usually issued to venture firms and other investors with registration rights like those discussed previously. This allows the investor to exercise the warrant and sell the common stock simultaneously, so the investor isn't "out of pocket" for the exercise price more than a day or two.

Warrants and options have two value sources: the time value and the fixed exercise price. The time value is based on how long the warrant can be exercised. Clearly, a one-year warrant has a lower value than a five-year warrant. During the exercise period, the fixed exercise price also gives the warrant value as long as the business's value increases.

Real World Example

One of our clients was negotiating a loan agreement with an institution that typically made large loans at interest rates in the 11 to 13% range. The management team proposed to the lender a "buy down" of the interest rate by giving the lender a warrant exercisable at $1.00. The management team suggested the lender get a four-year warrant in exchange for reducing the interest rate on the loan to 8%. After some hard negotiating, we successfully closed the loan, got an interest rate of 8.5%, and gave the lender a three-year warrant with a token exercise price. Even though the lender would own 15% of the business when it exercised the warrant, the management team felt that having the lender as an investor, and the lower interest rate, more than compensated for the dilution they'd suffer.

Payment-in-Kind Securities

Many early-stage businesses don't have excess cash flow to pay cash dividends on preferred stock or interest on debt. A PIK security allows dividend or interest payments to be paid in more stock or promissory notes, which is where the name "payment in kind" originated. Sometimes the PIK feature will increase the liquidation preference of the preferred stock. For example, let's assume your business issues preferred stock worth $1.5 million over a period of four years to pay dividends to a venture investor. When your business is later sold or liquidated, the investor gets its $1.5 million in unpaid dividends, together with the rest of the liquidation preference, before common stockholders are paid. Sometimes PIKs are payable in new promissory notes that are convertible into stock. As dividends accumulate, the number of shares of preferred stock or common stock to be issued will increase. So while the payment of dividends or interest by issuing a PIK security can help maximize cash flow, you need to measure that savings against the dilution in your ownership.

WHO BUYS EQUITY?

Figure 1-2 illustrates the major categories of equity investors. As you can see, the base of the pyramid is built by the founders. Employees and consultants further expand the base until angels and institutional investors can be attracted. These investors fund growth until larger private placements and public offerings are closed. The pyramid structure also tells you something else about equity financing—the larger the financings get, the fewer are done. Put another way, many businesses get capital from their founders, employees and angels, fewer businesses get venture capital or private equity, and fewer still get institutional funding or go public.

The first three types of equity investors are self-explanatory. *Angel investors* are usually high net worth individuals with prior management and investing experience in your industry or in a related one. Venture firms and private equity groups are pools of capital invested by professional money managers. The capital comes from pension funds, institutional investors, companies, and high net worth individuals. Most venture and private equity groups invest in early-stage entities or in particular industries. Others provide financing for management buyouts or for mature-stage businesses. Strategic partners are usually companies that are in your industry or in a related industry that have some "strategic" reason to help finance your business. A good example of a strategic partner is a computer software business that invests in a hardware business to get exclusive rights

FIG. 1-2 *Major categories of equity investors*

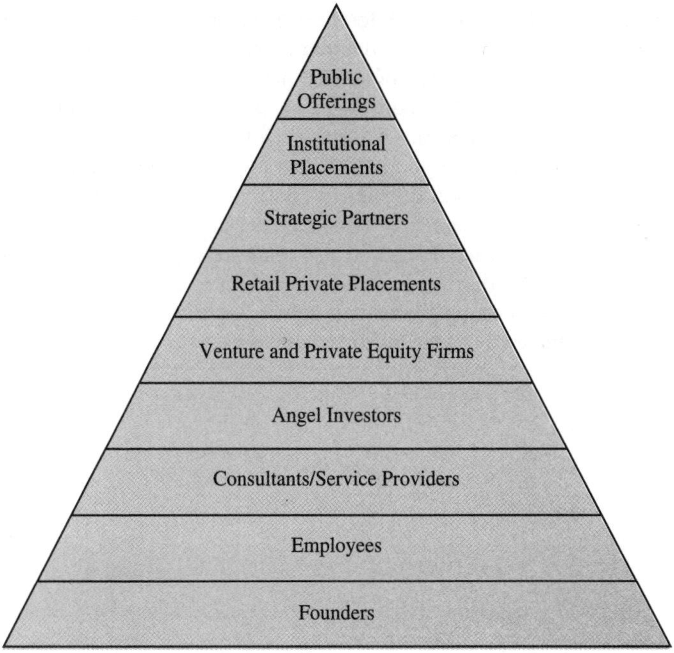
Public Offerings
Institutional Placements
Strategic Partners
Retail Private Placements
Venture and Private Equity Firms
Angel Investors
Consultants/Service Providers
Employees
Founders

to install software on each computer made. Institutional investors are pension funds, insurance companies, money management firms, mutual funds, and company-sponsored pools of capital that invest directly in public or private companies. Venture firms and private equity groups are institutional investors but aren't usually referred to in this more generic way.

CHAPTER PERSPECTIVE

Equity is made up of common stock, preferred stock, and hybrids like warrants, options, and PIK securities. Equity is ownership in your business and, unlike debt, shares in the earnings of your business. Common stock is the type of equity usually issued by small businesses and represents the most basic form of ownership. Common stock is typically sold to founders, employees, and other individual and institutional investors. Preferred stock can have a wide variety of rights, making it anything from straight equity to a debt look-alike. The most important preferred stock rights are its dividend rights, its rank above common stock in liquidating distributions, and its voting rights. The other preferences that a preferred stock investor wants, though, can have an enormous impact on your business's operations, financial condition, and control. You'll need to consider the funding needs of the business and balance those needs against the dilution in your ownership and other rights you'll give a preferred stock investor. Equity hybrids like warrants and PIK securities can dilute your ownership in the future. You'll need to weigh ownership dilution from these equity hybrids against savings you can get in interest costs and cash flow. You've been introduced to the different types of investors that buy equity in businesses like yours. We'll now consider debt financing alternatives before focusing on which financing type is more advantageous to you and why.

Debt Financing Alternatives for Your Small Business

INTRODUCTION AND MAIN POINTS

This chapter discusses different debt financings available to the small business during the corporate life cycle's four stages. Unlike equity financing, getting debt financing depends on having collateral to secure the debt and generating cash flow to pay interest and repay principal. This means that early-stage businesses will have fewer choices, and mature businesses will have more choices, among debt financing options. After studying this chapter, you will

▬ Learn what debt is and how it differs from equity
▬ See what debt financings your small business can qualify for at its stage of development
▬ Understand the common elements of most debt financings and how the lender documents them

WHAT IS DEBT—AND WHY USE IT?

Debt is financing for a business that must be repaid when it comes due. For making the loan, a lender receives a set rate of return (interest) and the business's pledge of collateral like inventory, receivables, or other assets. Debt can be

- Short term, or due in less than one year
- Long term, due in two to seven years or maybe longer

Short-term debt includes the *current portion* of long-term debt, or that part of long-term debt that is coming due within the next year. While debt is outstanding, it bears interest at a rate called the *stated rate*, which might be a fixed or variable rate. Most variable rates are based on the bank's prime rate or the London Interbank Eurodollar Market Rate (LIBOR). If there is a default, the stated rate typically increases to a *default rate* that usually ranges from 18 to 21%.

Debt has no ownership in the business and doesn't participate in its earnings. This is the biggest reason why a small business wants to get debt financing—the current owners keep their ownership and rights to the earnings. The small business also gets to deduct interest paid on loans as an expense on its tax return, but dividends paid to stockholders are not expenses that can be deducted on the corporate tax return—instead, dividends come from after-tax earnings. For these reasons, debt financing is a smart choice for the small business. However, since lenders want collateral to secure their loans and charge interest rates that reflect loan risk, development- and operating-stage small businesses aren't usually able to get all the debt financing they'd like.

WHAT DEBT FINANCINGS CAN MY SMALL BUSINESS QUALIFY FOR?

When considering debt financing alternatives, here's a simple formula to keep in mind. The three C's—*cash flow, credit quality*, and *collateral*—have a lot to do with your business's success in getting debt financing throughout the corporate life cycle. As shown in Table 2-1, early-stage businesses won't usually have the cash flow to pay interest on high-cost debt, so they'll rely on loans from friends and family, equipment vendors (using lease financing), and SBA guaranteed loans to meet their debt financing needs. As the business grows and its cash flow and collateral base increase, it will become attractive to traditional small business lenders like commercial banks that offer revolving lines of credit and asset-based loans. If credit quality remains high, the small business will eventually have access to low-cost debt financing using term loans, securitizations, and rated debt. Here is another good rule of thumb: the larger the business grows, the lower its debt financing costs are. Conversely, if the business starts to shrink because of declining sales or credit quality, debt financing costs are bound to rise as lenders react to changing business conditions by tightening credit availability or increasing interest rates.

Table 2-1 outlines for each stage of the corporate life cycle:

- Debt financing sources
- Debt financing types
- The documents you'll encounter when getting different debt financings

Like Table P-1, Table 2-1 presents good general guidelines, but each business's circumstances will affect a lender's willingness to provide

TABLE 2-1
Debt Financing Sources, Types, and Documents

Stage	Debt Financing Sources	Debt Financing Type and Documentation
Development	Founders, friends, and family	Loans—promissory notes and loan agreements
	SBA-guaranteed loans	SBA-guaranteed revolver or term note—notes and loan agreements
	Equipment vendors	Leases
	Hard money lenders	Promissory notes with high interest and collateralized by personal assets
Operating	Banks	Revolvers and term debt—loan agreements and promissory notes
	Institutional investors and private equity groups	Mezzanine debt, convertible debt, or securitizations—notes, debentures, loan agreements, conversion agreements, and warrants
	Equipment vendors and leasing firms	Leases
Mature	Banks	Revolvers, asset-based loans, and term debt—loan agreements and promissory notes
	Institutional investors	Mezzanine debt, securitizations, high-yield debt—notes, debentures, junk bonds, loan agreements, warrants
	Equipment vendors and leasing firms	Lease lines of credit
Liquidity	Banks	Revolvers, asset-based loans, and term debt—loan agreements and promissory notes
	Institutional investors	Rated debt, high-yield debt, and securitizations—notes, debentures, bonds, loan agreements

debt financing. Specific decisions about the loan size, interest rate, fees, collateral requirements, and restrictions on funding will depend on many factors, including the three C's.

LOANS FROM FOUNDERS, FRIENDS, AND FAMILY

Loans from founders, friends, and family are often the fastest, simplest, and most common way for early-stage businesses to borrow money and get into business. If you're lucky enough to have a rich uncle, your family connections can be just the ticket to reasonably priced debt financing. If you're not that lucky, the pooled resources of friends and family might be the solution to your early-stage debt funding needs. You should expect, however, that as your lenders and the amounts you borrow increase, people will ask for higher interest rates, collateral, or even stock ownership as the price for making more or larger loans. Since doing business with friends and family can be a quick way to ruin those relationships, you should consider using your personal resources and getting an SBA loan or a small revolving line of credit at a bank as soon as possible. Putting your company's debt financing on a "business" footing can save you plenty of aggravation—particularly if you find yourself at holiday dinners seated across from Aunt Mildred, who just can't wait to grill you about when her loan is going to be repaid or, worse yet, who continues to moan about the $5,000 loan that she wrote off when your business didn't make it.

SMALL BUSINESS ADMINISTRATION LOANS

To get a Small Business Administration (SBA) loan, you must first have attempted to get financing from a bank or other lending institution. If you haven't been successful, you may be eligible for SBA loan assistance. If so, you must prepare and submit the SBA loan application to a SBA-approved lender, which most often is a commercial bank. If the lender approves the application, it is submitted to the local SBA office. Once approved by the SBA, the lender closes the loan and disburses the funds. Although limited in amount, SBA-guaranteed loans offer lower interest costs than nonguaranteed loans and are an excellent low-cost debt financing source for early stage small businesses.

There are two basic SBA loans:

1. **Guarantee loans.** These loans are the most common SBA loan and allow

- Loans to be made by private lenders that are guaranteed up to 90% by the SBA

- A maximum guarantee of 85% for loans over $155,000
- A maximum total guarantee of $750,000 by the SBA

2. **Direct loans.** These loans

- Are up to $150,000 and are available only to applicants unable to get an SBA-guaranteed loan
- Require the applicant to first get financing from his or her bank and, in cities with over 200,000 people, from at least one other lender before applying for an SBA direct loan

SBA direct loan funds are limited and are often available only to businesses located in high-unemployment areas or those owned by low-income or handicapped individuals, minorities, or veterans.

LEASES

Equipment vendors are a great source for relatively low-cost financing for early-stage businesses. Although not debt financing in the traditional sense, lease financing is probably the closest thing to it, particularly when the lease has a buyout clause that lets you purchase the equipment for $1 at the lease's end. Lease financing is tied to specific equipment and so doesn't provide working capital for the business, but it reduces the capital you would otherwise need to operate. Lease financing is generally more expensive than revolving bank debt because lease payments have built-in interest of 12 to 14% included in the payment. Because leases are secured by the equipment or property being leased, many equipment vendors won't require personal guarantees or other collateral. The bottom line: lease financing is cost-effective and can play its part in financing early- and operating-stage small businesses, but it can't be your only debt financing source.

Larger businesses often use lease lines of credit, synthetic leases, and sale-leaseback transactions to finance equipment and facilities purchases. Synthetic leases and sale-leasebacks are referred to as "off-balance sheet" transactions because the equipment or property's purchase price moves from the company's balance sheet to a "remote" subsidiary or third party. These transactions and lease lines of credit are extremely cost-effective debt financings but are out of most small businesses' reach until much later in the corporate life cycle.

HARD MONEY LENDERS

These lenders are like the "payday" lenders of the corporate world. As you might guess from the name, these are "lenders of last resort" for most small businesses. Because usury laws only prohibit interest rates above 21% for consumer loans, hard money lenders can charge businesses interest of 25 to 40% per year, collect exorbitant up-front fees, and get personal guarantees or second home mortgages as collateral. If a small business is considering using a hard money lender for debt financing because no other financing is available, management should consider if the business plan is viable. While some small businesses have "outgrown" their hard money lenders and gone on to become wildly successful companies, you can safely assume that the businesses that fall in that category are far fewer than those that end up in liquidation or bankruptcy.

REVOLVERS AND SENIOR DEBT

The most common type of short-term debt is a revolving credit line, or "revolver" for short. A revolver

- Is usually secured by a first priority claim, or lien, on inventory, accounts receivable, or both
- Bears interest at a floating rate from just below a bank's "prime" rate or LIBOR to 4% or more above that rate
- Is due on demand or within one year
- Is usually funded by a commercial bank
- Is often repaid using a term loan or an equity financing

In addition to interest expense, there are two other significant costs to your business that are built into the revolver's structure. First, many banks require businesses to maintain a compensating balance, usually about 10% of the revolver's outstanding balance or the total committed credit line, which is held by the bank in a non-interest-bearing account. Second, draws under the revolver are limited to set percentages of the collateral's value based on differing "advance rates." For instance, inventory might receive a 50% advance rate on inventory value, while advances against receivables might receive an 80 or 85% advance rate. Advancing less than 100% against the inventory or receivables limits draws under the revolver and effectively increases the lender's collateral value. This is why a rapidly growing business is forced to use other debt or equity financings to fill the gap between advances under the revolver and inventory and receivables funding costs. As you can see, compensating balances and advance limits will result in a higher overall cost of capital for your business.

As your business builds a loan and repayment history, a revolver might be extended for a two- or three-year term before coming due, so long as there's no default. These extended revolvers are classified as long-term debt and are really "permanent" capital. Long-term revolvers and credit lines with first priority liens on inventory and receivables are generally called *senior debt*. The right to have first claim on inventory, receivables, or other collateral is what gives this debt its name.

Companies that aren't able to get senior debt because they don't generate sufficient cash flow are sometimes able to secure asset-based lines of credit. Like traditional revolvers, the asset-based line has advance limits, but these are based on a percentage of asset values rather than cash flow. Asset-based lenders focus on

- Collateral value
- Collateral audits
- Inventory turnover rates
- Orderly liquidation asset values
- Forced liquidation asset values

when deciding the financing's amount and structure. Since the lender is not relying on repayment from cash flow but is making a loan decision based at least in part on the worst-case liquidation scenario, advance rates under asset-based lines of credit are often just a fraction of the assets' market value. As we'll see later, several well-known asset-based lenders in the United States, such as Fleet Capital, Congress, and GE Capital, specialize in making loans to distributors, retailers and other industries that must maintain large inventories.

Senior debt includes credit lines and term loans that are used to fund operations rather than to buy capital assets. For this reason, a first mortgage on a production facility is not considered to be senior debt even though it has first claim on the production facility if the mortgage payment isn't made. Other long-term financings like sale-leasebacks and capital leases with first priority claims on land, buildings, or equipment aren't viewed as senior debt because loan proceeds don't fund operations.

SUBORDINATED DEBT

Debt that does not have first claim on the business's assets is referred to as "subordinated debt," meaning that its claim is ranked lower than a first-priority claim. Subordinated debt, or sub debt for short, can be

- Term debt
- Mezzanine debt
- Convertible debt

Term debt requires scheduled principal and interest payments over the loan's life or sometimes calls for a balloon principal payment at maturity. These loans are used for working capital, to finance a major facility expansion, or to buy another business. Coming due in 1 to 10 years, term debt is sub debt's most cost-effective form, but it is more expensive than a revolver. Lenders consider term loans to be riskier than revolvers because the loan is outstanding longer. They usually want a higher interest rate based on this perceived time-value-of-money risk. Commercial banks fund most term loans for their more creditworthy business customers who might, for instance, already have revolvers with the banks. For this reason, your small business will generally not qualify for term debt until you have a demonstrated earnings history.

Mezzanine debt is more accurately called mezzanine financing because "intermediate" capital usually finances a business through a debt and equity combination. This debt financing got its name from being "layered" between the senior credit facility and the business's equity. Debt mezzanine financing is higher risk debt that usually gets a second priority claim (below the senior debt) on inventory, receivables, or other assets or even just a general claim on the business's assets. This means the mezzanine lender has a much higher risk if the business can't repay its debts. Mezzanine lenders compensate for this risk by charging higher interest rates, often between 12 and 14%, and getting an ownership interest in the business known as an *equity kicker*. The equity kicker is often an option to buy common stock in the business, known as a *warrant*. Like an option, a warrant might be exercisable by the mezzanine lender in a 3- to 5-year period and represents the right to buy 10 to 20% of the business's common stock for a token purchase price. If the small business is more mature, you can sometimes get an exercise price for the warrant that is closer to the stock's fair market value.

From the lender's perspective, there is some tradeoff between the interest rate, the warrant's exercise price and the ownership percentage the warrant will buy. Because the lender considers all these factors when estimating its rate of return, you'll need to understand tradeoffs among them and how they can affect your business and its ownership. For example, if the mezzanine financing carries a 14% interest rate and the warrant has a token exercise price, the warrant might only buy a small interest in the business. Or, if the interest rate is 11% and the warrant will buy more ownership in the business, the warrant's exercise price is higher (usually close to your stock's fair market value). In later chapters, we'll consider the advantages and disadvantages of different mezzanine financings and analyze how different structures can impact your interests.

Businesses typically get mezzanine debt from nonbank sources like

- So-called mezzanine funds
- Private equity funds, including Small Business Investment Companies (SBICs)
- Institutional investors
- Strategic partners
- Unregulated subsidiaries of financial institutions

Convertible debt, as its name implies, is debt that converts into common stock or preferred stock; it is a type of mezzanine financing because the conversion feature builds in an equity upside for the lender. Convertible debt

- Gives the lender the right to convert all or part of a loan into stock at a fixed or variable conversion rate until the loan matures
- Carries a lower interest rate than nonconvertible debt, reflecting the potential upside for the lender from conversion
- Is subordinated to senior and term debt
- Tends to be used by smaller companies with high growth rates and more leveraged capital structures

A lender that wants ownership upside in the business but doesn't want to take an equity kicker can accomplish the same result by taking debt that is partially or completely convertible into stock. The loan agreement often says conversion is automatic if your business has a so-called *liquidity event*, like a sale, merger, or IPO, or the lender might have an option to convert anytime the debt is outstanding. Once converted, this debt dilutes the other stockholders' ownership and for that reason is much more "expensive" for the business's equity owners than debt with a fixed interest rate.

High-yield debt has an extremely high interest rate and is subordinated to virtually all other debt. Also known as junk bonds or junk financing, high-yield debt is unrated or receives the lowest non-investment-grade ratings from bond-rating agencies. The lack of an investment-grade rating and any meaningful collateral means that companies selling junk bonds have to offer exorbitant interest rates to attract lenders. The sizeable cash flow needed to pay the high interest rates charged on junk financing prevents most small businesses from using junk debt.

Rated debt is debt that has been graded by rating agencies like Standard & Poor's, Moody's, or Duff & Phelps. Rated debt sold with an investment grade rating carries a lower interest rate that makes this debt financing more attractive than many other debt financings. An investment grade rating is also important because some institutional investors are limited to buying investment grade debt. Unfortunately, most small businesses lack the

- Operating history
- Information and other systems
- Capital strength
- Profitability
- Needed collateral or *collateral enhancements* like insurance policies or third party guarantees

to get an investment grade rating. For this reason, only larger small businesses will be successful in getting their debt rated and sold with an investment grade rating.

Securitizations are similar to synthetic leases and sale-leaseback transactions because they are another type of off-balance-sheet financing. Given a bad name by Enron, securitizations are actually very common financings for companies that originate mortgages, auto loans, consumer loans, credit card debt, and other receivables. In a securitization, the company creates a "bankruptcy-remote" subsidiary and transfers a receivables portfolio to it. The subsidiary then issues to a third-party purchaser, often an insurance company or other institutional investor, trust certificates that entitle the purchaser to receive the cash flows generated by the receivables portfolio. In exchange, the purchaser pays the subsidiary a lump sum that represents the receivables' present value, discounted by some additional amount for a loss reserve. This amount is then upstreamed to the parent company to pay for the original portfolio purchase by the subsidiary. Like rated debt, the receivables portfolio is almost always graded by a rating agency, meaning that the insurance company or institutional purchaser gets investment-grade trust certificates. The effective interest rate charged in the securitization transaction, referred to as the *implicit cost of capital*, makes securitizations among the lowest cost debt financings available.

Securitizations have many different structures and can be far more complex than the simple outline given above. For example, rating agencies often require the business to get an insurance policy covering the financial performance of the receivables portfolio. These policies, or financial performance guarantees from the parent company, are called *credit enhancements*. Credit enhancements can be expensive and can require the parent company to substitute performing receivables owned by it for nonperforming receivables in the portfolio. If the parent company remains "on the hook" for the portfolio's financial performance, you can see that financing costs can increase considerably if economic or industry conditions worsen.

Real World Example

One of my clients was a startup formed to provide equipment lease financing to small and mid-sized businesses. The management team had been in the leasing industry for many years and had come to know independent lease originators across the country who were among the largest equipment lease "originators" in the United States. One cofounder contributed about $2 million in equity as startup capital and the business was able to secure a bank credit line that it used to begin funding leases. Before this business completed its IPO, it received a letter of intent from a well-known financial institution that agreed to "place" the first securitization with an insurance company purchaser. At only $25 million, the amount securitized was small, but the business was able to increase its lease funding volume quickly as its lease originator network expanded. After its IPO, the business completed more securitizations and established an excellent track record. When the business was sold after having been public for only 2 years, the founders received stock in a New York Stock Exchange-listed company that was worth many millions, and the public investors had tripled their investment. This was a fantastic result for all, but it was one that could not have been realized if securitization financing hadn't been found!

In the next two chapters, we'll discuss how to identify debt financing sources, including senior and subordinated debt, and the advantages and disadvantages of different debt financings. Before getting to these topics, let's first review debt financings' common characteristics you should expect to see when you're negotiating for senior or sub debt.

COMMON ELEMENTS OF DEBT FINANCING

Debt financings are typically governed by a loan agreement, but the "promise" to repay the debt is usually in a promissory note or a debenture. A debenture is a bond backed by the business's earning power or general credit. Whether your business is less than a year old or has operated for a decade, loan agreements with senior and subordinated lenders share many common characteristics. This is because lenders share the same objectives: setting the debt's amount and rate of return, being adequately secured, getting repaid, and determining what happens if there's a default. You can expect to see most, if not all, of the following terms in senior and subordinated loan agreements:

▬ A fixed credit limit or a formula that sets available borrowings based on a percentage of receivables, inventory, or other assets

▬ A statement on how the debt proceeds will be used

▬ A collateral description, including whether personal guarantees are required

▬ The initial interest rate, an adjustment formula if the interest rate is variable, the default interest rate, and any minimum interest charges

▬ Fees charged by the lender, including

- Commitment fees
- Fees on any unused debt
- Annual or periodic fees for making funds available to your business
- The lender's closing and legal fees your business will pay
- Fees for auditing collateral or appraisal costs if the collateral has fluctuating values
- Letter of credit fees, if you do business overseas and issue letters of credit to your suppliers
- Prepayment fees
- Early termination fees if you pay off the loan before it's due

▬ The loan's time period, whether principal is paid in a balloon payment or amortized over the loan's term, and payment dates for principal and interest

▬ Expenses payable by your business, including

- Appraisal fees
- Uniform Commercial Code (UCC) search and recording fees
- Credit report costs
- "Lockbox costs," if the lender collects payments for you at a P.O. Box and applies them to the loan as collected
- Real estate title policies and recording fees
- Environmental survey costs

▬ Whether you're required to give monthly, quarterly, or annual financial reports and whether an audit or a review by an outside accounting firm is necessary

▬ *Representations and warranties*—statements that confirm historical facts about your business to the lender, like

- The business's organization and good standing as a corporation in its home state
- The right to do business in other states
- Authorization by the board of directors and/or stockholders to get the loan
- No litigation and regulatory proceedings concerning your business
- No environmental issues in your business or at its facilities
- No undisclosed liabilities
- The lender's lien priority on the collateral
- Good title to the pledged collateral

▬ *Covenants*, which are promises about what your business will do (or operating goals it will meet) in the future, including

- Financial covenants like total debt to equity, tangible net worth, debt to EBITDA, interest coverage, loan to value, and similar ratios
- Nonfinancial covenants addressing reporting requirements; limits on compensation, dividends, or distributions; limits on asset acquisitions or sales; restrictions on stock buy backs or redemptions; notices when management changes, capital expenditure limits, and limits on, or approval requirements concerning, related party transactions

▬ Events of default like

- Nonpayment
- Noncompliance with warranties or covenants

- Insolvency or bankruptcy
- A change of control not approved by the lender
- Cross defaults caused by violations of other agreements that are part of the loan agreement
- Judgments and similar events

■ Signed subordination agreements that are satisfactory to the senior and sub debt lender or a signed "intercreditor" agreement that says what collateral priority each lender has and how they can assert their rights

■ What legal opinions, audit opinions, and appraisals you have to get before closing or while the loan is outstanding

Loan agreements also give the senior or subordinated lender every possible remedy and protection from liability that the lender or its lawyers can dream up. Following a default, the lender generally has the right to hold or dispose of collateral, recover a deficiency from any personal guarantors, get its legal fees and other costs paid, be indemnified from claims by stockholders or third parties, and be held harmless by the company. As you might expect, lenders are unwilling to negotiate any substantive changes to these rights. Their position is that these rights are what they need and deserve in exchange for accepting a fixed return on their "investment" in the business.

CHAPTER PERSPECTIVE

Debt is a financial obligation that, unlike equity, carries a fixed return and does not participate in earnings. Interest expense and out-of-pocket costs to get debt financing are deductible expenses for tax purposes, but dividends on equity are not deductible. For these reasons and to limit ownership dilution, consider debt financing options when developing a financing plan for your business. As your business grows, improving the three C's—cash flow, credit quality, and collateral—will open up more debt financing options and reduce debt financing costs. Early-stage businesses often use loans from founders, friends and family, leases, and SBA-guaranteed loans for debt financing. Graduating to a revolver helps create a banking relationship that can later expand to include term debt for growth or acquisition financing. Subordinated debt financings like mezzanine or convertible debt are excellent sources for growth capital but are more expensive than traditional senior debt. Most mezzanines are really combined debt and equity financings. The mezzanine lender gets a healthy interest rate but also wants an equity kicker to compensate the lender for being in "second position" behind the senior debt. As your business matures, you'll want to use lower cost debt financing options like lease lines of credit, securitizations, sale-lease-backs, and other off-balance sheet financings. Using these financing methods and rated debt will give your business access to the most cost-effective debt financing available in today's markets. Whether you're getting senior debt or sub debt, loan agreements with your lenders will share many common elements. The major categories covered in almost every loan agreement include the terms, fees and expenses, representations and warranties of historical facts, covenants (or promises) about future events, the lender's collateral and claim priority, and what happens if there's a default. Now let's consider the advantages and disadvantages of different financings and how timing issues can influence what type of financing is right for your business.

Advantages, Disadvantages, and Timing Issues of Different Financings

INTRODUCTION AND MAIN POINTS

This chapter covers the advantages and disadvantages of different equity and debt financings. It also considers timing issues that can delay or accelerate the financing's closing. Since there are trade-offs between financing availability, cost, and timing, you'll need to understand what you are trading off when you select one type of financing over another. After studying this chapter, you will

▬ Know the most important advantages and disadvantages of different equity and debt financings for your business

▬ Understand critical timing issues that can affect when your business gets financing

▬ Be able to anticipate events that can help or hurt your chances of attending a closing

Too often, small business owners don't plan ahead or allow enough time for the financing process to proceed at a normal pace. Instead, managing day-to-day operations gets priority and not enough planning goes into deciding what financing is best for the business at its current stage of development. The result is a rush to find and close a financing on an unrealistic timetable that often antagonizes the investor or lender and undermines the business's negotiating position. To avoid this, you'll need to know:

- The financing options realistically open to your business
- Why one financing might be better or worse than another
- The time you'll need to negotiate, document, and close the financing
- What roadblocks to anticipate

No one—from investors or lenders to management and stockholders—involved in a financing likes surprises. It also goes without saying that you won't be able to predict every issue that can affect a financing or its timing. However, one of the key themes in this book is that planning and preparation can reduce the chances of a "surprise" that prevents a financing from closing. Let's start this effort by looking at what financing is best for your business today.

OVERVIEW: ADVANTAGES AND DISADVANTAGES OF DEBT VERSUS EQUITY

Consider the following points as to why debt or equity is best for your business. As you'll see, many of these points relate to issues covered in Chapters 1 and 2.

Advantages of Debt Over Equity

▬ A lender has no direct claim on future earnings.

▬ The lender is only entitled to repayment of principal and interest.

▬ Interest on debt can be deducted on the business's tax returns. This lowers your "real" debt cost.

▬ Debt does not dilute the stockholders' interests since the lender has no claim to the business's equity.

▬ Interest and principal payments are typically a known amount that can be forecast.

Disadvantages of Debt When Compared to Equity

▬ Interest is a fixed cost that raises your business's break-even point. If your business is too highly leveraged, it may not be profitable enough to fund more growth.

▬ There are practical limits to how much debt your business can carry. The larger the debt-to-equity ratio, the more risky the business is considered to be and the less a lender will advance.

▬ Cash flow is necessary for both principal and interest payments.

▬ Debt is not permanent capital because at some point it must be repaid.

▬ Debt instruments often have restrictive covenants that limit future financings or how the business is managed.

Now let's examine your financing alternatives within the four stages of the corporate life cycle, keeping in mind the points we just touched on.

DEVELOPMENT STAGE: EQUITY AND DEBT ALTERNATIVES
Equity Financing Options in the Development Stage

In the development stage, equity financing is often the only financing you can get. The business usually lacks cash flow to repay or assets to secure debt financing except in isolated instances. Equity investors at this stage include

- The business's founders
- "Friends and family"
- Angel investors

- Venture capital firms
- Private equity groups
- Early stage IPOs

Founders, friends, and family. Founders, friends, and family typically purchase common stock for cash or services. The investment is described in a subscription agreement signed by the investor and the company. The subscription agreement describes the shares being purchased, lists the purchase price, and contains some representations by the company (e.g., that the company is a formed corporation, has sufficient authorized shares to sell the investor his or her shares, and that the investment is high risk). The investor also has to make some representations in the typical subscription agreement. These include that he or she understands the risks of investing, that there is no public market for the stock, and that the investor can afford to lose the investment. A copy of the business plan usually accompanies the subscription agreement, at least for investors who are not employed by or familiar with the business.

Real World Example: Watch Out for Lurking Tax Issues

Anytime a business issues stock for services, the stock's value might be taxable income to the recipient when it's received. Options that are issued with a below-fair-market-value exercise price can create similar tax headaches for the option recipient. Even though this may not be a problem if the stock has little value, the Internal Revenue Service (IRS) can look at stock sales to third parties that occur around the same time to set the stock's fair market value and calculate taxes. Also, if your business issues stock for services, the stock's value must sometimes be included as compensation expense on the financial statements. In an extreme case, one of my clients issued stock right before an IPO that had to be valued at the IPO price (since the IPO was right around the corner). This caused the business to record over $7 *million* in compensation expense, resulting in the business going from being profitable to showing a significant loss. You can imagine the reaction this got from management when they found out that their financial statements were going to show a large loss rather than a profit!

Angel investors. Angel investors are usually high net worth individuals who invest in early-stage businesses and who look for high returns (and are willing to take high risks) not available in later stage investments. Angel investors are often entrepreneurs who know or have been previously involved in your industry and who were fortunate enough to "cash out" in a sale or IPO. Angels are interested in serving as mentors or even board members, if the business is private or has director and officer liability insurance.

Most angel investors want to buy stock in your business before a venture capital firm or institutional investor has invested, but angels expect to pay more than the founders, friends, and family. Sometimes angel investors will invest at the same time and at the same price as an institutional investor. This not only reduces the risk of investing in an undercapitalized business but also lets the angel investors ride on the institutional investor's "coattails." This means that angel investors know an institutional investor will do a complete review and investigation (before investing) of

- The business
- Its industry
- The business's financial performance
- Its operations
- The management team and their backgrounds
- The current financing structure and proposed investment terms
- Projections for future performance

This review is known as *due diligence*. Even if the angel investors don't see and can't use the institutional investor's due diligence, they'll know that the institutional investor is reasonably comfortable with the results if it invests. If the institutional investor pulls out before funding, angel investors will understand this is a red flag and could mean the due diligence review surfaced negative information about the business or its management. Here are some other benefits angels get from investing alongside institutional investors:

■ If the angel investor invests on the same terms given to the institutional investor, the angel investor will benefit from the institutional investor's financial acumen, negotiating skills, and "deep pockets." In other words, the angel investor can leverage the institutional investor's resources and influence and get better terms than he or she would otherwise. Knowing this, many institutional investors discourage businesses from letting angel investors invest alongside the institution. Of course, exceptions are occasionally made for angel investors who have a prior relationship with management or the institutional investor, or for angel investors with name recognition or industry prominence.

▰ In the best case, the institutional investor agrees to let its lawyers represent both the institutional investor and the angel investor(s) and to share costs like background investigations, audit fees, legal fees, title searches, environmental surveys, and other out-of-pocket expenses. This can save the angel investors a considerable sum of money because they split due diligence and other expenses.

Angel investors invest anywhere from $10,000 to $2 million or more. More sophisticated angel investors who invest larger amounts usually purchase preferred stock with the same protections given to venture capital firms and private equity groups. Depending on the amount invested, angel investments are documented by simple subscription agreements accompanied by a business plan or a lengthy and complex stock purchase agreement. Angel investors don't usually provide debt financing because the returns are limited. In cases where they provide debt financing, the angel investors want warrants to purchase stock so that they can participate in the upside if the business succeeds.

Venture capital firms. Venture capital firms are usually the largest cash investors in early-stage entities. Venture firms raise their capital from pension funds, insurance companies, and institutional investors that set aside part of their funds for investment in early-stage businesses. These investors pool their investment dollars and rely on the venture firm to do due diligence, negotiate investment terms, and oversee their investments. This lets the institutional investors diversify their portfolios and outsource the primary responsibility for investment oversight.

Venture capital firms generally have

- Minimum investments of $100,000 to $4 million and maximum investments of $250,000 to $50 million
- Specific industries or markets like technology, healthcare, or consumer goods where they invest
- Time horizons to liquidity of five to seven years;
- Annual return targets ranging from 30 to 40% or more
- Policies about participating on the board of directors and/or board committees
- Contract terms that increase their control over the business if financial goals aren't realized

Some venture investment firms are organized as Small Business Investment Companies. SBICs are licensed by the SBA but are privately owned and managed firms that make their own investment decisions. When licensed, an SBIC is eligible to receive long-term, low-interest loans from the SBA that mature in 5 to 20 years from funding. The loans are two to three times the SBIC's equity. SBICs invest in startup and early-stage enterprises but cannot invest in

- Nonmanufacturing companies with a net worth over $6 million or average net income after tax for the previous two years over $2 million
- Manufacturing companies with more than 250 employees unless the business is below the net worth or net income amounts described previously
- Other investment companies or lending institutions

If you approach a venture firm that is an SBIC for funding, you'll want to be sure that your business meets these SBIC investment criteria. Most SBICs note their SBIC status on their web site or in their firm brochures.

Private equity groups. Private equity groups are usually hedge funds or other private capital pools that are funded by pension funds, money management firms, other institutions, and select high net worth investors. Some private equity firms are funded from family fortunes like those of the Hunt brothers, the Bass brothers, and the children of Sam Walton, Wal-Mart's founder. These families have numerous partnerships and limited liability companies that buy equity or debt in small and mid-cap companies.

Private equity groups usually fund:
- Early-stage investments similar to those made by venture capital firms
- Operating- and mature-stage businesses needing mezzanine financing
- Mature companies' buyouts in management-led transactions and leveraged "recaps"

Leveraged recaps. Leveraged recaps are structured similarly to management-led buyouts. However, instead of the management team increasing its ownership, it reduces its ownership. The private equity group simultaneously buys equity that effectively replaces the equity cashed out by the management team. The private equity group's equity is also used to meet minimum equity requirements imposed by outside lenders. Outside lenders provide the "leverage" part of the recap by funding revolvers or term loans used for growth capital. Some private equity groups provide both the equity and debt needed in a leveraged recap or guarantee the debt financing provided by outside lenders.

Many private equity groups finance:

- Leveraged recaps of family-owned businesses or large ownership stakes in private companies
- ESOP and employee-led buyouts of retiring management
- Management-led buyouts
- Startup and early-stage companies with some infrastructure, a strong management team, and good business fundamentals

Typical Preferred Stock Terms for Venture and Private Equity Investors

Most venture or private equity investors don't purchase common stock or will put only a small part of their investment in common stock. This is because preferred stock can be "customized" to include terms that give the investor greater downside protection and more upside participation than common stock. So, preferred stock sold to venture or private equity investors usually includes

▬ *Conversion rights* into common stock if the business gets an IPO done or is going to be sold or merged

▬ *Optional conversion rights* at the investor's discretion

▬ *Mandatory redemption rights* that kick in if an IPO or a sale doesn't occur within three to seven years—once triggered, the redemption terms say the business must repurchase the preferred stock in annual increments over two or three years. Redemption rights often include a *redemption premium* that gives the investor some additional return that's a "penalty" for the business's failure to complete an IPO or sale. If the business doesn't have cash to redeem the preferred stock, it converts into a controlling common stock position.

▬ *Antidilution rights* for specified events (stock splits, dividends, mergers) and *price antidilution rights* that kick in if the business sells common stock below the price at which the preferred stock converts into common stock

▬ *Cumulative dividends* payable in cash or a PIK security (i.e., by the business issuing more preferred stock) that must be redeemed with the rest of the preferred stock and that's part of the liquidation preference

▬ *Liquidation preferences* that give the investor back the amount invested plus some minimum return before the common stockholders get any dividends or sale proceeds—some liquidation preferences have a *ratchet clause* that automatically increases the liquidation preference if the preferred stock hasn't been redeemed or converted by specific dates.

■ *Voting rights* that let the preferred stockholder vote on an as-if-converted basis on all matters voted on by the common stockholders

■ *Approval rights* under which the preferred stockholders can approve or disapprove

- Acquisitions
- Change of control transactions
- Sale of new preferred stock
- Changes to preferred stock rights
- Changes in use of proceeds from the financing
- Fundamental changes in the business
- Changes in the number of directors unless the preferred stockholders add directors because the business hasn't met financial targets
- Transactions with officers or directors not approved by independent board members
- Changes in compensation for executive officers
- Options or warrants granted over predetermined amounts
- Modifications to the articles of incorporation or bylaws

■ *Rights of first refusal or preemptive rights* to purchase additional equity or debt that the business sells, subject to a standard exception for sales to strategic partners

■ *Standard tag-along and drag-along rights* and, in some situations, an *equity claw-back* for senior management's benefit

■ *Registration rights* for common stock that's issued when the preferred stock is converted, including *demand and piggyback rights*, with all expenses paid by your business

■ *Language* about board representation, financial reporting, budget review, operational issues, inspection rights, key man life insurance, and management continuity

■ *Payment of all legal fees* for the preferred stock purchasers and indicating which side's lawyer will first prepare the investment documents

■ *A "sunset" provision* that automatically terminates most preferred stockholders' rights when an IPO is completed.

Preferred stock terms are first described in a term sheet prepared by the venture or private equity investor. The investor and the business sometimes sign a version of the term sheet or negotiate terms and then sign a letter of intent.

Real World Example

One of my clients received a term sheet from a venture investor that appears in the appendix. As you'll see, this term sheet has many of the terms and conditions in it that have already been discussed. Even though each venture or private equity investor has its own term sheet form, this sample is fairly typical of what you would expect to see in a proposed venture financing. (*Note*: The names and investment amounts have been changed to ensure confidentiality.) If you want to know what you'll get when negotiating terms with a venture or private equity firm, spend some time reviewing the appendix.

Early stage IPOs. An early-stage IPO occasionally offers a financing option for development-stage companies when the market window opens. The most recent example of this phenomenon was the IPO boom for dot com companies in 1998 and 1999. You should know this event for what it is: a speculative bubble that inevitably disappears as values go back to traditional models. This doesn't mean that you should disregard opportunities for financing created by market forces, but an open IPO window for early-stage companies can't usually be planned for. The early-stage IPO's principal advantage is that the business will be valued by investment bankers based on trading prices for public companies considered comparable to yours. Public companies trade at earnings or EBITDA multiples that are considerably higher than private company multiples paid in private financing or sale transactions. So if your business can get an early-stage IPO done, the valuation you get will be higher than in any other financing. However, the IPO process is time consuming and expensive, and if the market takes a turn for the worse, your IPO might not get done.

Table 3-1 lists the relative advantages and disadvantages for the most common early-stage equity financings. As discussed earlier, there are some tradeoffs among different financing options, including

- Time it takes to get funding
- The business's valuation

TABLE 3-1

*Early-Stage Equity Financing Sources—
Key Advantages and Disadvantages*

Common Sources for Early-Stage Equity Financings	Key Advantages	Key Disadvantages
Founders, friends, and family	Speed; simple documents; higher valuations often acceptable	Limited funds availability
Angel investors	Funding availability; typically simple documents; valuation more favorable than institutional investor	Time to find; funding amount per investor usually limited; structure may be variable, requiring more documents and adding to cost
Venture and private equity firms	Capital availability—both time to funding and amount	Control issues; valuation usually lower; high returns required for investment; complex documentation; higher expenses to document; limits on future operations and funding
Early-stage IPO	Valuation is unbeatable	Time to complete an IPO and the cost can be serious obstacles; market downturn risks IPO being called off

- Cost (in dollars and/or control)
- Funding availability

For example, venture financing can be gotten quickly once terms are agreed upon (since venture firms can "write the check"), but it takes longer to find and negotiate terms with multiple angel investors. The venture firm will, however, have restrictions on your operations and approval rights like those described earlier, while angel investors won't often bargain for similar rights. Also, friends and family might pay a higher price for stock in the business than, say, a venture firm, but friends and family probably have fewer investment dollars available. Again, the tradeoff between only getting enough funding for six months' operations versus getting enough for two years has a price: your business will get a higher valuation from friends and family, but the venture firm's funds give you more time to implement your business plan. As you think about funding options for your business, keep these tradeoffs in mind.

Debt Financing Options in the Early Stage

Debt financing in the development stage is very limited since the business doesn't have cash flow to service the debt. Most early-stage funding sources aren't interested in making loans to your business unless the loans are accompanied by an equity kicker. Let's briefly consider the advantages, disadvantages, and timing issues of early-stage debt financing.

Advances from founders, officers, and directors. Advances from founders, officers, and directors are often made to meet working capital needs in a business's early years. These advances sometimes are non-interest-bearing or pay interest using a PIK security and are often due on demand. The loans are usually tied to warrants or options that allow the lender to buy common stock in the business at a token exercise price. The most common issue in "insider" debt funding is deciding if the founders, officers, and directors will simply buy new stock in the company or loan money to it. Unless all founders, officers, and directors are investing additional funds in the business in amounts proportionate to their existing ownership, loans can be a better way to meet short-term capital needs because

- Loans won't have an immediate impact on ownership percentages if the equity kicker isn't exercisable for some minimum time
- Loans at the development stage can be secured by a first lien on the business's assets because the business doesn't have bank debt
- If the lenders want to get an early, partial return of their "investment" in the business, they can ask that some proceeds from the next financing be used to repay outstanding loans
- if the business generates cash flow and qualifies for bank debt, the bank is often willing to fund insider loan repayments if the founder or officer gives the bank a personal guarantee

SBA loans. As previously discussed, the most common SBA debt financing is the *SBA-guaranteed loan*. These loans are limited in amount and are often available only to startups or early-stage businesses that are not eligible for other debt financing. Where available, SBA-guaranteed loans are a great financing option because they have low interest rates that reflect the credit enhancement offered by the SBA (the guarantee). The limits we've discussed on *SBA direct loans* are such that these loans aren't available to most businesses. Since the business has to be turned down for an SBA-guaranteed loan and the loan amount can't exceed $150,000, only the smallest businesses and startups will get SBA direct loans. This limited availability means that these loans can't be counted on to meet most businesses' financing needs.

Lease financing. Lease financing has a higher cost than bank financing but is available for equipment types and small businesses that wouldn't qualify for bank financing. For example, while banks might be reluctant to make loans to buy special-purpose medical imaging equipment, lease financing is often available from medical equipment manufacturers for specialized surgery centers that use this equipment. Because the manufacturer usually sells supplies, servicing contracts, and add-on equipment to its customers, growing its installed equipment base is in its financial interest. For this reason, the manufacturer will assume more financing risk than a bank. The manufacturer also has contacts among its other customers that make the equipment's resale, or re-lease, more likely if the equipment is repossessed. Manufacturers that don't do their own lease financing sometimes outsource financing to specialty finance companies that give businesses favorable lease rates. These lower rates are often based on the manufacturer's agreement to buy back the equipment for preset prices during the lease if the equipment is repossessed.

Because lease financing is based primarily on the equipment's value, you can often get lease financing without providing a personal guarantee. If personal guarantees are needed, the guarantor is usually responsible for any deficiency after the equipment is sold or re-leased. Banks do not typically provide early-stage lease financing and are reluctant to make loans to buy equipment that is not readily salable. Banks are also more focused on cash flow and are not as willing to assume high use rates for "income producing" equipment as manufacturers or specialty finance companies are.

Hard money lenders. The final source of debt financing for the development-stage small business is hard money lenders. These lenders are

- Bridge capital lenders
- Angel investor groups
- Unregulated specialty finance companies
- Small private equity investors

that engage in highly risky lending transactions. Between exorbitant interest rates, collateral requirements, and fees and expenses charged by hard money lenders, this is the most expensive debt financing a business can get. Because hard money lenders also want personal guarantees from management, getting this financing can result in personal exposure too.

Real World Example

A husband and wife team ran a business that experienced good growth over several years but then saw its sales decline as technology in its industry changed. As sales slowed, the bank got more nervous and finally asked the business to find another financing source. The husband and wife explored setting up a bank line with several other local banks but couldn't get a new credit line that would come close to replacing the old one. Finally, they learned about a hard money lender with a history of financing businesses using high interest rate debt and applied for a loan. The hard money lender offered to replace the existing revolver with a slightly larger credit line, but also asked for a second mortgage on the owners' house. The loan documents had so many covenants and financial ratios for the business to meet that it was almost certain the lender would end up with the business if *anything* went wrong. In spite of these facts, the husband and wife decided they had no choice but to go ahead with this lender. They were also convinced that the greater availability under the new credit line would give them breathing room to turn the business around. After getting the loan, sales continued to fall, and the lender later foreclosed on the business's assets. The husband and wife team had to sell their house to avoid foreclosure and pay off the deficiency owed to the lender. They clearly would have been better off if they had simply sold the business's assets and paid off the old bank line.

Instead, by taking on higher cost debt that contributed to the business's failure, the husband and wife were left with a smaller house and a higher mortgage. As the old poker saying goes, "you got to know when to hold 'em, and when to fold 'em." Think twice before going to a hard money lender!

Table 3-2 shows the key advantages and disadvantages for the most common early-stage debt financings. As with equity financing, the principal advantages and disadvantages revolve around the cost and time to get financed, although collateral is another issue to consider.

TABLE 3-2

Early-Stage Debt Financing Sources—
Key Advantages and Disadvantages

Common Sources for Early-Stage Debt Financings	Key Advantages	Key Disadvantages
Founders, friends, and family	Speed; simple documents; loan repayment may occur earlier than equity sales; collateral often not an issue	Limited funds; dilution from an equity kicker; possible ownership percentage changes if equity kicker exercised
SBA-guaranteed loans	Low cost; no equity kickers; SBA guarantee enhances collateral; relatively low exposure on personal guarantees	Time to get; conditions to qualify; limits on loan amounts
Equipment manufacturers/ lease financing	Typically fast; equipment is primary collateral; expenses are low	Higher cost than bank debt; limited equipment types qualify; may require supply or service contracts
Hard money lenders	Funds availability when other sources are tapped out	High cost; exposure on personal guarantees; expenses to close and keep financing in place

OPERATING STAGE: EQUITY AND DEBT ALTERNATIVES

In the operating stage, your business has many more financing options to choose from. This blessing, however, can be mixed. The simple decisions you made when choosing among different financings in the development stage are now much more complex, and the factors that affect your decision aren't reducible to numbers in all cases. Consider the following issues that come up in operating stage financing:

▬ You can finance the business by selling stock to many retail investors in a private placement or by getting one or two large institutional investors—each with its own positive and negative considerations

▬ You can get financing from a strategic partner, but the partner can end up controlling your business or competing against you using the knowledge it gets from the partnership

▬ If you try to calculate your business's cost of capital, the financing options will differ so much that you can't always make direct comparisons (*e.g.*, you can't directly compare the cost of warrants or preferred stock)

▬ Market conditions can have a big (and unforeseeable) impact on IPOs and follow-on public financing

▬ It's hard to quantify and compare valuation and control issues in equity financings against limited availability and personal exposure that comes with debt financing

Selecting operating-stage financing is often not about making the right choice but rather deciding what financing option appears better than others. You can choose a financing that is based on assumptions about

- Market or economic conditions
- Addition of key management
- Relationships with financial institutions, investors, or strategic partners
- Factors that affect the business that are outside of your control

only to later find out that your assumptions have to be tossed out the window. Without a crystal ball, making the correct choice sometimes involves guesswork that isn't based on known facts—and may even require a little bit of luck!

Real World Example

One of my clients was told that it would receive a term sheet from a merchant banking firm that would provide all the financing the business could use over the following two years. While the merchant banking firm was conducting due diligence and talking with management, the president continued to pursue other financing options through two strategic partners. When the merchant bank's term sheet arrived some weeks later, the terms were so one-sided that the management team would have given up control for far less money than was initially discussed. Fortunately, the president's continued discussions with the strategic partners resulted in the business getting a term sheet a week later from one potential partner that was clearly more favorable. The moral of the story—when permitted, most operating-stage small businesses are best served by simultaneously negotiating with several alternative financing sources. Exploring different financing options is not difficult since the same business plan, with minor modifications, can be used to present your business to both equity and debt financing sources. Having a backup plan you can use if a particular financing isn't available or is too expensive is just good business.

Equity Financing Options in the Operating Stage

The operating-stage business usually gets equity financing from the same investors that finance early-stage businesses, as well as

- "Retail" private placements
- Institutional investors
- Public offerings
- Strategic partners

Retail private placements. A retail private placement is a private sale of common or preferred stock to many individual, or retail, investors. The terms *private placement*, *placement*, or *private offering* are used interchangeably to describe stock that is sold privately and not in a public offering. Your small business can conduct its own retail private placement, called a *self-underwritten placement*, or can hire an investment banking firm to sell stock to retail investors. In a self-underwritten placement, the officers and directors typically sell stock to friends, family, and associates. The securities laws let the business's officers, directors, and employees sell stock without being registered as brokers so long as no commissions or other compensation is paid for making sales. Some retail private placements are hybrids that let the company sell stock through its officers and directors but also pay commissions to investment banking firms that get investors to buy stock.

When a retail private placement is being sold by an investment banking firm, it agrees to solicit retail investors on a *best efforts* basis. This means the investment banker is obligated to use only its best efforts to find retail investors, and the banker doesn't guarantee, or underwrite, the placement. There are two types of best efforts placements: the all-or-none and the mini-maxi. If a $2 million offering is structured as a best efforts, *all-or-none* placement, the investment banker will use its best efforts to find retail purchasers for $2 million worth of stock. If the offering expires and less than $2 million has been collected, the investment banker must refund the money it collected and won't get any commissions for the stock sales. If the offering expires and $2 million in stock has been sold, a closing is held, and the company gets the placement's proceeds, minus commissions and any expenses it owes the investment banker. In a *mini-maxi* placement, some minimum amount, like $1 million, and a maximum amount, like $2 million, are disclosed in the offering document. The offering document is known as a *private placement memorandum*, a *placement memorandum*, or simply a *memorandum*. The memorandum says that if the placement proceeds exceed $1 million, a closing can take place because the minimum has been exceeded. The private offering usually continues until (i) the offering period expires or (ii) the full $2 million is raised, when a second closing takes place.

The mini-maxi placement has some obvious advantages:

■ If the sales effort falls short of collecting $2 million, the business will still receive some capital, even if this is less than the optimal amount

■ Offering expenses like legal, accounting, printing, and roadshow costs are covered if at least $1 million is collected

■ The company and/or the investment banker can continue the selling effort after the initial closing

■ If the sales effort is successful, the business can still close on the full $2 million

A retail private placement might set the minimum investment per investor at a small amount like $10,000 or at $50,000, $100,000, or more. We'll discuss later why minimum investments and an investor's financial status, sophistication, and investment history are critical to deciding what disclosure you have to give to potential and actual investors. For now, though, remember this guideline:

- The lower an investor's net worth
- The less his or her financial sophistication
- The shorter his or her history of investing in similar companies or stock

the more disclosure your business must provide to potential and actual investors before you accept an investment.

Institutional investors. Institutional investors often invest in operating-stage companies. In contrast to a retail private placement, an *institutional placement* is a private stock sale to one or several institutional investors. Institutional investors are typically

- "Second-stage" venture investors
- Private equity groups that offer growth capital to operating-stage businesses
- Company-organized funds that are designated for investment in strategic partners or industry opportunities
- Pooled investment funds managed by a money manager or investment advisor

Few institutional investors are willing to buy equity in an operating-stage private business unless the business has a clear exit strategy already planned, like an IPO or sale. Also, institutional investors are likely to demand too much ownership and to give the business too low a value for you to consider an equity investment acceptable. If equity is purchased, it will probably be preferred stock with characteristics similar to preferred stock sold to first-round venture investors. For these reasons, it is more common for institutional investors to fund operating-stage companies' debt that is partially convertible to equity or is accompanied by an equity kicker.

Public offering. A public offering for an operating-stage business should be considered if market conditions are receptive to IPOs or follow-on offerings. A follow-on offering is a "second," "third," or other additional public offering by a company that is already public, as opposed to an initial public offering. In the operating stage, public offerings are usually small (from $5 million to $20 million) and are sometimes called *public venture capital*. Just as we saw in early-stage IPOs, the valuation an operating-stage business will receive in an IPO or follow-on offering is far above the valuation arrived at by any other equity investor. This must be balanced against the time and cost of pursuing a public offering that isn't completed because market conditions deteriorate or for other reasons.

Retail public offering. A retail public offering is almost always a *firm commitment* offering that is sold to individual investors by investment bankers. The "lead" investment banker for a retail public offering will often have several offices staffed by brokers and usually recruits other investment banking firms to join the selling "syndicate." In a firm commitment retail offering, the investment banker underwrites the offering and agrees to deliver the proceeds to the company three days after the stock begins trading. Bankers that underwrite firm commitment offerings must have minimum capital levels and meet regulatory guidelines that apply to underwriting activities.

It is important to understand that firm commitment offerings are not guaranteed offerings because

▬ The company and the investment banker only have a letter of intent between them until the offering is cleared by the SEC, or "declared effective." The letter of intent is cancelable at any time by the company or the investment banker, which means that either can walk away from the offering at any time.

▬ When the SEC declares the offering effective, the company and the investment banker sign a contract, known as the *underwriting agreement*. Even after the underwriting agreement is signed, the investment banker can still cancel the offering if there is a natural disaster, war, large decline in the market, key management member's death, or other significant negative event. (This is known as the *market-out clause*.)

Institutional public offering. Institutional public offerings of $40 million to $100 million or more that are sold mostly to institutional investors are also firm commitment offerings and can be canceled just like retail public offerings. Even the largest investment bankers sometimes cancel an offering before the SEC declares the offering effective. This usually happens when the investment banker has taken the business on a roadshow and has gotten feedback from institutions or the investment banker's own institutional sales force indicating that there isn't enough interest for the offering to be successful. Put another way, if the investment banker doubts that demand for the stock will keep the trading price above the offering price, the banker might cancel or postpone the offering until market conditions improve. When you see references in the media to companies that have withdrawn their offering or that have withdrawn the registration statement that registers stock and is filed with the SEC, the withdrawal has usually been prompted by the investment banker canceling the letter of intent because they don't believe the offering can be sold.

If the lead investment banker has very limited capital, the lead investment banker will want to sell the public offering on a best efforts basis. This means that the investment banker doesn't put its capital at risk but rather attempts to fund the all-or-none or mini-maxi public offering just as if it were a retail private placement. Few investment banking firms do best efforts public offerings in today's financing environment.

Strategic partners. Strategic partners offer another financing alternative that is sometimes available to operating-stage businesses. Strategic partners will sometimes buy a minority ownership stake that comes with licensed technology rights, exclusivity for specific markets or guaranteed access to key products. These partnerships are *strategic* because the investor is not merely a financial partner but is usually in a business or industry that's related to yours. Strategic partnerships became common in the late 1990s as a financing tool for small businesses that were mostly in the technology industry. Among the higher profile partnerships were those between

- Routing and switching equipment manufacturers and small high-speed Internet access providers
- Telecommunications infrastructure companies and small voice and data carriers
- Larger Internet search engines and e-businesses offering products or services targeted at specific markets
- Software companies getting access to particular products like video or sound technologies or new sales channels

Strategic investments take various forms, but they almost always involve equity purchases in the small business. This is because the strategic investor getting a technology license or new sales channel wants to capture part of the business's increased value that comes from its use of the technology or new sales. This is particularly true if the strategic investor is a large cap company whose association with the small business will validate the small business's technology for sale to other customers. The savvy small business owner will look for the strategic partnership to

- Increase the business's equity capital base
- Validate its technology
- Create a marketing "buzz" to attract new strategic partners

Strategic partners often invest by buying new preferred stock that has more favorable conversion terms than preferred stock sold to financial investors. This reflects the nonfinancial benefits the small business plans to get from the strategic relationship. Strategic investors often will accept a lower dividend or interest rate than financial investors because they are more focused on the long-term benefits of the relationship and equity investment. If the strategic investor is not sure about the prospects for the small business's technology or sales to a new channel, the strategic investor might tie the preferred stock conversion rate to sales or other targets. This is how a performance-based conversion would work: if sales from the technology fell short of expectations during specific periods or the small business couldn't meet implementation or customization deadlines, the conversion rate would "rachet" down to a lower level. Like rachet clauses used by venture and private equity firms, these clauses are powerful ways to tie your technology's performance or market penetration to the strategic investor's ownership.

Special note. Strategic partners have nonfinancial as well as financial goals. So, their goals are not based solely on the financial returns on the investment over a specific timeframe. For this reason, an investment proposal from a strategic investor will typically be more favorable to your small business than a proposal for the same investment amount from a so-called financial investor. When considering equity capital alternatives at this stage, you should review potential strategic investors and consider how your technology or product can be partnered with other products, services, or distribution channels in ways that would benefit a potential strategic partner. Some creative thinking could open up investment possibilities that are far better for your business than more traditional financing options.

Table 3-3 shows the relative advantages and disadvantages for the most common forms of operating-stage equity financing. Notice that you have many more financing options at this stage in the corporate life cycle than what's available to the early-stage business.

TABLE 3-3
Operating-Stage Equity Financing Sources—
Key Advantages and Disadvantages

Common Sources for Operating-Stage Equity Financings	Key Advantages	Key Disadvantages
Founders, friends, and family	Inexpensive; few limits; little documentation	Availability often restricted
Angel investors	No high fees; may give loan guarantees; eager to help management make business successful; usually simple documents	May be limited follow-on money; expect big returns; difficult to find
Venture capital firms	Funding availability; prefer to invest large amounts; industry knowledge	Expect big returns; expect some control; difficult to find the right firm; extensive documentation
Private equity groups	Availability; often fund when other sources will not; will customize funding proposals; industry knowledge	Expect big returns; control issues; difficult to find; extensive documentation
Private placements	Generally inexpensive and fast; structure and valuation often under business's control	Limited funding; compliance with SEC and other documentation requirements may increase legal, accounting, and other expenses; need for investment banker to assist in sales can increase cost
Institutional investors	Funding availability; experience in the industry or market may benefit business	Expensive; complex documentation; valuation often an issue
IPOs and follow-on public offerings	Valuation higher than all alternatives; funding availability in good market	Accountable to new shareholders; must adhere to complex SEC regulations; relatively slow process; expensive
Strategic partners	Less expensive than financial investments; promotes working together to make business grow	Complex documentation; possible restriction on technology or products sales to others; conflicts of interest can complicate investment

Debt Financing Options

As the small business reaches the operating stage, debt financing options become realistic (and good) alternatives to equity financing. Debt financing from banks and equipment vendors or leasing firms is very attractive because

- These financing sources do not demand equity
- Interest costs and fees associated with operating stage revolvers and term loans are usually reasonable
- The expenses (legal, filing fees and other) for revolvers or leases are low

Operating-stage companies can usually negotiate revolvers from local banks or local branches of larger banks and are not condemned to dealing with hard money lenders or friends and family to get debt financing. Institutional investors and private equity groups will also make mezzanine loans to select small businesses in this stage, although these loans will be coupled with warrants or conversion features that increase the "true" cost well above traditional bank debt or lease financing.

Banks. Bank financing for operating-stage companies are usually revolvers with the characteristics described in Chapter 2. Revolvers are usually an operating-stage business's senior debt. The revolver is documented using promissory notes, credit, and security agreements or line-of-credit notes that are usually renewed annually if the business is in compliance with the financial and nonfinancial covenants. Smaller revolvers are sometimes documented in as little as five or six pages and are usually quick to negotiate and close. As the revolver's size goes up, the documents' complexity will also increase as the bank

- Imposes more covenants or reporting obligations on the business
- Puts more limits on advance rates by, for instance, adopting different advance rates for raw material, work in process, or finished goods inventory
- Gets notice of changes in key management personnel
- Offers you alternate rate structures, like interest based on the bank's prime rate or LIBOR

Almost without exception, banks will get personal guarantees from the business's founders or largest stockholders. While many guarantors don't have the net worth or assets to pay off the revolver if the business gets in trouble, banks often want the guarantee anyway to have leverage if things get difficult. With larger revolvers, banks usually ask the founders or management team to sign support agreements that force these individuals to help the bank sell collateral and collect accounts receivable for up to 12 months after a default.

Institutional investors and private equity groups. Debt financing for operating-stage companies from institutional investors and private equity groups is often called debt but, as discussed earlier, will come with conversion rights or warrants to increase the return to an "equity equivalent" level. Mezzanine debt generally comes with terms that are close or identical to preferred stock bought by a venture or private equity investor. Many mezzanine debt facilities do not require personal guarantees from the founders or management team because the investor's focus is on the equity kicker's upside as opposed to the strict collateral and credit analysis performed by a bank.

Securitizations. Securitizations are used by many operating-stage businesses to fund their financing requirements if their operations generate consistent and predictable cash flows from accounts receivable. These receivables come mostly from mortgages, credit card transactions, equipment leases, and auto loans or leases. As we saw earlier, the business usually funds the loan or lease transaction from a so-called warehouse line of credit that is then repaid from the securitization proceeds. Securitizations typically carry a low all-in cost of capital. For businesses with access to the asset-backed securities markets, securitizations are one of the most cost-effective ways to convert senior debt to low-cost, longer term debt financing.

When credit quality and business conditions decline, securitizations are difficult to complete, and the obligation to substitute performing leases or loans for nonperforming ones reduces cash flow. Before pursuing a securitization, you should consider conditions in the asset-backed securities markets, general economic factors, industry developments, and the credit quality of your business's receivables.

Table 3-4 shows the advantages and disadvantages for the most common forms of operating-stage debt financing.

MATURE STAGE: EQUITY AND DEBT ALTERNATIVES

As your business matures, it can access many different financing alternatives and is usually in the enviable position of choosing

TABLE 3-4
Operating-Stage Debt Financing Sources—
Key Advantages and Disadvantages

Common Sources for Operating-Stage Debt Financings	Key Advantages	Key Disadvantages
Banks	No ownership dilution; continuing credit availability; fewer reporting responsibilities and requirements than mezzanine alternatives	Requires collateral or personal guarantees; loan agreements include restrictive covenants; interest payments; must have cash flow to repay
Institutional investors and private equity groups	Availability	Expensive; extensive documentation; cash flow necessary to pay debt; ownership dilution from equity kickers
Equipment vendors and leasing firms	Down payment usually smaller than equity needed to buy; simple and quick; can often be modified	Cost over time usually higher than buying or senior debt; cash flow needed to service lease payments; limitations on eligible equipment types
Commercial finance companies	Availability; willing to take more risks than traditional banks	Higher interest rates than banks; cash flow needed to service debt
Securitizations	Low cost of capital; frees up bank lines of credit; speed good when the business has been rated	Rating requirement; cost of substituting performing loans or leases for nonperforming; extensive documentation; credit enhancements usually necessary

among alternatives that all offer low costs of capital. Now, though, you'll consider issues other than the cost of capital when deciding on a particular financing. These other issues include

- Management's wanting some liquidity means that either a public offering or a leveraged recap is the right choice

- If a sale transaction is planned, you'll want to set the stage for a better sale price by getting into a strategic partnership or doing a public offering
- Getting an institutional investor to provide mezzanine financing to demonstrate credibility and help you enter new markets without overcommitting your financial resources.

Equity Financing Options

The mature small business is usually able to get equity financing from many sources. Taking advantage of less-expensive equity financing options means the mature-stage business will pursue:

- Public offerings
- Retail private placements
- Institutional investors
- Strategic partners

The discussion of these financing alternatives under "Operating Stage: Equity and Debt Alternatives" is generally accurate for mature-stage companies, with a few differences:

▬ The mature business's operations are usually large enough to get interest in a public offering from regional and national investment banking firms. Your business might get bids from several investment banking firms and end up with a more competitive price and other terms for a public offering.

▬ The public offering's size is likely to be $30 million or more, meaning that management and the founders are often selling shareholders in the offering.

▬ The retail private placement will still be a best efforts placement, but your business can now get a larger investment banker to assist in the selling effort, increasing chances for a successful closing.

▬ Institutional investors are more likely to invest in a mature-stage business than one in the operating stage. Because the mature business has reached critical mass, institutional investors will view the investment as less risky and will give it a higher value.

Table 3-5 shows the advantages and disadvantages for the most common mature-stage equity financing alternatives.

Debt Financing Options

As with equity financing in the mature stage, debt financing is available to the mature business from many sources at considerably less cost than what an operating-stage business pays. Debt financing has a lower all-in cost when compared to equity financing; however,

TABLE 3-5
Mature-Stage Equity Financing Sources—
Key Advantages and Disadvantages

Common Sources for Mature-Stage Equity Financings	Key Advantages	Key Disadvantages
Public offerings	Valuation; liquidity for management and founders	Expensive; responsible to stockholders; compliance cost with complex SEC regulations; competitive information and compensation disclosure; potential class action litigation risk
Private placements	Quick; relatively inexpensive	Documentation for disclosure and SEC regulation compliance is complex
Institutional investors	Funding availability; speed	Expensive; reduction in control
Strategic partners	Funding availability; work together to develop business	Time to negotiate; possible conflicts between business and investment goals; reduction in control

(1) interest expense reduces available cash flow, and (2) debt financing offers no liquidity for management, making debt financing less attractive. This is even more the case when equity financings are done through selling non-dividend-bearing common stock. Keep in mind, though, that bank revolvers and term loans for companies in the mature stage will probably come without personal guarantees and the rate charged will often be below the prime rate.

One debt financing that offers the best of both worlds is a leveraged recap. As we've already mentioned, many institutional investors, principally investment funds and private equity groups, fund these transactions. In general, a leveraged recap usually involves

- An "old line" manufacturing, distribution, or service business controlled by one owner or a small stockholder group

- Highly stable and predictable cash flow
- Stockholders who want some personal liquidity while keeping daily operating control and a large ownership stake
- Stockholders who want more capital, director-level expertise, and to acquire complementary companies in the industry

Equipment lease financing is available from more lease finance companies when a business reaches maturity. In some cases, you can set up a leasing credit facility with a bank, insurance company, or equipment vendor that will finance equipment purchases on an ongoing basis. At this level, some lease credit facilities are competitive with, or cost only slightly more than, bank financing. Businesses with major capital equipment needs can use a lease credit facility to finance longer term capital expenditures rather than tying up part of their revolver for these long-term commitments.

Table 3-6 shows the advantages and disadvantages for the most common forms of mature stage debt financing.

TABLE 3-6

Mature-Stage Debt Financing Sources—
Key Advantages and Disadvantages

Common Sources for Mature-Stage Debt Financings	Key Advantages	Key Disadvantages
Banks	Lower interest rates from proven track record; quick; less documentation because relationship is in place	Debt service cost
Institutional investors	Availability; may add to credibility and increase value for next round	Debt service cost; equity kicker might still be needed; board membership and more restrictive covenants than banks
Equipment vendors and leasing firms	Quick; simple documents	Over time, lease credit facility often more expensive than buying

LIQUIDITY STAGE: EQUITY AND DEBT ALTERNATIVES

The liquidity stage is reached when you decide that liquidity for the stockholders is the objective that now outweighs all others. When you reach this stage, the cost of capital becomes irrelevant because you'll be focusing your efforts on creating a liquidity event. Nonetheless, *how* the liquidity event is funded can have great influence on the benefits for the stockholders as well as the costs incurred by the business.

Equity Financing Options

A follow-on public offering is the most common way for the business to get liquidity for the stockholders and management. At this point, the business has typically been public for several years and the stockholders and management have sold small amounts of their stock into the market under Rule 144. But, because

- Volume limitations apply to quarterly Rule 144 sales by officers, directors, and 10% or more shareholders
- Rule 144 sales are public and get negative attention from analysts and institutional investors
- Investment bankers usually discourage large, continuing Rule 144 sales because of the real or perceived impact on the market

most officers and directors of public companies get only limited liquidity through Rule 144 sales. The successful liquidity-stage business should be able to complete a follow-on public offering that includes stock being sold by selling shareholders, including management. A follow-on public offering that includes selling shareholders offers a number of advantages:

■ Officers, directors, and founders will have substantial liquidity in one transaction.

■ The stock sale won't have the kind of negative impact on the market that continuing Rule 144 sales might have.

■ Institutional investors can increase their ownership stake in the business without "chasing" the stock and causing a large run-up in the stock price.

■ The business usually pays the registration costs for the selling stockholders, at least for the officers and directors who want to sell stock.

■ The sales by officers and directors will typically not result in a change in management (other than a planned change), meaning that the follow-on offering will generate liquidity without causing management to lose control. For this reason, follow-on offerings are like management having its cake and eating it too; compare this to a sale transaction where management loses control or ends up working for a different management or ownership team.

A follow-on public offering includes stock sold by the company, the selling shareholders, or a combination. If the business is performing well and has no need for capital, the officers, directors, and founders might be the only sellers. The board of directors decides who will sell stock in the offering unless a selling shareholder has registration rights that force the business to register its shares.

In the liquidity stage, companies will typically consider selling the business. A well-run and profitable small business will often get to choose among buyers from two groups: financial buyers and strategic buyers. As you'd expect, *financial buyers* are private equity groups and institutional investors that purchase companies for investment purposes. *Strategic buyers* usually operate in the same industry as your business or in a related industry. They also believe that combining operations will lead to increased revenues, earnings, market share, or other synergies. This is why strategic buyers are usually willing to pay a premium over the price that financial buyers want to pay.

Special note. A financial buyer will sometimes pay a purchase price equal to that offered by a strategic buyer. This usually happens when the financial buyer has another business in its investment portfolio that would be a strategic buyer if it purchased your business directly. This financial buyer can be the ideal buyer for your business because it usually has substantial financial resources and is willing to pay a "strategic" price. When deciding what buyers you or your banker will approach if you're selling your business, don't overlook financial buyers that have portfolio companies in your industry!

Strategic partners are logical candidates to purchase a business because they usually know the business and did some due diligence when they first invested. The strategic partner is often in a unique position to close a purchase quickly, if speed is important. This must be balanced against a reluctance to inform the strategic partner that you're thinking about selling if you think a sale to a third party could hurt your relationship.

Businesses that want to maximize stockholder value are sometimes forced to auction themselves in a limited or full auction conducted by an investment banking firm, particularly if the business is public. The auction process can be time consuming and expensive and result in early disclosure of the proposed sale, which can hurt relations with customers, suppliers, and employees. While you can take steps to prevent disclosure of sensitive or competitive information until late in the auction process, the fact is that a full auction will often result in competitors finding out information about your business while posing as strategic buyers. For this reason, some businesses instruct their investment banker to conduct a limited auction that excludes actual or potential competitors.

A liquidity discussion would be incomplete without considering the stock versus cash issue. When a private buyer is buying the business, you would naturally insist on a cash purchase because (i) you and the other stockholders would otherwise end up as minority shareholders in a private company, and (ii) a stock transaction with a private company gets you no liquidity. A public company buyer, on the other hand, might purchase your business for stock in a tax-free exchange at a more favorable value than it would pay in cash. Consider a number of factors in this situation, including

- The premium offered to the stockholders for taking stock rather than cash
- The trading history, volume, price range, and other statistics about the buyer's stock, including how many investment bankers (and who) make a market in the stock, institutional investors that own the stock, and research coverage for the company
- Whether other companies have been bought by the public company for stock and, if so, when shares previously sold become freely tradable
- The lock-up period's length when you and the other officers, directors, and principal stockholders can't sell stock or are prevented from doing so by tax regulations
- The state of the industry, general economic conditions, the state of the stock market as a whole, and other "macro" economic factors that affect the stock's value.

If you're approached by a public company buyer with an all or partial stock offer, get advice from your professionals, particularly your tax advisors, about the transaction's impact on you and the other stockholders. The previously listed factors, as well as how these factors affect other objectives, need to be well understood by you and the management team before proceeding. A stock-based offer can be attractive and offer the highest value, but you may also decide that an all-cash offer is better even if that offer puts a lower value on the business. This usually happens when management concludes that the certainty of an all-cash transaction outweighs the tax

TABLE 3-7
Liquidity-Stage Equity Financing Sources— Key Advantages and Disadvantages

Common Sources for Liquidity-Stage Equity Financings	Key Advantages	Key Disadvantages
Public offerings	Substantial liquidity possible in one transaction; no direct impact on market; continued control	Expensive; time consuming; can be stopped by changes in market or business conditions
Strategic partners	Prior business knowledge; often willing to pay premium	Possible negative impact on business relationship; confidentiality issues
Financial buyers	Capital availability; portfolio investments are a reason to pay premium	Lengthy due diligence process; usually unwilling to pay as much as strategic buyer
Strategic buyers	Strategic nature of investment equals higher prices; industry or business knowledge can speed up due diligence	Competitive facts disclosure; negative impact on employees, customers, or suppliers if sale process and possible buyer are disclosed

benefits and any premium the buyer will pay in a tax-free stock exchange.

Table 3-7 shows the sources, and advantages and disadvantages, for the most common forms of liquidity stage equity financing.

Debt Financing Options

In the liquidity stage, debt financing is limited to loans from banks, other financial institutions, or institutional investors that are used to buy back stock. If the debt financing is being used to finance a founder buyout, banks and other financial institutions sometimes insist on getting personal guarantees from management or other credit enhancements. This is particularly true if the bank believes the exiting founder will be difficult to replace or if the remaining management doesn't have as much experience in managing the business.

TABLE 3-8
Liquidity-Stage Debt Financing Sources—
Key Advantages and Disadvantages

Common Sources for Liquidity-Stage Debt Financings	Key Advantages	Key Disadvantages
Banks	Low cost; speed	Need for credit enhancements and continuity in management
Institutional investors	Funds availability	Equity participation nearly always a condition to loan

Institutional investors are sometimes more willing to make loans for a founder's exit if they are able to purchase equity in a leveraged recap or if the other management team members will give the investor an equity kicker. Again, institutional investors in these transactions will be looking for "equity equivalent" returns that make a straight debt financing unlikely.

Table 3-8 sets forth some sources, and the relative advantages and disadvantages, of the most common forms of liquidity-stage debt financing.

CHAPTER PERSPECTIVE

Once you've considered the financing alternatives available in your business's stage of development, you'll need to refine your search by considering how specific issues will affect your selection. These include whether equity or debt is best, the financing needs, how much each source can fund, the cost of different financings, and each source's advantages and disadvantages. The time to close each financing must be considered, and your planning should take into account both unforeseen delays in the process and backup plans in case a particular financing becomes unavailable. There will continue to be tradeoffs between cost, the time necessary to get financing, valuation, and ownership dilution. Preferred stock is the most common form of equity bought by venture and private equity firms, institutional investors, and many strategic partners. Bank and mezzanine financing are the most common debt financing sources. As your business grows, you'll have a greater number of choices for financing that become progressively less costly.

When the business reaches maturity, you'll need to consider financing alternatives that will maximize value in later sale or public offering transactions and meet your liquidity goals. While there is often no one "right" choice for a financial partner along the way, your plan should be to review the most likely financing alternatives for your business at its stage of development. Concentrate on those sources that are best suited for helping the business reach its goals—lowering capital costs, creating liquidity, and maximizing value for the stockholders. Now let's talk about how you actually find financing sources that fund the equity and debt needed to grow your business.

Finding Financing Sources and Understanding Their Goals

CHAPTER 4

INTRODUCTION AND MAIN POINTS

This chapter covers how to find funding sources offering equity and debt financing that is right for your business's stage of development. It lists web site addresses for investor and lender databases that offer specific financing types like early-stage equity or mezzanine debt, and others that can help you find financing sources that specialize in funding early-, operating-, mature-, or liquidity-stage businesses. For each financing source, we've discussed their key goals to help you understand what the investor or lender is looking for when they're first approached by a business looking for financing. After studying this chapter, you will

▬ Know how to locate investors and lenders that are right for your business, whatever its size

▬ Understand the motivations and goals of different investors or lenders

▬ Be comfortable in choosing potential investors or lenders to go to with your proposal

Special note and disclaimer. The publisher and the author do not endorse or recommend, and are not affiliated with, any of the web sites or search engines mentioned in this chapter. These web sites and search engines illustrate how you can find and learn about investors and lenders interested in funding your business, but this information can be found on other web sites and in nonelectronic media. The publisher and the author expressly disclaim any liability or responsibility for use of the listed web sites or search engines, including any express or implied warranties of any kind. The publisher and the author have not investigated or analyzed the information on these web sites and search engines and make no representations that the information contained on them is complete, correct, reliable, or current. Before using these web sites or search engines, you should conduct your own due diligence and make an independent decision about whether to do business with, or use, any of the web sites and search engines that are named in this chapter.

FINDING EARLY- AND OPERATING-STAGE INVESTORS

Founders, friends, and family. Founders, friends, and family usually have preexisting relationships with you or other members of management. This means that you and the other officers and directors each have your own contacts who might be potential investors or lenders for your early-stage business. Most founders lack the net worth to finance the business on their own, so it's not unusual for early-stage businesses to get financing from friends and family. In fact, sometimes friends and family are eager to "buy into" your concept if they believe you've got a home run on your hands. But, having friends and family members as investors or lenders can leave you open to a barrage of questions about how the business is doing at every family get-together, holiday meal, and party. If you expect and can deal with this, the price is sometimes worth the financing you get for the business. If not, be cautious about how much financing you look for from friends and family. It's ironic that when some friends and family invest, they begin to think you owe them a weekly update that they wouldn't dream of asking for from management of a business run by nonfamily members. If you believe in the old saying that money doesn't belong between friends or family members, be selective when you're looking for funding close to home.

Real World Example

One of my clients came up with an interesting approach to handling the friends and family issue when going out for early-stage funding. Because the two founders had some contacts among friends and family, they decided each of them would talk to the other one's friends and family about investing in the business. Their theory, which actually worked fairly well, was that it would be easier for each founder to discuss business and financing issues with non-family members. So, each founder talked to the other's friends and family about investing. The founders had a great relationship and trusted each other, so there wasn't any concern between them about what was said to the other's friends and family. Each founder also asked those they spoke with to call him with questions, rather than asking their relative about the business. Most of the friends and family who bought stock respected this request, and the business went on to be funded by a venture firm in the following round. While this approach won't work for every business, it's one way to deal with money issues that might otherwise get in the way of relationships with friends and family.

Angel investors and lenders. Angel investors and lenders are the next funding sources for early- and operating-stage businesses. Angel investors and lenders are often found through

- Prior personal and business relationships
- Industry or professional organizations
- Industry conventions and conferences
- Business incubators and business networking groups
- Contacts made through friends, accountants, lawyers, investment bankers, or even commercial bankers

Angel investors who are on boards of directors and advisory boards can sometimes be found through public filings, fellow entrepreneurs, and professionals.

Angel investors can also be found through the following web sites.

■ *The ACE-Net (Access to Capital Electronic Network),* http://acenet.csusb.edu. This web site lets small businesses and angel investors exchange information; it is set up to match businesses to angels, venture firms, and SBICs that can fund between $250,000 and $5 million. The business fills out an application and pays a $450 subscription fee, at which time its information goes into the database. Angel investors can scan the database and contact companies directly if they want to get more information or begin doing due diligence. The network was organized in 1997 and indicated in 2002 that it had helped businesses get over $700 million in financing with an average transaction of $1.2 million. The network was first set up by the University of New Hampshire and is now partnered with California State University at San Bernardino.

■ *BusinessPartners.com*, www.businesspartners.com. This web site offers services similar to those of ACE-Net, but postings are less expensive at $50 per month or even $20 for one day.

■ *CloudStart.com*, www.cloudstart.com/site1.php. This web site says it has 3,000 accredited investors and will post a summary business plan on its site for viewing by angels for $99 for 12 months.

■ *Garage.com*, www.garage.com. Garage Technology Ventures says that it directly invests venture capital in early-stage businesses and offers a matching service for angels and companies in the technology and medical science markets.

■ *Ground Floor Finance.com*, www.groundfloorfinance.com. This matching service lets your business post its information for six months for $199 or for 12 months for $299. It offers free registration for accredited angel investors who want to browse business listings.

■ *Vfinance.com*, www.vfinance.com. This web site features AngelSearch, a search engine that says it gathers information from public records about angels' investment history, industry preferences, and stock positions. The site also says you can buy all or some records that match your search criteria for a per-record fee.

For venture capital and private equity groups, you can find these investors through the following sources.

■ *The Venture Capital Database*, www.findingmoney.com/vc. This web site has a complete, alphabetized listing of active venture capital firms throughout the United States. The database is organized by office locations, principals, investment preference, minimum investment, transaction size, and fund size. The directory of 630 venture firms and funds is available by e-mail for $147, on CD-ROM for $247, or in a soft cover edition for $42.95.

■ *Vfinance.com*, www.vfinance.com. This web site has a free listing of the venture firms in the United States on its site. This listing does not have the contact information and other facts available on the Venture Capital Database, but you can find specific facts using the search engine on the site for $1.00 per listing.

■ *VcPro Database*, www.vcaonline.com. This web site has a downloadable directory of 3,000 venture firms and funds worldwide, including contact information and investment criteria. The database can be purchased for $99 (downloadable) or on CD-ROM for $112 plus shipping. This database includes listings for 1,700 U.S. firms and funds, 700 European firms and funds, and 460 Asian firms and funds.

■ *Directory of Venture Capital*, found on www.Amazon.com and authored by Kate Lister and Tom Harnish, is a soft cover book that includes contact facts and investment criteria for over 600 U.S. venture firms and funds. The book is available for $27.96.

■ *Private Equity*, http://privateequity.com. This web site contains a list of 1,345 private equity firms, with each listing linked to the private equity firm's own web site. Through each site, you can get contact information and investment criteria. Some of the firms listed also appear in the venture capital directories listed earlier. This is because many venture firms also offer private equity for leveraged recaps, buyouts, and mezzanine financing.

■ When searching "private equity" on the Internet, most search engines will direct you to web sites of "major bracket" investment banking firms like Credit Suisse First Boston, Merrill Lynch, J.P. Morgan Chase & Co., Bear Stearns, and Wachovia. Most large investment banking firms have affiliated private equity funds that manage the firm's own investment capital and also have relationships with independent private equity groups.

■ You can find several of the largest private equity firms like GE Equity Capital Group and Hunt Private Equity (affiliated with the Hunt family of Texas) through search engines including MSN and Google. Use "private equity group" or "private equity groups" as the key search words and then go to the web sites to get contact information and investment criteria.

■ Several well-known private equity groups have gotten considerable media attention for their high-profile transactions or from the returns they generated when an investment was sold or taken public. These firms include The Shansby Group; Trivest, Inc.; Patricof & Co. Ventures, Inc.; Golder Thoma Cressey Rauner (GTCR); Bain Capital; Weiss, Peck & Greer; Hicks, Muse, Tate & Furst; and EOS Partners, L.P.

Retail private placements and early-stage public offerings.

Retail private placements and early-stage public offerings are typically marketed through retail and regional investment banking firms. Rather than concentrating on the individual investor, let's focus on how to find investment bankers that specialize in these placements and offerings. When searching "private placement" on the Internet, most search engines will send you to private equity groups and angel investors' web sites rather than to investment banking firms that help raise retail private placement financing. Instead of searching that term, you should look at the investment banking firms' web sites that you find through the following sites to see if a firm is active in funding retail private placements.

■ *IPO Underwriter Search*, www.ipo.com. This web site contains a list of investment banking firms in the U.S. that are the "managing" bankers, co-managers or syndicate members in public offerings. This list does not appear to have been updated recently as several firms listed are no longer in business. However, you can use the listed phone numbers and office locations for each firm to check their status.

■ *Investment Banks*, www.vfinance.com. This web site gives a more updated but smaller list of investment banking firms that are underwriting initial public offerings.

■ Recent IPO filings, including the name of the managing underwriter and the comanagers, can be accessed through a variety of web sites, including Nasdaq's web site at www.nasdaq.com and the SEC's web site at www.sec.gov.

■ *Hoover's*, www.hoovers.com. This web site has a list of the most recent IPO filings and also lets you search IPOs in the "premium" section by the managing underwriter's name. The "name" listing includes completed offerings and those that are not trading, which is helpful in seeing how many offerings the investment banking firm got done and how many it didn't.

Keep in mind the distinction between a retail private placement (small, probably $2 million or less) and an institutional private placement (large, probably $5 million to $10 million minimum) when looking for private funding. Many investment banking firms say that they help fund "private placements," without clearly describing what type is being referred to. It's safe to assume that the larger the investment banking firm, the more likely the firm gets involved in institutional placements rather than retail placements.

When looking for investment bankers for a retail placement or an IPO, pay special attention to recent filings for IPOs by companies that compete with yours or that are in your industry. If the investment banker is a larger firm, it usually has one or several analysts in-house or knows independent analysts who will provide research coverage for your competitors. If the investment banker employs or uses outside analysts who cover an industry, it is more likely to be interested in providing financing for other companies in that industry. If the investment banking firm believes that it can get the lead underwriting position in a later IPO, it will often help fund an earlier private placement. Some bankers will even ask for a right of first refusal to do the IPO if they help you get your placement funded. Make sure you carefully consider this, though, because you might be precluded from negotiating with other investment bankers who could help you raise more capital or offer better terms.

Real World Example

Another way to spot an investment banker that's a good potential lead underwriter is to get your competitors' stock symbols and search them on the Nasdaq or NYSE sites. Once you put in the stock symbol, you can "click through" to a list of firms that offer research coverage on the competitor's stock. These firms are excellent prospects to fund an IPO, retail private placement, or institutional placement for your small business because they'll have analysts that already cover the industry. One of my clients used this tip to find a larger investment banker when it came time for the business to do an institutional placement about a year after its IPO. As it so happens, the firm's analyst had begun to follow my client's business informally some time before the financing, so she was familiar with the business when the president called. Within a few months, my client had signed an investment banking agreement with the investment banker, and they had their first meetings with potential institutional investors. Shortly afterward, the business got $8 million in additional equity from an investment fund that held interests in several companies with complementary businesses!

Strategic partners and institutional investors. Strategic partners and institutional investors are often more difficult to find because these investors are more company specific. However, if you're looking for these investors, keep a few points in mind:

▄ Strategic partners are often your suppliers, customers, or even integrators that put your business's product into theirs. If you find potential strategic partners that need access to your products or technology, your chances of getting funding get better.

▄ Investment banking firms you find for private or public offerings will often have on-going client relationships with large companies and institutional investors. These relationships are the strongest argument for retaining an investment banker, even if you must pay more for funding. Bankers with direct access to the decision makers at a large company or institutional investor can save you lots of time and money you would otherwise spend searching for strategic and institutional investors. Also, well-connected bankers can get you audiences with investment and financial officers that are typically beyond the reach of all but the most attractive (and persistent) businesses needing funding. While this access comes at a price, you should consider these relationships when deciding whether to use an investment banking firm to approach a strategic partner or institutional investor.

GOALS OF EARLY-STAGE AND OPERATING-STAGE INVESTORS

Early-stage investors who invest in your business are looking for the chance to generate above average returns. While this is a common expectation among early-stage and operating-stage investors, different investors sometimes have secondary goals that are important to their investment decisions. Angel investors, for example, typically invest in

- Businesses that they understand well or industries in which they had previous management or investment experience
- Companies that need informal advisors and board members, or young management teams needing mentors, who know the issues the business will face
- opportunities with returns of 10, 20, or even 30 times the investment, depending on the investment's timing and amount (e.g., if an institutional investor has already invested, an angel might accept lower returns if the institution's investment validates the business or its products).

Angel investors often invest based on their intuition and the commitment the founders have to the business. If angels believe that

- The business plan is compelling
- Management is committed to the business through investing its personal assets, time, and energy
- The technology or product has sales potential to deliver high returns

the angel investor will usually be more inclined to invest. This is often quite different from how institutional investors approach their investments, where having professional management is sometimes one of the deciding factors.

Venture capital and private equity firms typically invest in businesses that meet the following investment goals:

- The business must be in an industry in which the venture or private equity firm has investments or, if not, there has to be a coinvestor who has analysts to assess, recommend, and monitor the investment
- The investment must be over a minimum amount without the investor owning 75% or more of the business
- The venture or private equity investor can get annual returns of 35 to 45% or more in a five- to eight-year window
- The business's prospects and projections support a value that generates the targeted returns in the time window
- The investor participates in management or on the board and gets more control if the business doesn't meet its financial or operating goals

Investors in retail private placements might expect returns like angels get, but these investors usually get returns closer to those offered early-stage public offering investors. If your business is going to raise funds on its own and without an investment banker, you'll set your own price for the placement stock. A good general guideline is to give the placement investors a 20% or greater annual return, and to base this on your financial projections with some "fudge factor" built in. Of course, if your business is wildly successful, you'll probably be able to sell equity with returns of 12 to 15% built into the purchase price. If you use an investment banking firm to market the placement to its customers, the banker will have a direct role in valuing the business and setting the stock's price. Some good general guidelines for retail private placements that are sold through investment bankers:

▬ Investment bankers like to see private placements priced at a level that, once your business is public or sold in a year or two, will get placement investors a 100 to 200% return over the amount they invested.

▬ Most bankers prefer to sell placements for businesses in an industry covered by the banker's analysts.

▬ Some bankers want the placement investors to get an early "window" to register and sell all or some stock into the public market, or at least before insiders can sell when the lock-up expires.

▬ A company should have growth prospects that support the business's value in the placement.

▬ A management team that understands the business's fundamentals and has successfully grown the business should be on board.

Real World Advice

Investment banking firms, like venture investors, believe that management is the single most important ingredient to a business's success or failure. If you're on an early-stage management team that lacks "professional" management, angels and retail placement investors are probably your best target investors. But, you shouldn't assume you can't get institutional investors just because you don't have professional management. Remember that your business's performance and growth prospects can outweigh a "novice" management team. The larger your business gets, though, the more likely it is that an investment banker or venture investor will insist on professional managers filling key posts. Planning ahead for management additions and letting the bankers or venture investors know about your plans is a good idea if you think lack of professional management might be an issue.

WHO ARE MATURE- AND LIQUIDITY-STAGE INVESTORS?

As noted in Chapter 2, investors in mature- and liquidity-stage companies are typically

- Institutional investors
- Strategic partners
- Private placement investors
- Public offering investors
- Financial buyers
- Strategic buyers

The immediately preceding section covers how you can find venture and private equity firms, strategic partners and investment bankers that market private placements and public offerings. Now let's consider financial buyers and strategic buyers of mature and liquidity stage companies.

Financial buyers are usually private equity groups and buyout firms that specialize in funding management buyouts, going private transactions, or "roll-ups" of related businesses that can be sold or taken public. Strategic buyers are like strategic partners—they are usually in the same business as you, but they might also be a supplier or customer that wants to buy your business because it's a strategic fit.

Most investment banking firms have relationships with buyout firms that are active financial buyers. Also, many private equity groups allocate some investment funds to buyout transactions meeting specific criteria. If you search "buyout group" and similar terms on the Internet, you'll find that most listings are for private equity groups. Many of the best known private equity groups—Shansby Group; Trivest; Patricof; GTCR; Bain Capital; Weiss, Peck & Greer; Hicks, Muse, Tate & Furst; and EOS Partners—are active financial buyers.

Strategic buyers are usually found through investment banking firms, but if you have good relationships with your customers and suppliers, it's possible to find strategic buyers on your own. The greatest difficulty in approaching a potential strategic buyer on your own is the potential to "scare away" a good customer or perhaps lose a good supplier. If the customer or supplier isn't interested in buying your business and doesn't want to "break in" a new business owner, they might decide to replace you as their supplier or customer if they find out you want to sell. Also, disclosing confidential financial and operating data to someone who knows your business only as a customer or supplier could backfire too. For example, a customer might find out that your margins are better than theirs, and a supplier might find out that your business isn't as strong financially as it thought. For these reasons, many small businesses use investment bankers or business brokers to "shop" their business to strategic buyers. If you have confidentiality concerns, you can instruct the banker to approach only strategic buyers with which you don't have an existing relationship. Even though this might narrow your potential buyers' list, the peace of mind might be worth it!

GOALS OF MATURE- AND LIQUIDITY-STAGE INVESTORS

A mature- or liquidity-stage business is attractive to investors because of

- Predictable returns
- The business's size
- Market share
- Possible synergies with an existing business or investment
- Expansion opportunities

Investors in mature- and liquidity-stage businesses are "return" driven and focus on investing in or buying the business for the best price. They'll give you some credit for the factors listed here, but price negotiations usually boil down to how your business is valued. You clearly have some control over pricing, as your asking price is usually where negotiations begin. But, if your price is completely unrealistic, investors are sometimes turned off to the point that they don't even bother making an offer. This means that you, like potential investors and buyers, need to understand how to value your business. Determining your business's value is also what an investment banking firm does when it prices a public offering and proposes what percentage of your business it wants to sell to the public. The valuation process is discussed in detail in Chapter 6 because it's important to every equity financing you'll ever do.

Private equity groups sometimes fund leveraged recaps or management buyouts for liquidity-stage businesses. In these scenarios, the private equity groups look for

- Market dislocations, consolidations, and industry changes that create opportunities
- A business with a strong management team
- A highly developed infrastructure and strong fundamentals in the business
- New sales opportunities through acquisitions, the addition of complementary product or service lines, or the development and licensing of new technologies
- Potential returns of 25% or more over a three- to seven-year window from the funding date

DEBT FINANCING

You've probably noticed that the options we've discussed don't cover debt financing. There are several reasons for this:

■ Banks are easily identified through many sources, including your personal banking relationships, Yellow Page ads, local newspapers or business weeklies, and the Internet.

■ Lease financing is usually found through equipment vendors, local commercial finance companies, and searches for "lease financing" through the Internet.

■ Some institutional investors that buy equity in your business also make loans to it. If the investor is getting convertible debentures or notes, or its debt comes with warrants, the investor focuses less on the interest rate and more on its total return (Expected equity value + interest on the debt). So, if you're thinking about getting institutional debt, you'll often find yourself negotiating a simultaneous equity sale unless your business has plenty of excess cash flow and collateral.

The venture firms, private equity groups, and buyout firms identified in this chapter usually fund mezzanine and other debt financings. You'll find these lenders by using the resources suggested earlier for finding equity investors. Look for guidance on each firm's web site for the debt financing they provide. For example, if you look at Softbank Capital Partners, you'll see that it specializes in late-stage mezzanine funding of $10 million or more for Internet businesses, while Pacific Mezzanine Fund funds $1 million to $3 million for middle-market companies located mostly in the western United States. If you review information you've developed through the sources we've covered, you can develop a debt financing source list that fits your business's needs and stage of development.

CHAPTER PERSPECTIVE

The Internet has placed a powerful information source at your fingertips that you can use to find equity investors, lenders, and investment bankers that represent institutions and retail investors. Equity financing sources include angel investors, venture and private equity firms, strategic partners, and other institutional investors. Investment bankers can offer you retail private placements, institutional placements, and public offerings that appeal to retail investors, institutions, or both. You can get information about equity investors and lenders from the search engines and web sites we've discussed, from books and CD-ROMs you can buy, and through referrals from your board members, professionals, and existing investors. You can use the Internet, local advertising, and news stories to find banks and commercial finance companies that provide senior debt to businesses like yours. Because lenders that fund sub debt treat this debt like equity, you'll want to look for sub debt lenders that are active equity investors in your industry like venture firms, private equity groups, and institutions. Investors are "return" driven no matter what your business's stage of development. As your business grows, investors and lenders will accept lower returns, but issues like management's experience, opportunities for growth, cash flow stability, and collateral become more important. Now that you know where to find financing, the financing your business is likely to get, and investors' and lenders' goals, let's consider the next step: how to approach possible financing sources and get a preliminary commitment.

Starting the Process: From Business Plan to Term Sheet or Letter of Intent

INTRODUCTION AND MAIN POINTS

This chapter focuses on how to get a preliminary financing commitment from investors or lenders and reviews several samples so that you'll know what a term sheet or letter of intent looks like. It also discusses what happens before you get a term sheet or letter of intent, and the issues that investors and investment bankers will concentrate on in negotiations. After studying this chapter, you will

■■■ Know what your business plan should include to interest potential investors and lenders

■■■ Understand what investors and lenders want to know about your business at this point in the financing process

■■■ Learn what preliminary financing commitments look like and what to watch out for

Figure 5-1 presents a quick overview of events that occur in the preliminary financing process and some average times to completion. You can see that getting to a term sheet or letter of intent can sometimes take up to 13 weeks, so planning ahead is important if you want funding by a certain date.

THE BUSINESS PLAN

The following discussion focuses on preparing a business plan in a form most useful to angels, venture and private equity investors, and investment bankers. As you know, entire books have been written on how to prepare a business plan. The following summary isn't meant to replace these resources, but it is designed to highlight points that deserve special attention.

FIG. 5-1 *Stages in the preliminary financing process*

Events	Average Time to Complete
Business Plan Preparation	2–3 weeks
Conference Calls and Meetings	3–4 weeks
Due Diligence	1–2 weeks
Exploring and Negotiating Key Issues	1–2 weeks
Review and Finalize Term Sheet or Letter of Intent	1–2 weeks

Real World Advice

Keep this old saying in mind when you put together your business plan, which a more experienced banker I know tells her analysts: "you bet on the jockey, not the horse." This saying emphasizes that management is the most important ingredient in a business's success. Your business plan should focus on your team's experience, background, and qualifications when talking about why the investor or banker should invest in your business.

A common question many entrepreneurs ask is how long the business plan should be. Having seen plans that are as short as 12 pages and as long as 200, a good rule of thumb is to ask yourself which plan you would rather read. Most people believe that they can grasp the business's basics in 15 to 25 pages of text and 10 pages or so of financial statements and/or projections. Even though this isn't a hard and fast rule, it's good to keep in mind that your audience has limited time to review business plans, and quality is more important than quantity.

Real World Advice

If you send out a business plan that's too long or detailed, you'll slow down the investor's or banker's analysis. You can also discourage financing sources from entering into discussions with you on the phone or in person. This is especially true when dealing with investment bankers because many bankers will give your plan only a cursory review until their analyst has given a "thumbs up." Think of the business plan as a marketing tool to help you get your foot in the door. It isn't a top-to-bottom review of your business and it's not a disclosure document. A good rule of thumb here is "the more to the point, the better."

Here are some other guidelines to keep in mind:

■ Most investors and investment bankers have an "intake" analyst read the plan or executive summary and pass interesting plans up to the managing directors or principals. The intake analyst also checks to make sure that the business is in an industry that the firm knows and needs funding that's within the firm's parameters.

■ If the plan piques the firm's interest, a financial analyst will review and analyze the financial projections and assumptions in the plan.

■ If the projections are supportable, the firm will then review management, industry data, competition, marketing and sales, production, supply, and other information both in the plan and from other sources to try to verify what's in the plan.

These reviews will develop information that the investor or banker will want to cover with you in the next step in the process, the question-and-answer sessions.

THE PLAN'S CONTENTS

The well-prepared business plan will have

■ A two to five page executive summary with

- A brief overview of your business
- Factors driving growth for your business and its industry

- Historic sales and profitability growth and its impact on operations
- Factors that differentiate the business from competitors and a brief competitive overview
- Key management resumes
- Historic and projected financials
- Funding requirements
- Use of proceeds
- Contact information for you or other officers

■■■ An industry overview, including what drives growth, market share data, sales and marketing channels, and where your business fits in the industry

■■■ A business section that talks about your strategy, products, sales and distribution channels, marketing, customers, production, trademarks and service marks, facilities, employees, and competition

■■■ Management resumes for officers, directors, and key employees, as well as information about their ownership in the business

■■■ An operational analysis that explains variations in past results and highlights industry or business-related events that were particularly important

■■■ Both historic and projected financials—the projections should come with assumptions that you or your chief financial officer used to prepare the numbers.

Most investors and investment bankers are satisfied if the business presents projections covering three years. The projections should have monthly operating results for the first year and cumulative annual operating results for the next two years. Because some financing sources want five-year projections, it doesn't hurt to prepare annual summaries for the next two years so that you have them in case you're asked. Even though you'll find it difficult to project out five years, the investor or investment banker sometimes asks for five-year projections to see if you and your chief financial officer (CFO) use reasonable assumptions when you put the projections together.

Most investors and investment bankers are good at questioning assumptions that underlie projections. You should expect the firm's principals and analysts to have "done their homework" when they sit down with you, meaning that they'll know the "metrics" that your business is built on. *Metrics* are operating data commonly used in your industry to measure how the business is performing. For example, if you sold golf equipment to consumers over the Internet, a potential investor or investment banker would want to know the number of click-throughs to your web site, sales per hit, and the dollar amount per order for your site compared to your competition. If your projections have assumptions about these metrics that are wildly optimistic and haven't been achieved by your competition, you'll need to support why your business is different or you'll lose credibility.

Real World Advice

It's important to remember that the typical venture or private equity investor is very experienced in evaluating projections and assumptions. Because most investors and investment bankers specialize by industry and have funded companies like yours, they'll often understand your business better than you do. Take some extra time when you're putting together or revising your projections to review the metrics and assumptions, and then question them. Are they supportable? Did you assume growth that's never been seen in the industry before? Are your margins realistic? Have you factored in more competition in later years if your technology will lose patent protection? Have you added in some key employees that you'll need as you grow? Even though you'll want to finish the business plan and get the financing process started, your prospects will improve by taking a little extra time to question and revise the projections and assumptions. If you show investors that you know your industry and its important metrics and have the people and other resources to be successful, your chances of getting funding will increase geometrically. This doesn't mean, though, that all good management teams with excellent projections and supportable assumptions receive funding. Investors and bankers must still be convinced that you can build a successful business, your product or service has a market, and the market is large enough to deliver sales and returns that justify their investment.

WHO IS THE DECISION MAKER?
Once your plan has been sent and the intake analyst has sent your plan up the chain of command, you'll want to know who to focus on

when you begin discussions with the investor or banker. Large investors have investment committees that decide if the firm will make an investment. The committee's decision usually rests on the senior analyst's or junior partner's recommendation, but one or several general partners must agree to a preliminary commitment. Funding over specific amounts often requires agreement by a majority of the partners. For investment banking firms, identifying the decision maker can be more difficult. Is it the corporate finance officer, the analyst, the senior executive officer, or some combination? Here are some guidelines:

■ The larger the banking firm, the more likely the firm has a commitment committee. This committee usually includes the senior executive officers, senior corporate finance officers, and sometimes a senior analyst or two. The committee must evaluate funding opportunities and decide if the firm will issue a letter of intent. Commitment committees decide if the firm will be the lead or comanager for public offerings and if it will help sell a private placement. The bankers and analysts who reviewed the business plan and met with you will usually prepare a written summary of your business for the committee. They'll then make an oral presentation explaining why the firm should do the funding, in what amount, and the firm's expected compensation.

■ Most smaller investment bankers that don't have a commitment committee will let the chief executive officer, president, or vice president of corporate finance issue a letter of intent. The vice president must usually get the chief executive officer's approval before the letter of intent is delivered.

■ Despite the numerous news articles, criminal investigations, and civil lawsuits about analysts' compensation and conflicts of interest, analysts are still the key players in a public offering. The analyst's view of your business and his or her write-up for the commitment committee is relied on to a greater extent than other information given to the committee. Some investment banking firms have informal policies that say at least one analyst must agree to begin research coverage after the offering if the commitment committee will issue a letter of intent. For firms without these policies, analyst coverage is still very much desired. This is because some institutional investors won't buy your stock in the market unless your business is covered by an investment banker or independent analyst. It's wise not to underestimate the analyst's importance in the financing process.

THE NEXT STEP: INTERVIEWS AND DUE DILIGENCE

Once the investor or investment banker has gotten the business plan and you've passed the initial review, most firms will ask to have a conference call or face-to-face meeting with you and the other key managers. The purpose is to get answers to questions about the business and make an early assessment of your team's experience. At this stage, the analyst is still looking over your projections, and the questions you'll get are regarding what bankers call "30,000-foot-view" issues. Some investors and bankers get preliminary background checks on your management team or contact a customer or investor to get early insight into your operations. Most firms wait to get background checks done until right before a term sheet or letter of intent is issued, and won't do significant due diligence until after the term sheet or letter of intent is signed.

After the first conference call or preliminary meeting, most investors and bankers will set a face-to-face meeting to discuss your business, operations, management, and financial results in more detail. This meeting is usually attended by the analyst who has studied your financial model, but you probably won't get detailed financial questions at this point. Investment bankers and investors will also ask for your judgment about what issues pose the greatest risk to your business.

Real World Example

One investment banker I knew went into management meetings and almost invariably would conclude the meeting with one question: "What issue about your business keeps you awake at night?" He was always very interested in the businessperson's answer, as it told him a lot about how he or she looked at their industry, business, and future prospects. So, when a client I had introduced to this investment banker asked me for some advice about what to expect in a meeting with him, I warned the client he should expect this question when the meeting was about to end. Sure enough, when the meeting was about to wrap up, the banker asked the question, and my client answered in a very thoughtful and complete way that really impressed the banker. My client got the first draft letter of intent a few days later and was really glad that he had time to develop a response to the question over a few days instead of a few seconds!

Investors usually do more due diligence than bankers do before sending out a term sheet. This is because an investor's preliminary commitment is coming directly from the funding source, while the bankers admittedly have to go to retail or institutional investors to get funds. Also, because institutional investors are occasionally sued for failing to close a financing after giving out a preliminary commitment, institutions are reluctant to send out term sheets without having done some due diligence. We'll explore the due diligence process in more detail in Chapter 9.

Term sheets and letters of intent say that funding depends on due diligence being satisfactory to the investor or banker. If your business is enjoying record earnings and the investor or banker knows that you're talking with other investors or bankers, they sometimes won't do much due diligence before sending you a draft term sheet or letter of intent. A good rule of thumb here is that preliminary due diligence will vary by business type, stage of development, financial needs, management qualifications and experience, and the investor's or banker's comfort level.

CONFIDENTIALITY ISSUES

Business plans as a rule don't include confidential information about the business, its technologies, or its products. When due diligence begins, investors and bankers ask about your customers, suppliers, technology, or production processes. Before disclosing this information, you'll want your attorney to put together a confidentiality agreement that will

- Broadly define confidential facts, including all written materials, oral discussions, and any studies prepared by the investor or banker using confidential facts
- Make the investor or banker keep the facts confidential for one or two years after you give them the information, even if the funding doesn't close
- Release the investor or banker from confidentiality once an authorized disclosure has taken place
- Include nonsolicitation clauses that prevent the investor or banker from soliciting your business's employees, customers, or suppliers for one or two years
- Limit the use of confidential facts to the potential financing only
- Make them return all confidential information to you if the financing doesn't close

Experienced investors and bankers are accustomed to signing confidentiality agreements that cover these issues. You should still be alert, however, for investors or bankers that have an inordinate interest in getting your confidential information. You won't necessarily know when an investor owns a portfolio company, or a banker represents a business that's a competitor of yours.

Real World Example

One of my clients retained a large regional investment banker to help him sell his business. He was very concerned about putting his customer names in the so-called pitch book that the banker put together to describe his business. He was afraid that the pitch book would fall into his competitors' hands, and that they would find out who his best customers were. He and the banker agreed to include a customer list in the pitch book that gave customers code names (Customer A, Customer B, etc.) and that gave sales amounts in the last two years for the top 20 customers. When a private equity group offered a term sheet for a buyout, we negotiated a clause that said the customer names would be given to the private equity group only right before closing. Knowing my client was sensitive to this issue, they agreed to this, and my client slept better knowing that he could keep this information close to the vest until it looked like the buyout would close. The private equity group's only concern was that they could have time to verify the customer information before the closing by reconciling the customer list to the financial statements. This was agreeable to my client, and the buyout closed successfully after he gave them the customer names right before closing and the verification was done.

CRITICAL ISSUES IN THE TERM SHEET OR LETTER OF INTENT
When negotiations with an investor or banker get serious, you'll start discussing the most important issues that the term sheet or letter of intent will cover. In other words, you won't have to wait to get the

term sheet or letter of intent to know what the big issues are. These issues will come up because the investor or banker wants some assurance that you and they are "in the same ballpark" before they put a term sheet or letter of intent together. Also, many investors or bankers avoid putting together a term sheet or letter of intent until they have a sense that you won't "shop" the term sheet or letter of intent with other investors or bankers to get better terms.

Here are the issues investors and investment bankers will be most concerned about when negotiating the term sheet or letter of intent, in order of importance:

Investors	Investment Bankers
1. Value	1. Value
2. Rank/Structure	2. Compensation
3. Transferability	3. Future dilution
4. Liquidity	4. Liquidity/Insider lock-ups

Let's briefly cover each issue, keeping in mind that later chapters will discuss these issues in more detail and give you negotiating guides to deal with investors or bankers.

Value. For you, investors, and bankers, value is the defining issue. An investor will be focused on valuing your business using EBITDA, discounted cash flow, or net income multiples or another valuation method. Sophisticated investors will develop financial models they can manipulate to look at different operating results and investment levels based on your projections. Investment bankers will have analysts go through the same financial modeling process and then compare actual and projected operating results to comparable public companies in your industry. In each case, once investors and bankers arrive at a preliminary value, they'll discount your business's value by some small amount to give them some negotiating room or, as bankers say, to "leave something on the table for the public."

Rank/structure. Venture and private equity investors are focused on limiting downside risk where possible. They do this by structuring their investment using promissory notes, debentures, or preferred stock with first claims on dividends and liquidating distributions. These investors will also structure the financing to give them downside protection if you sell more stock or issue more debt. This is done by getting antidilution protection, limiting options or warrants you issue, preventing you from selling debt that's senior to theirs, and making you get their consent before adding debt that's junior to theirs.

Compensation. Investment bankers want to have some understanding with you about their compensation before you get the letter of intent, if for no other reason than they don't want you to be surprised. In public offerings, the underwriting discount, nonaccountable expense allowance or success fee, and underwriter's warrants are the most common forms of bankers' compensation. The National Association of Securities Dealers (NASD) oversees investment banking compensation in public offerings but has no oversight responsibility for investment banking compensation in private placements. This is why banking compensation in private offerings can vary, sometimes widely.

Transferability. The venture or private equity investor is very interested in being able to convert debt or preferred stock into common stock once you've completed an IPO. They'll want to use conversion and registration rights, tag-along rights, and redemption rights to get liquid when opportunities arise.

Future dilution. Investment bankers want to know what options, warrants, or rights you've issued and any preferred stock or convertible debt you've sold that might increase your outstanding stock. They'll want to factor in the dilutive effect on expected earnings and sometimes ask that future option grants, warrants or rights be limited for six months or a year.

Liquidity/insider lock-ups. Venture and private equity investors want to know they can get liquidity when you sell all or part of your business, go public, or sell some personal stock. For investment bankers, they'll want to understand the insiders' liquidity needs and will focus on the lock-up period when insiders can't sell.

THE TERM SHEET

Venture, private equity, and other institutional investors use term sheets to set the financing offer's preliminary terms. You usually get the term sheet once the investor is comfortable with your business plan, projections, and management. This follows preliminary due diligence and discussions about the major issues we've already touched on. A term sheet is like a letter of intent, but it usually describes the investment terms in a shorter, summary format. If you look at the first three sample term sheets in the appendix, you'll see that we've included term sheets for

- A preferred stock financing from a venture or private equity investor
- A senior subordinated debt financing from an institutional investor
- A senior credit facility that includes a term loan and a revolver

Because these term sheets came from actual financings, you should study these so you'll know what to expect from an institutional investor. The first term sheet was put together by a venture firm for one of my private clients that was an early-stage business at the time. Let's consider a few points from this term sheet:

▬ Note that the investor focused immediately on the business's value and capital structure, describing the business's fully diluted ownership excluding options. The investor didn't ignore options; through due diligence, the investor knew how many were outstanding and what could be issued in the future.

▬ If you multiply the $2 offering price by 8,500,000 (the shares outstanding if the investor bought the maximum preferred stock offered and converted it into common stock), you can see that the investor valued the business at $17 million on a *post-money*, or after financing basis. This means that the business was valued at $12 million ($2 times the common stock outstanding before the financing) on a *pre-money*, or before financing basis. The pre-money and post-money valuation terms are used by institutional investors and investment bankers to tell you how they've valued your business before and after their money is invested.

▬ The investor included standard rank and structure language, as discussed earlier. The term sheet has antidilution protection, limits on future incentive stock (see the Negative Covenants subsection under section IV), and limits on issuing more preferred and other stock.

▬ Transfer issues have also been dealt with, including conversion and registration rights, tag-along rights, and redemption rights.

▬ Corporate governance is covered in detail throughout the term sheet. Clauses about board membership, employment agreements, key man life insurance, board committee membership, board meeting minimums, and votes needed to change charter documents deal with these issues.

▬ The term sheet calls for the business to pay a deposit to cover the investor's legal expenses and out-of-pocket due diligence costs.

The second term sheet was submitted by a financial institution to one of my public clients and describes a senior subordinated financing. This term sheet got its name from the fact that the debt is senior to all other debt, but junior (subordinated) to an existing senior bank line. You'll note that this term sheet is shorter than the first, partly because the public company already has many corporate governance controls in place. Key points in this term sheet include:

- A higher interest rate than what an early-stage business pays
- The investor's warrants, which buy a much smaller interest in the business than what the investor got in the preferred stock term sheet
- No board representation and no price antidilution protection
- An early out for the investor if the business completes a follow-on public offering
- Covenants that restrict a change in control, changes in the business, dividend payments, senior debt increases, or common stock redemptions without the sub debt's consent
- Reports to the sub debt holder consistent with reports given to the senior lender
- A right of first refusal for the business to buy back sub debt and the accompanying warrants

The third term sheet is for a senior credit facility that incorporates both a term loan and revolver. This term sheet was prepared by a large national bank for one of my clients that needed financing for several acquisitions and for working capital. Key points include

- A five-year term for both the term loan and revolver, but the term loan has principal payments that start immediately and continue for five years for 30% of the principal
- Term loan proceeds that finance acquisitions, with the remainder being escrowed and released when the business gets new equity funding or financial goals are met
- Revolver draws based on eligible accounts receivable and inventory
- Two interest rate options—the bank's base rate and a LIBOR option
- Commitment fees for unused debt
- The bank's legal and collateral audit expenses paid by the business, whether or not the financing closes
- Mandatory and voluntary prepayments, including mandatory prepayments using excess cash flow

- Lender's indemnification and its right to syndicate all or some of the loans

If you review these term sheets, you'll be prepared for what most institutional investors or lenders will put in a term sheet even though the forms vary slightly. If you're negotiating a smaller bank loan or equipment lease, you'll often find that these financings use short-form documents that don't need much negotiation.

Before we leave term sheets, one point about timing deserves mention. A debt financing through a bank or similar institution will close much faster than an equity financing because the bank is focused on collateral value, your business's credit history, and its lien priority. This means that a banker's due diligence will concentrate on historical financial performance, collateral value and audits, receivable collection rates, inventory turns, and lien priority issues. An equity investor is concerned with these issues and several others like management, operations, capital structure, and regulation. Because equity investors rank behind creditors and don't have any security, they'll do much more due diligence on your business and will usually take much longer to close a financing than a senior lender.

INVESTMENT BANKING COMPENSATION

Before looking at sample letters of intent for public offerings, you need to understand who regulates investment banking compensation and when and how bankers are compensated. You can use this knowledge to your advantage when negotiating with a potential banker, so that's why we've included it here.

Investment banking compensation paid in public offerings is regulated by the NASD. The NASD doesn't say how much a banker can or should make; instead, it says only that the total compensation can't exceed a maximum amount. In other words, don't rely on the NASD to negotiate or watch out for you—their job is only to make sure that the bankers don't go over the limit. There's often some negotiating room between what the NASD will accept and what you can negotiate, so compensation negotiations can return big dividends. This is particularly true if you're fortunate enough to have several investment bankers competing for the lead manager position. Remember, only a half percentage point reduction in the underwriting discount on a $20 million offering will save you $100,000.

Investment banking compensation includes:

- Underwriting discounts (commissions)
- Nonaccountable expense allowance
- Underwriters' warrants
- Success fees
- Consulting fees
- Rights of first refusal with respect to future offerings
- Rights to nominate or designate board members

Table 5-1 breaks out cash underwriting compensation into three categories based on offering size. Note that both the percentage and different types of compensation are highest in smaller offerings.

Unfortunately, the NASD does not publish a guide for what maximum underwriting compensation is for a particular offering size. If you look at offerings over $25 million, you'll find nearly all have a 7% discount and that the bankers don't get any other compensation. As the offering gets smaller, the bankers get more compensation including nonaccountable expense allowances, warrants, and consulting fees. The bankers can vary these elements within NASD guidelines, so long as they stay within the compensation limit. That's why you might see one $10 million IPO that has a 9% discount and a 3% nonaccountable expense allowance, where another might have a 10% discount and a $2\frac{3}{8}$% nonaccountable expense allowance. Some regional investment bankers won't ask for a nonaccountable expense allowance, but they will charge a "success fee" that's due at closing. The success fee's often used to pay legal fees, due diligence costs, travel, and roadshow expenses like a nonaccountable expense allowance.

Some smaller banking firms want more cash compensation when they underwrite an offering. These firms might ask for a $100,000 consulting fee *and* a 3% nonaccountable expense allowance. To avoid going over the NASD's limit, the firm might choose to increase the underwriter's warrant exercise price to 165% of the IPO price. At that level, the NASD says the underwriter's warrants are worth $0 in their compensation calculation.

Most bankers for IPOs of $15 million or less will ask for underwriter's warrants. An underwriter's warrant, like an option, gives the underwriter the right to buy stock from the company for a fixed price that's usually 120% of the IPO price. The warrant is exercisable for five years and is given to the banker when the IPO closes. The warrant will buy 10% of the stock the banker sold in the offering, without counting the overallotment option. The banker usually gets

TABLE 5-1
*Categories of Investment Banking
Compensation for IPOs*

Small Retail Offerings (<$15 million)		Mid-Size Offering ($15 million–$25 million)		Large Offering (>$25 million)	
Item	Amount	Item	Amount	Item	Amount
Underwriting discounts	8–10%	Underwriting discounts	7–8%	Underwriting discounts	$5\frac{1}{2}$–7%
Nonaccountable expense allowance	2–3%	Success fee	1%		
Consulting fees	1%	Underwriter's warrants	8–10% of stock sold		
Underwriter's warrants	10% of stock sold				

demand and piggyback registration rights for the stock underlying the warrant, but also gets "cashless" exercise rights. These rights let the banker turn in the warrant to the business and get a cash payment equal to the difference between the warrant's exercise price and the stock's market price. For example, if a banker got an underwriter's warrant to buy 100,000 shares of stock at $7 and the stock was trading at $12 when the cashless exercise right was used, the business would owe the banker $500,000 ($12 − $7 = $5 × 100,000 = $500,000). When a banker used to exercise its underwriter warrants, the business would get the exercise price paid to it in cash, which was always a welcome addition to equity. Because most bankers now use cashless exercise rights, you shouldn't count on your business getting more capital later on when the underwriter's warrants are exercised.

Finder's fees or financial consulting fees can be a huge stumbling block for businesses wanting to do a public offering. The NASD can classify *any* finder's fees or consulting fees that are paid in the 12 months before the prospectus is filed with the SEC as "investment banking compensation." *This includes fees paid or payable to finders or consultants that aren't investment bankers or even NASD members!* If your business pays a finder or "financial consultant," your investment banker is likely to back out of the offering because the banker's compensation is reduced by the fee paid to the finder or consultant.

Real World Example

A banker I represented had signed a letter of intent to do an IPO for a business with outstanding growth prospects. While doing due diligence, we found out that the business had entered into an agreement with a consulting firm for financial consulting services. The consulting firm had introduced the business to the banker, and it appeared that this is why they were being compensated. As noted earlier, the NASD counts consulting or finder's fees as investment banking compensation, even if the money is paid to a non-NASD member (in other words, not to a banker). When my client found out about the payment, it told the business that the consulting agreement would have to be canceled or the firm couldn't do the offering. Because the consulting fee was about $200,000, you can see why my client was concerned about losing this income. Ultimately, the business bought out the consultant's agreement by paying the consulting firm $75,000, an amount my client approved. The NASD deducted the $75,000 from my client's allowable compensation under the consulting rule—a result we expected and, despite some grumbling, the offering proceeded.

LETTERS OF INTENT

If you look at the next two samples in the appendix, you'll see that we've included:

- A letter of intent from an investment banker for a retail IPO
- A letter of intent from a regional investment banker for a larger follow-on offering

Again, each letter came from an actual financing and is similar to what you'll get if you hire an investment banker for a public offering. It's interesting to note that the longer letter of intent is for a small $9 million IPO, while the shorter letter is for a $26 million follow-on offering. The main reason for this difference is that a letter of intent for a small retail IPO must deal with several issues that only come up in an IPO. Let's start by considering a few points about the letters of intent, focusing first on the key issues we discussed earlier.

▬ On valuation, you need to refer to paragraphs 1 and 4(b) from the IPO letter of intent to figure out how the banker valued the business. Paragraph 1 tells you that the offering's price range is $8 to $9, and at the low end of the range the banker will offer one million shares at $8. Paragraph 4(b) says that five million shares will be outstanding before the offering, as well as $500,000 in preferred stock liquidation value. So, to calculate the business's post-money valuation, you'd take:

1,000,000 shares offered + 5,000,000 shares outstanding × $8 = $48,000,000 + $500,000 preferred stock value = $48,500,000

If the $500,000 in preferred stock liquidation value was convertible into 2,000,000 shares of common stock, the banker would calculate post-money value like this:

1,000,000 shares offered + 5,000,000 shares outstanding +
2,000,000 shares (assumed preferred stock conversion)
× $8 = $64,000,000

If the offering was priced at $9, the high end of the price range, the business's post-money value would be $54 million in the first example and $72 million in the second.

The second letter of intent has no price range and says in paragraph 4 that the offering will be priced based on market conditions. This is because there is already a public market for the business's stock, and the prevailing price is the biggest factor in the banker and the business negotiating a price.

Real World Example

Follow-on offerings are usually priced slightly below the market price so that investors have some incentive to buy in the offering, as opposed to the open market. Sometimes negotiations between the business and the lead investment banker can turn ugly, particularly if the market price has dropped while the offering is being reviewed by the SEC. In one situation where I was representing the lead investment banker, the company's stock price went down by $2 per share while the offering was in for SEC review. At the pricing conference, the banker told the chief financial officer that the offering price would be $0.75 below the prevailing market price because of weak demand for the stock. The CFO became incensed and told the investment banker (my client) that the business wouldn't accept a price that was now $2.75 per share below where the stock was when the offering got started. He proceeded to tell my client to do something that was anatomically impossible and left the pricing meeting in a rage. The company tried to get another banker to step in and get the offering done but wasn't successful; the offering was withdrawn and was never refiled. Later, the company ran out of working capital and filed for bankruptcy. The investment banker I represented wasn't pleased with losing the offering, but was glad they had stood by their guns when the pricing negotiations became rancorous.

■ As to investment banking compensation, you'll notice quite a difference between what's paid to the banker in the IPO and what's paid in the follow-on offering. The reason is twofold: bankers that underwrite IPOs are permitted by the NASD to charge more because it's assumed that marketing an IPO to retail investors calls for more selling effort and due diligence than for already-public companies. Conversely, bankers that market follow-on offerings usually sell large share allocations to institutions, meaning that the sales effort is not as extensive. In other words, there are some efficiencies realized in the capital-raising process as the offering size grows. You'll notice that the investment banker underwriting the small IPO in the first letter of intent gets:

- A 10% discount (Paragraph 13a)
- A 3% nonaccountable expense allowance (Paragraph 13b)
- Five year warrants to buy 10% of the stock sold in the offering, exercisable at 120% of the public offering price (Paragraph 6)

■ Compare that to what the investment banker gets for underwriting the follow-on offering: a 7% discount—and that's all.

One other point to remember about underwriting compensation is that it's public. Bankers that are involved in several public offerings know that their compensation is disclosed in offering documents that are filed with the SEC. This means that you and your management team, other investment bankers, and company counsel can (and will) review previous offerings to see what the banker's been paid for underwriting similar offerings. This is why bankers are reluctant to reduce their compensation beyond a certain point, knowing it might be used against them when they're negotiating to underwrite a later offering. If you sense that you're not making progress negotiating down a banker's compensation, this is often why.

■ On future dilution, notice that the retail IPO banker:

- Doesn't permit any other stock to be outstanding except what's disclosed or used for acquisitions (Paragraph 4b)
- Doesn't let the company issue stock for 12 months after the offering except for acquisitions and when options are exercised, unless the underwriter has agreed to the sale (Paragraph 16b)
- Doesn't let the company or its principals make offshore stock sales for three years after the offering (this is the reference to Regulation S that also appears in Paragraph 16b)

■ The investment banker for the follow-on offering has put no restrictions on the business selling more stock after the offering.

■ Wants all the company's existing stockholders to lock up their shares for nine months (Paragraph 16a). The banker for the follow-on offering has not asked for insider lock-ups, meaning insiders can sell stock into the market any time after the offering.

Now that we've covered the four most significant issues that bankers focus on, let's look at some other points in the IPO letter of intent.

■ Paragraph 2 gives the banker an option to buy additional shares from the business after the IPO is completed. This option, known as the overallotment option, lets the banker buy up to 15% of the stock sold in the offering for up to 45 days after the offering is completed. The exercise price is the same as the stock's IPO price. So, if the stock's market price falls below the IPO price, the overallotment option is worthless and won't be exercised. If the stock trades up in the aftermarket and the banker sees that there is demand for the stock, it will exercise the overallotment option. The banker would get the difference between the overallotment option's exercise price (equal to the IPO price) and the stock's market price.

Real World Example

One of my clients did a follow-on offering and gave the bankers an overallotment option. The stock traded up $2.25 within 45 days of the offering, and the banker exercised the overallotment option for 200,000 shares. If the banker sold the overallotment option stock for an average of $2 per share over the IPO price, it made $400,000. You can see why the overallotment option is highly valued by bankers!

■ Paragraph 13c lets the investment banker get an advisory fee if the public offering is called off because the business is merged or acquired.

■ Paragraph 14a says the banker can send an observer to board meetings and that the observer will get compensation just like the board members.

Paragraphs 4c and 18a cover the "cold comfort" letter to be delivered by the independent public accountants and the banker's right to approve the audit firm.

Paragraphs 13e, 18f, and 21a say that even though this is a "firm commitment" offering, the banker can terminate the letter of intent at any time because of market conditions, due diligence, and operational changes, among other reasons.

Real World Advice

Remember that your due diligence on investment banking firms needs to focus on the banker's track record in completing offerings that it signs up. There's no record of every letter of intent a firm signs, but once an offering is filed, you can see if it has started trading, where it is trading, and which banker was the lead underwriter. The Hoovers web site, at www.hoovers.com, has information in its premium section about offerings filed for lead underwriters that indicates whether the offering is trading or not.

Paragraph 20 is a performance escrow that makes the business's majority stockholder put part of its shares in an escrow account. The shares are released from escrow when the business hits the predetermined financial targets or at the end of seven years, whichever is first. Performance escrows are used to bridge a valuation gap between investment bankers, and businesses like equity claw-backs are used to bridge valuation gaps between venture firms and businesses. The main difference between a performance escrow and an equity claw-back is that stockholders who escrow their shares will eventually get them back, while management with a claw-back won't get their shares if they don't hit their numbers.

The letter of intent for the follow-on offering is noteworthy for these points:

Paragraph 3 says the bankers will pay their roadshow expenses. But, if the offering is pulled by the bankers for due diligence reasons or if the business terminates the letter of intent, the business must reimburse the bankers their expenses.

■ Assuming the offering is for a business with its stock listed on the New York Stock Exchange (NYSE), American Stock Exchange (AMEX), or Nasdaq's National Market, blue sky qualifications won't be a problem. If the business's stock is listed on the Nasdaq SmallCap Market, the offering must be qualified in enough states that the bankers can sell the offering.

■ The business must pay the banker's legal fees and out-of-pocket due diligence costs if the offering isn't successful for any reason. These fees and costs can be substantial depending on the offering's size, how far the offering process gets, and the due diligence that's been performed.

■ This letter of intent doesn't have many of the other rights and restrictions outlined in the IPO letter of intent. Sometimes, larger investment banking firms will cover these issues in drafting conferences with you and the management team. The bankers say this is because their firms want to create a trust-based relationship with the business. The management team shouldn't assume these issues won't come up in a follow-on offering, but they should keep these issues in mind as the offering proceeds.

NEGOTIATING TIPS ON LETTERS OF INTENT WITH INVESTMENT BANKERS

Here are a few tips to keep in mind when you're negotiating a letter of intent with a banker. We've saved valuation for the next chapter, but discuss these topics here:

- Options and warrants
- Insider lock-ups
- Management issues
- Share escrows

Options and warrants concern bankers because they consider these to be "common stock equivalents" if the exercise price is below the expected IPO price. Warrants outstanding before an IPO are typically issued in prior financing rounds to venture capital firms and private equity groups, mezzanine lenders and, occasionally, retail private placement investors. The concern about warrants doesn't extend to underwriter's warrants because these have an exercise price that's at least 120% of the offering price and, as you'd expect, the underwriter isn't eager to reduce its payday!

Most investment bankers won't object to your business having an option plan in place as long as the number of shares in the plan is reasonable. While there aren't any hard and fast guidelines about what's reasonable, if the plan's shares are less than 15% of the total stock outstanding after the offering, most bankers won't object.

The issue of how many options have been issued *prior to the IPO* is different from the stock set aside for future options. Most bankers take outstanding options much more seriously because your business can register the stock in its option plan with the SEC and option holders will get free trading stock. Bankers usually attack this two ways. First, they ask option holders to sign lock-up agreements so option shares can't be sold until the lock-up period expires. Second, the letter of intent includes the business's agreement that it won't register option stock for six to 12 months.

Even with these restrictions in place, investment bankers understand options will be exercised and increase the total outstanding shares, potentially diluting future earnings per share. Also, most businesses don't have a compensation committee of the board before the IPO, meaning that management has really been making option grants to itself. For these reasons, bankers will look at preoffering option grants more carefully. If the preoffering options look too high, the banker sometimes asks management to cancel part of its options or to postpone exercise until the business hits mutually agreed-on sales or earnings targets. If the outstanding options are reasonable, many investment bankers will exclude the options from your business's preoffering valuation. This is because management normally holds options for some time before exercise, particularly if they are incentive options with a ten-year exercise period.

Most investment bankers have a standard lock-up period when officers, directors, employees, and 5% or more stockholders aren't able to sell shares into the public market. This period is sometimes negotiable. If you're lucky, you might find recent offerings your banker funded that used different lock-up periods and be able to use this fact in negotiations. But don't negotiate this issue too aggressively—at some point, it can backfire. Here's why: bankers will ask why you can't wait to sell stock and will begin to wonder if you don't believe your own projections. The argument you'll hear is that if you believe in your projections, by waiting just a few more months (or quarters), you'll be selling stock at a much higher price.

If you have many nonemployee investors, the banker will likely ask for the lock-up to include all pre-IPO stockholders. A lock-up like this can raise several issues, including what to do when a nonemployee stockholder refuses to sign the lock-up. If your private placement documents included a power of attorney that lets you sign lock-ups for your investors, you'll be able to assure the banker that you've got this issue under control. It's a good idea to include powers of attorney in your private placement documents so that you can sign lock-ups for reluctant investors. This will prevent a situation where a large stockholder who refuses to sign a lock-up might actually cause a banker to walk away from your offering.

Sometimes you can negotiate a shorter lock-up period for investors who aren't officers and directors. These "two-stage" lock-ups are good for your investors, especially for those who own a small number of shares. If venture or private equity investors hold a significant position, they'll usually be asked to sign a lock-up for the same period as officers and directors. That doesn't hold true, though, if the venture or private equity firms have other business going with the bankers or are willing to use their bargaining power to leverage themselves into a shorter lock-up. If that happens, you can find yourself with a large amount of stock overhanging the market right when your lock-up expires. This means that your stock could be under price pressure right when you want to sell, so that's why your lock-up shouldn't be longer than the venture or private equity firm's.

Your management team is another issue that sometimes surfaces when you're negotiating the letter of intent. Sometimes the banker will tell you that a vacant position like the CFO or chief technology officer must be filled for the offering to go forward. When the market is tough, bankers will want to have a critical position filled before the roadshow starts to reduce any investor reluctance to buy in the offering.

A more difficult issue comes up when the banker informs you that a senior executive makes a "weak" impression and should be replaced. This conversation usually happens later in the offering process after the bankers have more knowledge about the management team. Bankers don't usually insist that an executive be let go absent some serious issue in his or her background, but your banker might encourage you to "strengthen" the team by adding to it. If your banker's opinion is shared by other officers or your investors, you might give further thought to this issue. If it's likely that other bankers would reach the same conclusion, you need to address the underlying issue or postpone your offering.

Smaller bankers use stock escrows to make management accountable for its projections. If a forfeiture escrow is used, management can lose its stock if it doesn't meet its projections. A forfeiture escrow will get management's attention since not making the numbers will directly impact management's ownership. The problem with forfeiture escrows is that if the stock is earned out, the business must book compensation expense on its financial statements. The compensation charge is equal to stock released from escrow multiplied by the stock's market price on the release date, so the charge can be substantial. Unlike a forfeiture escrow, a performance escrow still has financial targets, but if they're not met, the management team will get the shares back after seven years. Because management doesn't ever forfeit the stock, there is no "earn out" if the financial targets are hit, so there is no compensation charge if the stock is released from escrow early. You can see why a performance escrow is better for you and the other officers, and it's good to remind the banker that no stock forfeiture equals no compensation charge.

If you must put some stock into an escrow, make sure that you carefully evaluate the financial targets you have to meet. When you can, negotiate for alternate release triggers—maybe if the business meets EBITDA *or* pre-tax income targets, rather than both of these targets. Also, try to get a cumulative release provision included in the escrow terms. This clause says that if the business doesn't meet the financial targets in the first escrow year but meets the combined objectives of years one and two in the second year, you get stock released for both years.

Real World Advice

You'll also want to make sure any escrow gives you an early release if (1) your business is acquired or (2) your business's assets are sold. Bankers should agree to these conditions, but they might want your stock release to depend on the public stockholders getting some minimum price (or stock value) above the IPO price.

INVESTMENT BANKING ENGAGEMENTS FOR PRIVATE FINANCING

The engagement letter that follows the two letters of intent in the appendix is one that you'd receive from a banker who is offering to help raise private equity or debt. This engagement letter was received by one of my clients from a large regional banker that offered to help raise institutional equity or debt on a best efforts basis. The key points of this engagement agreement follow:

▬ The business can accept or reject a financing, but notice that paragraph 7c imposes a break-up fee that rises the further the process goes on. Also, there is a "tail" in paragraph 7d that gives the banker its full fee if an investor introduced by the banker funds the business during the 12 months after the engagement ends.

▬ The fee arrangements discussed in paragraphs 6 and 7 include a retainer and a contingent fee equal to a percentage of the funding. The contingent fee is higher for equity and convertible debt and lower for sub debt. This recognizes that equity is harder to come by than sub debt, and the banker deserves a bigger payday if it gets an equity investor. Also, all the advisor's expenses are reimbursed by the business.

▬ Paragraph 9 is very important because it gives the banker a right of first refusal to be a comanaging underwriter of any future public or private offering if this financing is done. The terms of the later engagement are to be "standard," leaving plenty of room for differing interpretations. Like the follow-on offering letter of intent described earlier, the investment banker is looking for a trust-based relationship that will reward it if the placement closes. The right of first refusal is a real "carrot" for the investment banker and could bring them a windfall if market conditions are good and the later offering gets done. If relations with this banker deteriorate after the placement closes, the business might offer to buy out the right of first refusal if that becomes necessary.

Real World Advice

The NASD defines any payments from your business to an investment banker, including a buyout of a first refusal right, as underwriting compensation. The only qualifications are that the payment is "in connection with" an offering and within one year before the business files its offering with the SEC. You should consult with your counsel and any new underwriter you want to use before making any payment to a former banker. If the new banker is forced to reduce its compensation because a payment was made to an old banker, it could lead the new banker to withdraw from the offering.

FIG. 5-2 *Stages in private financing with an investment banker engaged*

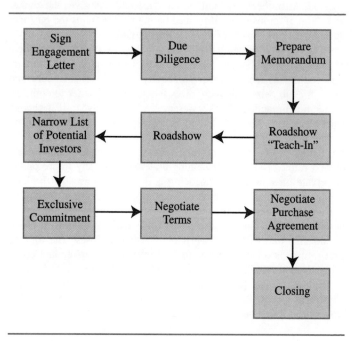

The process of getting private institutional investments through investment bankers is diagrammed in Figure 5-2. Much like a public offering, the process begins with engaging the banker and then goes on to preparing offering materials and a roadshow, narrowing potential investors, negotiating a term sheet and agreement, and a closing. The "teach in" that's referred to is a day or two when the banker and company get together for the banker to review the roadshow and critique it. The banker also gives you and the other key managers some tips about what questions to expect and hot buttons that investors will focus on in discussions.

CHAPTER PERSPECTIVE

To go from selecting possible financing sources to getting a preliminary commitment, you need to put together a top-quality business plan with compelling reasons why the investor or banker should finance your business. The plan is a marketing tool that needs to cover your operations, growth plan, management, finances, industry, and competition in a direct and concise way. If you've sent the plan to investors and bankers that have already funded businesses like yours in your industry or a related one, you'll soon start a dialogue with the investors or bankers. You'll get many questions about your experience, operations, products, and markets and should expect more attention on evaluating the projections and assumptions as the discussions continue. The financial analyst will play a key role in analyzing your financials and the assumptions you've used to build the projections. It's important for you and your CFO to know the metrics that are key operating points for your business so that you can defend your projections and assumptions effectively. Investors will do different amounts of preliminary due diligence, but bankers will usually hold off on doing much until after the letter of intent is signed. Once you've educated the banker or investor's personnel, they'll present a summary to the commitment committee or responsible officer, who'll decide if the firm will put together a term sheet or letter of intent. The key terms the investor or banker already discussed with you, including valuation, structure, compensation and liquidity, will be the focus points for investors or bankers in the term sheet or letter of intent. Having reviewed the samples in the appendix, you're now familiar with the different preliminary commitments used by investors and bankers for institutional investments, IPOs, follow-on offerings, private placements, and senior bank debt. Now let's turn our attention to valuation, since this is the biggest issue that you, investors, and bankers deal with when you're negotiating both the preliminary commitment and definitive agreement.

Valuation: The Key Issue for You and Investors

INTRODUCTION AND MAIN POINTS

Once you've found potential investors and bankers, given them the business plan, and successfully defended your projections, discussions will focus on how to value your business. Many management teams are at a disadvantage here—they don't know how valuations are done, and bankers aren't eager to share how they do this "magic." Valuation is the single most important issue for your stockholders in any equity financing or debt financing with conversion rights or warrants. It determines your post-money percentage ownership of the business and is as important for you to understand as it is for the bankers or investors to understand your projections. After studying this chapter, you will

■ Understand basic valuation methods used in financings and business sales

■ Know how private companies and public companies are valued by investors and bankers

■ Learn strategies to negotiate valuation issues with investors and bankers

WHY THE CORRECT VALUATION IS IMPORTANT

Getting to the correct valuation when you're negotiating a financing or a sale is critical. Here's why:

■ A "sky high" valuation might look good on paper, but once investors react by refusing to buy your offering, you'll quickly realize that your financing is in jeopardy.

■ A rich valuation can scare away buyers for your business even before they know anything about it.

■ If you're offered a lowball valuation by a banker or investor, you'll usually walk away, wonder if the banker really wants to do a financing, or suspect the investor is not serious.

For these reasons, you need to know how valuations are done and how to judge if they're in the ballpark. You also need to understand valuation to argue for a higher one or to know when a banker is overpromising. Some bankers want to give your business the lowest possible valuation at your existing stockholders' expense. These bankers justify this approach by figuring they "represent" the next round's investors and aren't expected to look out for your stockholders. You'll want to know how to differentiate aggressive and realistic valuations so that you maximize value for your existing stockholders but aren't locked into a banker or buyer who can't (or won't) perform.

HOW A BUSINESS IS VALUED FOR A PUBLIC OFFERING

Let's assume that you're in discussions with a knowledgeable banking firm that's expressed an interest in taking your business public. The banker has your historic financials and projections, and the analyst has looked closely at the business's operating metrics and has concluded that your projections are supportable. How does the analyst reach that conclusion? He or she has probably compared your metrics to other public companies in your industry. If you think back to our earlier example of a business selling golf equipment over the Internet, the analyst will have compared:

- Click-through rates
- Sales per web site hit
- Sales dollars per hit

to other public golf equipment sellers. Since not every business sells primarily through the Internet, the analyst will probably look at golf equipment sellers that go through off-course retailers and golf pro shops. For those businesses, the analyst might be looking for other metrics he or she can compare to yours, like sales per employee, sales per advertising dollar spent, or earnings per advertising dollar. The analyst will narrow down the list to businesses with metrics closest to yours in size (sales), market share, earnings, marketing costs, and other important factors. This list is known as the "comps," or companies the analyst believes are most comparable to yours.

As you've already guessed, the comps list might include several companies that aren't remotely like yours. For example, if your business is generating $10 million in sales, it seems unlikely that your business would be comparable to Callaway ($800 million in sales) or to a startup with $400,000 in sales. So even though Callaway's sales per employee might be close to yours, or the startup's sales per advertising dollar might be like yours, those comps won't be used by the banker. Other businesses with metrics that don't resemble yours in size, market niche, profitability, and other factors will also be thrown off the comps list.

After this process, the banker should end up with a comps list that most closely resembles your business based on the metrics chosen. Within the comps list, the banker now looks at what metrics determine the trading price for public companies in that industry. For example, banks trade at multiples of book value, while casinos trade at multiples of cash flow. Businesses in the oil and gas exploration and production industry (known as e&p companies) trade based on multiples of EBITDA, proved reserves, and probable reserves. Many companies trade at a multiple of earnings, EBITDA, or operating cash flow, while a few businesses even trade at multiples of sales.

Occasionally a business is so unique that few if any comps can be found. In these situations, the banker will develop comps from companies in similar industries and then apply some adjustments to the available comps. For instance, if your business makes DNA decoding software that is so advanced that it has no direct competition, the banker might look at metrics from niche software manufacturers, scientific software developers, and other leading edge software makers to value your business. Business multiples and valuations also fluctuate in the market based on industry trends, interest rates, general economic conditions, and other factors. When irrational exuberance takes over, valuations like those given the dot com companies in the bubble of the late 1990s bear little or no resemblance to traditional values.

WHAT A COMPS ANALYSIS LOOKS LIKE

Comps are values given by the market to companies in a particular industry. However, comps are subjective in the sense that no two companies are exactly alike. For this reason, valuation is more of an art than a science. A banker must use some judgment in arriving at comps for your business, but this means that the comps list can intentionally or unintentionally arrive at a value that understates or even overstates how the market will value your business. For this reason, you need to review the banker's comps and the metrics the banker used in arriving at your business's value.

The difficulty in developing proper comps is illustrated by the comps analysis in the appendix. This analysis was prepared by a large investment banking firm for a client of mine that analyzed seismic data using proprietary software developed by the management team. At the time the client was considering a public offering, there were several e&p businesses in the oil and gas industry that processed seismic data, but none that did so for outside customers. In other words, the e&p companies that processed this data were captive subsidiaries of large multinational firms, so the subsidiaries' financial results were not separately reported. There were also several public companies that collected seismic data for analysis by the e&p companies and my client, but the data wasn't processed by the companies that collected it. The business had no significant domestic competition because the last stand-alone seismic data processor had been acquired by an e&p firm three years before. My client's only international competitors were private, so there were no comps available outside the United States.

The question was which companies would the bankers use when developing comps—software developers, outsourced software service providers, seismic-data-gathering firms, oil and gas companies, or some combination? The banker used information from a business that was acquired three years before, a seismic data collection company, and a company that made instruments that collected and processed seismic data. I argued that the metrics used to measure my client's performance more closely resembled software companies—and if you look at the gross profit margin, EBITDA margin, and net income margin for my client and compare that to the comps, I think you'll see why. Whether the banker was correct in choosing these comps, you can look at the metrics that the banker considered important in this comps analysis and see where my client ranked. You can also see that the banker focused on comps values based on multiples of revenue, EBITDA, EBIT, net income, and book value.

If you look at the revenue numbers for my client on the bottom of the first page, you'll notice that my client was quite a bit smaller than the comps. This is one reason that their return on equity was so high. If you were considering whether these comps were fair ones, one question you would need to ask is how you would adjust for my client's smaller size but higher profitability.

Looking at the second page of the comps analysis, you'll see that the median multiple at which the comps traded was 12.2 times net income. If you assumed the banker was willing to use this median in valuing my client, do you think the banker offered to price its IPO at 12.2 times its net income? Unfortunately not—the banker wanted the offering priced at something less than this multiple in order to "leave something on the table for the public." Not coincidentally, this gives support to the stock in the aftermarket. The bankers tell their investors that the pricing values the business at less than comparable companies so they should buy it both in and after the IPO!

DOES YOUR VALUATION INCREASE FOR PROJECTED PERFORMANCE?

When you've looked at the banker's comps and the valuation negotiations are intensifying, you'll want to discuss with the banker how much weight is being given past versus future performance. Most bankers will give your valuation a boost for how you're doing in the current year, assuming results are better this year than last. Some bankers will even weight the current year's results, including estimates for the next six to nine months, at 33% of the business's total value, with historic results accounting for the other 67%. If your business is having a great year, you'll want to highlight that when you're talking about multiples of EBITDA, income, or other metrics that will help the valuation. The bankers will respond by focusing on ways to bring the valuation down, like including warrants and options with below-IPO exercise prices as part of outstanding stock. Put another way, the bankers will calculate pre- and post-money valuation on a per-share basis by assuming that all your options and warrants with low exercise prices have been exercised. Don't let this frustrate you, though. Remember that the valuation you'll get in the public market will still be much higher than the value you'll get in a private financing or sale.

VALUING THE PRIVATE BUSINESS IN SALE TRANSACTIONS

Private business values for sale transactions are easier to calculate than those we've already discussed. Most private company buyers price acquisitions at a multiple of EBITDA. Private companies in low-tech or old-line manufacturing activities typically get multiple ranges from 3 to 3.5 times EBITDA on the low side to perhaps a high of 4.5 times EBITDA. High-tech private businesses might change hands at multiples of 5.5 or 6 times EBITDA. It's rare to see multiples higher than 6 times EBITDA unless the business has extraordinary margins or proprietary technology that can't be duplicated.

One key issue to negotiate in valuing your business in a sale is what the addbacks and deductions are to, or from, EBITDA. When positioning a business for sale, many entrepreneurs will limit discretionary expenses and take other steps to improve the bottom line. Sharp buyers will identify these changes and insist that they be deducted from the purchase price. The business might also

TABLE 6-1
*Sample Addbacks and Deductions
from Purchase Price*

Addbacks	Deductions
Legal costs	Reduce marketing expenditures
Accounting fees	Reduce advertising costs
Difference between owner-	Reduce excess reserves
distributions and expected salary	Increase rents to market rates
	Increase salary costs for new employees

want expenses paid to prepare for the sale added back to the purchase price. Table 6-1 lists some typical addbacks and deductions that are negotiated between buyers and sellers when a business is being sold.

Earnings for the business might increase in the future when owner's distributions are replaced by fixed salaries, so that is also an addback to EBITDA. Negotiations surrounding these points are long and contentious and are often among the "deal breakers" we consider in Chapter 9.

You should consider one other point when planning your business's sale. Many investment bankers have databases about prices paid in private business sales in which they were involved. While confidentiality restrictions prevent disclosure of the purchase price in a particular sale, bankers are usually at liberty to discuss multiples paid in groups of sales. Other bankers can access sale information that's gathered from filings by public companies that acquire private companies. This knowledge can be critical to maximizing your sale price and to setting an asking price that's likely to generate buyer interest.

Real World Advice

Sale prices will vary, depending on whether the price is paid in cash, stock, or some combination. If you get all cash, the price you'll get will typically be less than the seller who takes all stock. The reason is that a seller who takes stock from a public company can lose out if the public company's stock price falls—and during the first year after the sale, tax laws can prevent the seller from selling stock. Private companies won't sell to other private companies for stock because being a minority shareholder in a private company and having no market for the stock is the worst of all worlds.

MY BUSINESS IS EARLY STAGE—HOW IS IT VALUED?

This question is difficult to answer because you almost need to throw out everything we've learned so far. With no earnings, limited capital, and no comps to refer to, a private business that's doing a private financing doesn't have many valuation guides to look at. Unless you're lucky enough to know another company with similar prospects and funding needs that recently got financed, valuation is often just a guessing game. Here are a few suggestions to keep in mind if you find yourself in this spot.

▬ Getting competing financing sources to put bids on the table is sometimes the best way to find out your business's value. Your business is worth what someone will pay!

▬ Resolve doubts by looking at debt or raising less money now. If you can limit ownership give-ups until you've proven out the product or concept, you'll get more value for the equity dollar you take in.

▬ If you have a hard time valuing your business, investors will too. When in doubt, ask a higher price but be flexible when it's time to move ahead. Remember that the objective is to get enough financing to grow your business to the next level.

VALUATION NEGOTIATING STRATEGIES

When you sign the letter of intent or term sheet, you and the investor or banker agree on your business's initial value. The final value

varies based on
━ The investment's form (e.g., whether you issue common or pre-ferred stock) or if the purchase price is paid in cash or stock
━ Due diligence results
━ Financial projections being met before closing
━ Market values of comparable companies
Consider the following strategies when you're negotiating valuation.

Managing the Financial Model
Most investors and bankers put together financial models that shave 20% or more from your projections by

- Reducing operating results across the board
- Developing their own projections

Investors and bankers that develop their own projections selectively reduce the metrics you give them. If the investor's metrics are different from yours, ask the investor to share its financial model and consider what changes were made. Most investors will share their model with you on request.

━ When you know the investor's metrics, show they are inconsistent with your metrics or the industry's. For example, if your business consistently has 20 click-throughs per 100 web site visits and the investor used an industry average of 12 click-throughs in its model, focus on this metric. Explain why your business performs better than the competition and why this will continue. Superior knowledge of the business and its metrics will pay dividends!

━ If you can live with the investor's metrics but the value still seems low, ask for an equity claw-back or more stock options. As previously discussed, a claw-back lets you and the other officers earn out more equity when the business meets preset revenue, income, or EBITDA benchmarks. The downside to a claw-back is that the value of the "earned" shares is taxable income to you. The business also has to report compensation expense equal to the stock value, so income falls. This is self-defeating because your higher earnings are offset by the compensation expense. You could also be forced to register and sell your shares to pay a sizable tax bill triggered by the earn-out. If the market is not liquid, large sales can drive your stock price down and cause your stock's value to fall further. Here is a better alternative. If your business has a stock option plan, ask the board to grant you and the other officers more incentive stock options. If the investor treats options just like shares, suggest the options vest only when the business meets income or EBITDA goals. This is just like an equity claw-back—except the business has no compensation expense and you don't pay taxes until you exercise the options *and* sell stock.

Public Company Valuation

■■■ Always review the banker's comps to see if obvious comps were left out, or if other comps were included that don't belong. If the banker has used bad comps or left out good ones, you will get a lower value than you deserve. Ask the banker to explain if more weight was given to one comp versus another and why. When you know the banker's comps and the weight given each one, you can challenge an unfair value or one that is just plain wrong.

Getting new stock options or upping the size of earlier option grants is another way to increase your effective value, especially if the option's price equals the expected IPO price. Options with exercise prices at or above the IPO offering price are not dilutive for financial statement purposes, meaning these options don't affect your earnings per share until exercise or until your stock price rises. Investment bankers argue that options will eventually dilute earnings per share when they are "in the money" and exercised. You should reply that "in the money" options are valuable only when the business has on-going earnings to support the stock price. More options allow you to "claw back" hard-earned ownership without immediate tax consequences.

■■■ Performance escrows are another way to compromise on value without getting a large tax bill. As we've discussed previously, you and other officers put 15% or more of your shares in an escrow account when the IPO closes. The escrowed shares are stock you already own, not stock you will get in the future. If you hit financial goals like projected income or EBITDA in the first or second year after the offering, you get the escrowed stock back right away. If you don't make your numbers, the stock stays in escrow for seven years and is then released.

Since the shares come out of escrow, even if you don't make the first- and second-year financial goals, you owe no taxes because of an "early" release. Smaller investment banks like these escrows—the early release doesn't affect the company's bottom line, and officers are rewarded for making their numbers. Also, bankers like the fact you and the other officers can't sell the escrowed shares for seven years if you don't make your numbers. Obviously, you should set reachable income or EBITDA targets when you suggest or agree to a performance escrow. This is another good reason to avoid using sky-high projections in your business plan—the projections are sometimes used by the bankers to set the numbers that get you an early escrow release!

CHAPTER PERSPECTIVE

You need to know how to value your business and how others will do so. Valuation is the key to maximizing your stockholder returns, whether your business is doing an IPO, raising private equity, or selling. If you understand valuation, you can spot weaknesses in the valuations done by investors and bankers and can avoid aggressive overvaluations that lead to failed financings. Knowing the metrics and comps used by bankers, you can do your own comp analysis and evaluate the EBITDA, earnings and other ratios that tell you how companies in your industry are valued. If you decide to sell your private business, you'll need to consider what EBITDA multiples are attainable, the way you'll get paid, and what addbacks and deductions to watch for. Valuation isn't an exact science, so you'll want to get more than one financing proposal if comps or ratios don't give you much guidance. If you run into valuation disagreements, use your knowledge about metrics, comps, options, earn-outs, and escrows to give you and your stockholders the best shot at higher returns.

Finalizing Terms: The Purchase Agreement

INTRODUCTION AND MAIN POINTS

You've now reached the point in the financing process where you are close to your objective. You signed a term sheet or letter of intent and reached preliminary agreement on major issues like valuation, structure, and compensation. Due diligence is ongoing, and you're now free to focus on getting the purchase agreement put together. Regardless of the financing you're working on, you'll find that agreements to buy euqity or debt are actually very similar. In this chapter, we take stock purchase agreements, loan agreements, and mezzanine finance agreements and focus on the six major sections that these and all other finance agreements share. After studying this chapter, you will

■■■ Know the common elements of debt and equity purchase agreements

■■■ Understand the key parts of all purchase agreements

■■■ Be able to analyze issues affecting your business or the financing in key parts of the purchase agreement

WHAT IS A PURCHASE AGREEMENT?

Often referred to as a definitive agreement, a purchase agreement is a contract between your company and a financing source. The contract says that your business will deliver a note, debenture, or stock certificate for the funds from your lender or investor. If you've seen stock purchase or loan agreements before, just the length alone might have intimidated you—these agreements are often 50 or 75 pages long. But when you boil these agreements down to their essence, they're not hard to understand. These agreements are broken down into the six categories they share in Table 7-1. For each category, we've listed what's covered in that part of the agreement or defined what's being asked for.

If you compare purchase agreements, you'd find that most are organized from front to back in this order, other than exceptions. Exceptions are either written into the agreement in the appropriate

TABLE 7-1
Major Categories of Purchase Agreements

Category	Description
Investment or Loan Amount and Terms	What's being invested or borrowed; dividends or interest; collateral; due date or redemption date; price
Representations and Warranties	Confirmation of historical facts, including operating, financial, legal, and management information
Covenants	Promises about future events or performance; ratio compliance; approvals; delivery of information
Exceptions	Facts that do not comply with reps and warranties or covenants; highlighted disclosure of known facts or events
Defaults, Remedies, Indemnities	What constitutes a default; notice and cure rights; penalties and expense allocation; rights when default not cured; investor or lender rights to be indemnified and held harmless
Closing Mechanics	What each party has to do for closing to take place; location; certificates from officers and others; documents to be delivered; notice, applicable law, and legal clauses

location or are put in a separate schedule or exhibit to the agreement. Now let's discuss the key parts of the purchase agreement other than exceptions, which are dealt with in Chapter 8.

INVESTMENT OR LOAN AMOUNT AND TERMS
The first part of every purchase agreement says the amount of capital that's being invested or lent and the instrument your business is

selling to the investor or lender. A stock purchase agreement says the investor is buying X number of shares for Y price, while a debt purchase agreement says the lender is loaning X and getting a note or debenture from your business for that amount. A purchase agreement for preferred stock might include a description of the preferred stock's rights or will refer to a statement of rights that's attached as an exhibit. Purchase agreements for common stock usually say that the investor is getting common stock with the same rights as the outstanding common stock. Debt purchase agreement will cover terms like interest rate, maturity, amortization of principal, and prepayments. Many debt purchase agreements include the note or debenture as an exhibit and refer to it when discussing the loan terms.

REPRESENTATIONS AND WARRANTIES

Every purchase agreement contains representations (or reps for short) and warranties. Reps and warranties are historical statements of fact or promises that a condition exists. Investors and lenders put reps and warranties in purchase agreements to get assurances that facts or conditions that are covered in due diligence are true. One key issue here is who gives the reps and warranties—your business, you, or both? Most banks accept reps and warranties from the business, but tie you to those reps and warranties by requiring a personal guarantee. This means that if the business violates a rep and warranty, the bank can still hold you personally responsible. As investors don't get personal guarantees, they usually want reps and warranties from you and the business so that they can go after you personally if the business's condition has been misrepresented. By the time your business is in the mature or liquidity stage, most financings are large enough that lenders and investors won't look for your personal signature on reps and warranties.

Nearly all lenders and investors write reps and warranties so that they are unconditional. This means that your business (and maybe you) is saying, for example, that your business has disclosed all liabilities to the lender or investor. If you wanted to qualify this rep and warranty so it wasn't unconditional, you would say that your business has disclosed *to the best of its knowledge* all liabilities or *all known* liabilities. You also might say that you've disclosed *all material liabilities* to the lender or investor. Alternatively, you might qualify the rep and warranty with a dollar threshold (*e.g.*, your business has disclosed all liabilities *over $50,000* to the lender or investor).

Lawyers call these knowledge, materiality, or dollar threshold qualifiers. You'll spend time adding (or trying to add) these qualifiers when you're negotiating the purchase agreement. The reason is that if your business violates a rep and warranty, the lender can declare a default and call the loan due. Investors might be able to sue for breach of contract if a rep and warranty's been violated. So using qualifiers gives you some "wiggle room" if something comes up after the financing that would have violated a rep and warranty. For example, if your business says it's not in default in any material contracts, a failure to deliver products due under a small contract that's not important to your business wouldn't trigger a loan default or give an investor indemnity rights.

Equity purchase agreements usually have more reps and warranties than loan agreements. This is because a lender is more concerned with what happens after the loan is made, which is when covenants apply rather than reps and warranties. Investors are more concerned if historical facts are correct because they rely on these in making their investment decision.

COVENANTS

Covenants are promises about future events. Covenants come in two forms, affirmative and negative covenants. *Affirmative covenants* say what your business agrees to do in the future, while *negative covenants* say what it won't do.

Affirmative covenants usually remain in force as long as the debt is unpaid. In an equity financing, these covenants remain in force until the investors have sold enough stock that their ownership falls below some preset percentage. A liquidity event like an IPO or a sale will also cause most affirmative covenants to expire. Some examples of affirmative covenants are agreements to give investors or lenders financial statements, get audits performed, comply with financial ratios, keep insurance and licenses current, have supply or customer agreements, and comply with laws and regulations.

Negative covenants usually remain in force until a time period expires or until a minimum percentage of equity or debt holders agree to release the business from the covenant. Examples of negative covenants are agreements not to merge with or acquire other businesses, make distributions to stockholders, declare dividends, sell more debt or equity, or make capital expenditures over a certain amount.

When you negotiate covenants with an investor or lender, focus on two issues: how you'll comply and the time given to comply. For example, if you've agreed to a covenant to deliver audited financial statements but haven't had an audit done before, build in extra time in the covenant to get the first audit done.

Covenants are like reps and warranties—you can qualify covenants using knowledge, materiality, and dollar thresholds to give yourself more flexibility. For example, if you've been asked to agree to negative covenants that restrict distributions or dividends, negotiate for dollar thresholds so that you can pay distributions to your stockholders that fall below the threshold. If you have to go back to your lender or investor for covenant waivers every time you want to accomplish something, you can see where this leads. Not only is it cumbersome, but you'll feel like you don't control your business. Lenders and investors don't want this either, unless they have the right to charge you for every covenant waiver they give and consider covenant waivers to be a profit center!

HOW COVENANTS AFFECT CONTROL OF YOUR BUSINESS

One of the most common issues that comes up when you're negotiating covenants is control and what happens if there's a change in management. This issue is key to equity and debt financing sources: they consider your stock ownership and that of other officers as the primary motivating factor for your involvement. Here are some examples of covenants that deal with control.

▬ In early-stage companies getting equity, most venture and private equity firms insist on a buy-back agreement between the business and key officers that's triggered if an officer leaves. You and other officers will often negotiate for less than 100% of your stock being covered by the buy-back right and will want to limit the buy-back to situations where you're fired for cause. Many investors want the buy-back triggered if you resign without cause. The other question that comes up in negotiating this covenant is how to value the shares that are covered by the buy-back. Many buy-backs have valuation formulas that set the price based on multiples of EBITDA or earnings, while others base it on the most recent price paid by outside investors. Still other buy-backs base the price on a value set by one or several outside valuation firms.

▬ Tag-along rights given to early stage investors are included in covenants. If you or another manager find an investor to buy part of your stock, the investor with tag-along rights can sell a pro rata portion of its stock too.

▬ In early-stage companies, the purchase agreement or an agreement among the stockholders will have a covenant that prohibits stock transfers to your competitors.

▬ In public companies getting private equity or mezzanine financing (sometimes referred to as PIPEs, Private Investment in Public Entities), covenants say that management's ownership will not fall below some preset percentage. You'll want to negotiate a clause that allows you to sell shares under Rule 144 or sell shares you get when you exercise options.

Rights of First Refusal and Preemptive Rights

Covenants that give investors rights of first refusal or preemptive rights also need special attention. Here's how these covenants can work against you.

■■■ If an investor has a right of first refusal to fund your next round, you'll find it difficult to get interest from other potential investors. You can understand that other potential investors will consider it a waste of time and money to start due diligence once they find out about the right. If you can't get other investors interested, you might get a lower valuation in the next round unless you've got a preset valuation formula in place. If you do give a right of first refusal, limit the right to the investor's pro rata share of the next round. This converts the right of first refusal to a preemptive right, which is better for you and your other stockholders because it doesn't lock you into one investor for future funding.

■■■ Preemptive rights let an investor buy stock in later rounds so that the investor can keep its percentage ownership of the business constant. You should focus on limiting the time that preemptive rights exist or eliminating them after your business raises more than some threshold in additional funding. Here's why:

- If preemptive rights are given only to one investor and the business does two or three more financing rounds, the investor's ownership will remain undiluted if it continues to exercise its preemptive rights. This is just like having antidilution rights, with the only difference being that the investor will pay the prevailing price in each later round. Unless you and your team also have preemptive rights and can afford to exercise them, the investor that exercises preemptive rights in multiple rounds can quickly gain effective control of your business.
- If you negotiate to get preemptive rights to try to keep up with an investor, your success in operating the business is the very reason that later rounds will have a higher price. Unless you and your team have deep pockets, you won't be able to keep ownership parity with an institutional investor. One way to deal with this is to put dollar or time limits on preemptive rights. If this doesn't work, consider negotiating for new options that'll become exercisable if preemptive rights are exercised.

DEFAULTS, INDEMNITIES OR HOLD HARMLESS LANGUAGE, AND REMEDIES

Equity and debt purchase agreements differ in how they treat a default. In a debt financing, a default will trigger a notice from the lender, and, if it's not cured, the loan will be accelerated, and the principal will be declared due. There are two types of defaults in debt financings: payment or nonpayment defaults. *Payment defaults* typically have shorter notice times and opportunities to cure than nonpayment defaults. Although breach of a rep and warranty is a nonpayment default, most *nonpayment defaults* are covenant violations. These include

- Default in other debt payments
- Transfer or sale of collateral without the lender's consent
- Bankruptcy, reorganization, and similar proceedings
- Loss of licenses needed to operate the business
- Entry of a judgment that remains unpaid or that's not appealed
- Consent orders or other regulatory actions
- A change in control, sale of assets, merger, acquisition, or similar transaction
- Noncompliance with financial and net worth ratios

When a default is declared and is not cured in the notice time, a lender has broad power to take and sell collateral, foreclose on real and personal property, and even operate the business. This is the main reason why you want the longest notice and cure times you can get when you're negotiating the debt purchase agreement.

In an equity purchase agreement, "default" is not an issue unless the business doesn't meet financial targets that give the investor more ownership, or the right to elect more directors or change management. These clauses are limited to early- and operating-stage entities that get significant funding from venture or private equity firms. If an investor decides after closing that a rep and warranty wasn't true, the investor's recourse is probably limited to going to the board of directors and getting the responsible officer fired. If the untrue statement was covered by an expert's opinion, like an audit opinion on the financial statements, the investor could seek recovery from the expert. Absent filing a lawsuit, however, an investor doesn't have much recourse. Investors get higher rates of return than lenders because the risks they assume are higher. This is also why due diligence is so important to investors: once the money's spent, an investor's remedies are usually limited or non-existent.

Lenders typically get broad indemnity protection from the business for any damages, expenses, and costs that relate to a loan or its collection. The only exceptions to this indemnity are the lender's gross negligence or willful misconduct. The lender will also get a broad environmental indemnity covering any facilities that are owned or leased by the business. Lenders seldom negotiate their indemnity language; instead, they have the attitude that indemnity is their right, and your obligation.

Investors aren't usually indemnified by the business for covenant violations or breaches of reps and warranties. If the investor's own funds that are invested in the business are the best source of recovery, you can see why investors don't usually care too much about being indemnified. Some investors want indemnity protection against third-party claims, like those from stockholders, in the purchase agreement. If the investor has a net worth that's far more than the business's, though, indemnity from the business won't mean much. The bottom line is that indemnification is not usually an issue with investors like it is for lenders.

Penalty Clauses

In equity purchase agreements, remedies given to investors are called penalty clauses. These clauses can take several forms.

■ Adjustments to the preferred stock or convertible debt conversion rate, or adjustments to warrant exercise prices that are sold with debt. These adjustments typically give the investor a bigger ownership percentage of the business if the business doesn't hit financial targets. Also, if the investor's shares aren't registered to become free trading in the time specified in the registration rights agreement, the investor sometimes gets penalty stock.

■ Voting trusts or irrevocable proxies that give the investor voting rights over your stock if the business doesn't meet performance benchmarks

■ Preferred stockholders that have a veto power over most, if not all, corporate decision making by requiring high stockholder approval percentages for most issues

■ Interest rate increases for debt that's sold with equity, and acceleration of the principal under some circumstances

■ An automatic increase in the board of directors' size that gives the investor control of the board

■ Loss of unvested options or stock in a claw-back if vesting or performance criteria aren't met

You need to review and negotiate penalty clauses carefully because a change in control, reduced board representation, or a major loss in stock value can have an enormous impact on you and your team. For financial targets in particular, take the time to consider worst case scenarios and what will happen to you and your team in these circumstances. You'll also need to explore what happens if your next financing round is delayed and, for that reason, you don't hit your financial targets. If you stand to lose ownership or control, try to negotiate performance clauses that specifically depend on your getting more funding when it's needed.

CLOSING MECHANICS

The last part of equity and debt purchase agreements covers closing mechanics. These include what conditions you need to fulfill before the investor or lender must close, what the investor or lender must do, and what has to be delivered by everyone at the closing. Lenders and investors usually want certificates that the reps and warranties are true, consents of government agencies or regulators, officer certificates, signatures on all exhibits and schedules called for by the purchase agreement, legal opinions, and a cold comfort letter from the audit firm.

Real World Advice

The one condition to closing that you'll need to review and discuss with your team is any requirement that the lender or investor must complete due diligence to its satisfaction. A condition like this is very dangerous because it gives the investor or lender a right to walk away from the financing at any time right up until closing. When an investor or lender asks for a "due diligence out," as these are known, try to get a time limit of 20 or 30 days after the purchase agreement is signed when the "due diligence out" will expire. You can also ask the investor or lender to accelerate their due diligence and get it done before you'll sign the purchase agreement. This will at least give you the right to keep talking to other investors and won't give the investor or lender the feeling that they've got you committed without having committed themselves.

CHAPTER PERSPECTIVE

Purchase agreements for equity and debt financings share much of the same language. These agreements cover financing terms, historical facts through reps and warranties, future issues through covenants, defaults, indemnities and remedies, and closing mechanics. Reps and warranties are statements of historic fact that are an investor's main protection. Lenders focus more on affirmative and negative covenants that promise what your business will or will not do in the future. Investors rely on covenants to exercise control over the business or your management team, get rights of first refusal or preemptive rights for future financings, and penalize you or your business if operating targets aren't met. Indemnities are standard in both equity and debt purchase agreements and indemnities for lenders are almost always nonnegotiable. Closing conditions are what you and your lender or investor must each do for a financing to close. Standard closing conditions call for officers' certificates, consents of other lenders, regulatory consents, legal opinions, audit firm cold comfort letters, and signed employment agreements, investor rights' agreements, and other exhibits to the purchase agreement. If the conditions to closing include a due diligence out, you'll need to understand what due diligence the investor or lender has yet to do and how long it will take. Try to get a time limit on any due diligence out; otherwise, your financing commitment will be a one-way street. Before we leave purchase agreements, let's look at exceptions and the schedules and exhibits that go with the purchase agreement.

Preparing Disclosure Schedules and Exhibits

INTRODUCTION AND MAIN POINTS

While you and the investor or banker are working on the purchase agreement, due diligence and discussions with the investor or banker will cause issues to surface. These issues have to be covered somehow in the purchase agreement. But if you changed the purchase agreement for these issues, you could end up with a 200-page purchase agreement. So instead of using the purchase agreement, you'll put together disclosure schedules and exhibits to the purchase agreement to disclose these issues, called exceptions. Exceptions can make an investor or lender uncomfortable and if an exception isn't handled correctly, it could cost your business its financing. The key to dealing with exceptions successfully is knowing what they are, how they're disclosed, and when they're disclosed. After studying this chapter, you will

■ Know what an exception is and why it's important
■ Learn where exceptions are disclosed
■ Understand that your financing depends on handling exceptions carefully

WHAT IS AN EXCEPTION AND WHY IS IT IMPORTANT?

Most exceptions are "carve-outs" from reps and warranties. This means that what's described as an exception is excluded from what's stated as a fact or a promise. Most exceptions are from reps and warranties that you give in the purchase agreement. These exceptions are usually disclosed in a disclosure schedule or exhibit to the purchase agreement. Occasionally you'll disclose an exception to a covenant, but most covenant exceptions are written into the covenant and not separately disclosed. For example, assume your business is a Subchapter S corporation for tax purposes and has covenanted that it won't make stockholder distributions. An exception would typically be put in the purchase agreement to let you distribute enough income to your stockholders so they can pay their taxes.

Exceptions in financings are important because lenders and investors pay attention to issues that appear in disclosure schedules and exhibits. If the issue is important enough, the lender or investor can ask for more due diligence and hold up the closing while it reviews more information. If the exception relates to a significant issue, the investor or lender might ask your attorney to give an opinion on the issue. In a public offering, a significant exception is a disclosure issue and will likely be highlighted in the prospectus. That's why most IPO prospectuses have long "Risk Factors" sections—the company is disclosing issues that might hurt its business. In a purchase agreement, you use disclosure schedules and exhibits to accomplish the same thing.

Even though each business has its own issues, some exceptions appear more often than others. Table 8-1 lists the common exceptions and the reason why the exception is disclosed.

Real World Example

One of my clients was negotiating a mezzanine financing with a commercial finance company and gave the mezzanine lender the most recent collateral audit done by their senior lender. The collateral audit had found a few inventory discrepancies, and the dollar amount involved was enough that it caused some concern for the potential lender. The client assured the mezzanine lender that all was well, but the loan officer decided that the lender would be better off waiting for a schedule of inventory adjustments. When the mezzanine lender got the schedule, the loan officer decided that my client's inventory controls needed to be beefed up before funding the mezzanine. The financing closed after four months, but by that time my client had spent over $50,000 putting new inventory controls in place and paying overlimit fees on its senior credit line. This really brought home for my client why exceptions are important.

TABLE 8-1
Common Exceptions to Purchase Agreements

Description	Nature of Exception
Litigation	Amount claimed is over dollar threshold
Taxes	Audit or appeals ongoing for income taxes, sales, use and property taxes
Changes in liabilities, assets, or debt	Change is "material" and over dollar threshold
Environmental issues	Use, storage, or disposal of environmentally sensitive products
Material contracts	Those in dispute or over dollar threshold
Inventory	Write downs or other adjustments
Material suppliers and customers	Identities, whether contracts exist, and term
Accounts receivable	Disputed, denied, or written off

DISCLOSING EXCEPTIONS: THE WHEN AND THE HOW

The cardinal rule when dealing with exceptions is to avoid surprises at all costs. A practical way to deal with a possible exception is to tell the investor or lender about it well before they see the first disclosure schedule. By "managing" the disclosure, you'll avoid surprises later on when the exception pops up on your disclosure schedule. You don't have to put the issue on the table in your first meeting with a prospective investor or lender, but you'll need to discuss the issue when your relationship has advanced and a good opportunity for disclosure appears.

Real World Advice

Do not adopt the *caveat emptor* approach, or let the buyer beware, and wait to see if the investor or lender discovers the issue in due diligence. When this happens, the investor or lender believes that they've been sand-bagged unless there's no way you could have known about the issue. If the investor or lender has any suspicion that you knew, they'll terminate the term sheet or letter of intent immediately. Even more damaging are situations where the investor signed a definitive agreement with a due diligence out and then refuses to close. Because the business probably hasn't continued discussions with other investors, the financing's termination means that the business must start the process all over again. The effect of a "busted" financing on management morale and the business's financial condition shouldn't be underestimated. Also, when word leaks out in the financial community that a bank or investor backed away from a transaction, the business might find it hard to get alternate financing.

The most difficult issue you can encounter in preparing disclosure schedules is when you, another officer, the lender, or the investor discover a disclosure issue during due diligence for the first time. This is a moment when the financing's future hangs by a slender thread, and the outcome often depends on how you respond. Although it's hard to generalize, many investors or lenders will use this situation to "take the measure" of management. If you respond in a thoughtful and measured way, making it clear that you're able to manage the issue and take appropriate action, your level-headed reaction can calm lenders and investors and reinforce their positive impression of your leadership.

PUBLIC OFFERING DISCLOSURE

A business doing a public offering has due diligence done by its own counsel, its auditors, the investment banker, the investment banker's counsel and even, to a very limited extent, the SEC and the stock exchanges. The SEC and the stock exchanges aren't responsible for doing due diligence. But with information widely available over the Internet, the SEC and the stock exchanges are taking a more activist role in questioning disclosure. They're also monitoring information appearing on the Internet about businesses that are doing offerings. That's why your lawyer will recommend that you clean and update your web site, remove questionable hyperlinks, and make sure that your disclosure and web site are consistent.

When your public offering becomes effective, you'll sign the underwriting agreement with the lead underwriter. Like any other purchase agreement, the underwriting agreement has the purchase terms for the stock, representations and warranties, covenants, indemnities, and closing mechanics. Instead of using a separate disclosure schedule, the underwriting agreement says that each rep and warranty is unqualified except for information disclosed in the prospectus. So the prospectus serves two purposes—giving full disclosure to investors and highlighting exceptions from reps and warranties that are in the underwriting agreement.

Underwriting agreements have most of the same reps and warranties, as well as covenants, that other equity purchase agreements have. That means you'll focus on qualifying reps and warranties and limiting covenants using knowledge, materiality, and dollar thresholds. A banker "represents" the public investors and is responsible for doing due diligence just like an institutional investor does due diligence for itself. The banker isn't responsible for the business's disclosure, but is expected to review and assist in preparing disclosure in the prospectus. The banker's main defense to a claim that the business failed to provide full disclosure to investors is its due diligence.

Failure to disclose issues in a public offering prospectus has far greater consequences than in a private financing. Officers and directors have very limited due diligence defenses. Class action lawsuits, civil action by the SEC or stock exchanges, and even criminal prosecutions are now possible if your business fails to make proper disclosure in a public offering. The dollar amounts and number of investors in public offerings mean bigger damages if things go wrong, so your best protection is making sure that all the issues that are important to your business are fully disclosed.

Like bank indemnities in loan agreements, the underwriting agreement gives broad indemnity protection to investment bankers. The underwriting agreement says the business will indemnify the bankers for everything that's in the prospectus except for the stock price, the bankers' names, and the name of their counsel. Just like bank indemnities, investment bankers won't negotiate their indemnities in the underwriting agreement. This means that you'll be better off spending your time reviewing your prospectus and its disclosure than negotiating indemnities with your bankers.

CHAPTER PERSPECTIVE

Exceptions are issues that you exclude from a rep and warranty or covenant so that your agreements and disclosure are accurate. Lenders and investors pay close attention to what's in your disclosure schedules and will do more due diligence if an exception raises questions. You need to take an active role in managing exception disclosure and to avoid surprises that might make a lender or investor uncomfortable. You also need to be proactive in making sure that exceptions are fully disclosed, particularly in public equity offerings. Although due diligence is the responsibility of investors, lenders, and investment bankers, indemnities shift the disclosure burden to your business. Failure to make full disclosure can trigger lawsuits and regulatory action, and the potential damages are extremely high. As your business's last "disclosure defense," you should personally review disclosure schedules and offering documents so that you're comfortable that each exception's been disclosed.

Exploring Deal-Breaking Issues

INTRODUCTION AND MAIN POINTS

In this chapter, we'll consider major issues that sabotage financings between term sheet signing and closing. These include

- Due diligence
- Antidilution
- Employment agreements
- Stockholder agreements
- Board membership and voting rights
- Major transaction approval rights
- Miscellaneous investment terms

We'll help you anticipate these issues and discuss strategies to deal with them without risking your financing. After studying this chapter, you will

▬ Understand the critical issues that stop financings from closing
▬ Grasp their impact on you, your business, and your stockholders
▬ Know negotiating strategies to create common ground with investors

As we've discussed, due diligence is proving facts in the business plan are true, and valuation is deciding a business's worth. Due diligence or valuation issues come up in all equity and convertible debt deals, and due diligence is part of rating every borrower's creditworthiness. You can deal with 98% of diligence issues if you ask the right questions and anticipate what investors/lenders need to know. If you fill in missing diligence before an investor's review, you'll save valuable time and eliminate potential surprises. Well-prepared management will close a financing faster by arming itself with vital information and due diligence that leaves nothing to chance.

Employment and stockholder agreements have great potential to stop your financing before closing. Most term sheets say employment issues and stockholder rights will be "customary" or "industry standard." Don't be surprised if the actual agreements use language that is anything but customary or industry standard. You and the other officers will face difficult problems like

- The time and territory of noncompete clauses
- How to define "cause" in your employment agreements
- Severance and benefits after termination
- Terms of stock buybacks or put options
- Limits on stock/option sales or gifts

A favorable answer to these issues can be the difference between financial success and losing your job or control of the company. That's why you must understand how employment and stockholder agreements work and how they can help or hurt you.

CONDUCTING DUE DILIGENCE: WHAT TO EXPECT
Due diligence is always business specific, but here are some broad categories.

1. **Operational**

- Business model: manufacturing, service, distribution, or other
- Products or services sold
- Growth drivers and strategy
- Industry or market studies
- Sales and marketing channels and methods
- Suppliers
- Customers
- Patents or trademarks (owned or licensed)
- Facilities
- Security
- Insurance

2. **Financial**

- Tax filings, disputes, and policies
- Liquidity sources, present and projected
- Borrowings and collateral
- Information technology and systems
- Intangible assets
- Known or contingent liabilities, including environmental issues
- Capital equipment and expenditures

3. **Legal**

- Articles and bylaws
- Board and stockholder minutes or consents
- Agreements of all types
- Pending or threatened litigation
- Purchases, sales, and mergers and acquisitions
- Indemnifications and guarantees
- Stock classes and features

4. **Personnel**
   - Board/committee's qualifications
   - Officers' qualifications
   - Background investigations
   - Compensation plans
   - Stock ownership and performance incentives
   - Employee relations
   - Related party dealings
   - Policies and procedures; code of conduct and code of ethics

5. **E-Business**

- Web site
- Hyperlinks
- E-Security/intruder protection
- E-Distribution or e-sales
- E-Employee recruiting

6. **Outside Stakeholders**

- Stockholdings/warrants or rights holders
- Relationships with stockholders and lenders
- Capital structure
- Investor relations practices and press releases
- Expansion possibilities through consolidation
- Exit strategies

When you put together due diligence for a potential investor, anticipate problem areas and cover them *before* you deliver due diligence.

DUE DILIGENCE TIPS
■ **Make an unbiased assessment of your team.** Investment bankers have an old saying about successful businesses: "It's the

jockey, not the horse." Are there holes in the organizational chart? If so, will investors spot those holes and say they justify changes in terms? Or perhaps give them an excuse to push "their" candidate for the job? To avoid this, fill these holes with new hires or ask prospective hires to come on board when you get funding.

Real World Example

A high-technology business pursuing $10 million from institutional investors had a capable controller, but no CFO. The founder knew the potential investors would want a new CFO hired before investing. The founder had several interviews and selected the ideal candidate who, unfortunately, was still employed at another company. The CFO candidate was reluctant to give up his existing job until the high-tech business got the $10 million, but he did want to join the company when the funding closed. Without his biography, the business plan's management section looked weak. The founder and the prospective CFO solved this by using a "no name" biography that summarized his experience without naming him or his present employer. This accomplished two goals: it told investors the business knew about the weakness and had proactively dealt with it before investors raised the issue.

■■■ **Have the CFO or an outside accountant review your accounting systems to spot weaknesses.** If the business has audited financial statements, the auditors must issue annual "management letters" that discuss weaknesses in your accounting systems. Your CFO should make accounting system changes suggested in the management letters before the business pursues a funding. If you need financing to upgrade your accounting systems, arrange to buy/lease the software or hardware contingent on funding. If the financials are unaudited, your CFO should get an outside accounting firm to look at your accounting systems before going after funding. Because investors in a post-Enron world are quick to focus on accounting issues, get ahead on this issue and do away with system weaknesses.

■ **Perform corporate cleanup; that is, review operating, financial, and legal papers to make sure your files are complete and updated.** "Corporate cleanup" is a common phrase that in medical terms would be a complete physical. Good corporate cleanup involves you, other senior officers, and your attorney thoroughly reviewing all the company's operating, financial, and legal documents. The review is used to spot expired or unsigned contracts, missing minutes or board consents, covenant violations, and many other issues. You and your attorney should work together to fill in missing information and update old materials so that an investor doing due diligence finds your files in perfect condition. For example, many private companies don't take board or stockholder meeting minutes, even when major issues are discussed. Fix this by reconstructing meeting minutes from notes or getting director consents that approve actions taken at the meetings. Table 9-1 presents common corporate cleanup items and suggests who should be responsible for getting these items completed. (References to COO are to chief operating officer; to CMO are to chief marketing officer; and to CTO are to chief technology officer.)

When corporate cleanup is finished, make a complete set of due diligence files for you, your attorney, prospective investors, and their counsel. Ideally, deliver due diligence files to the investor and its counsel when the term sheet is signed. This makes quite an impression on investors at this early stage!

■ **Consider your antitakeover measures before funding.** You should update your antitakeover measures before each funding round or ask that your attorney confirm the existing measures are still adequate. If you don't have antitakeover protection, get the stockholders to approve measures commonly used in your state (consult your attorney for specifics). Most companies use some or all of the following:

- *"Blank series" preferred stock* that has terms set by the board;
- Language in the *articles and/or bylaws* that allows the board to divide itself into three classes, with each class having a three-year term (referred to as a staggered or classified board); calls for a 66% or greater stockholder vote to remove a director or change the board's size; calls for advance notice and special procedures when board candidates are not board nominated; allows only the board or chief executive officer to call board meetings; and allows stockholders to remove a director only for cause

TABLE 9-1
Common Corporate Cleanup Issues

Who's Responsible	Corporate Cleanup Description
COO, CFO, and attorney	Contracts in your files are signed and in effect
CEO or COO and attorney	Employee handbooks and policies are done and cover topics like discrimination, sexual harassment, and drug or alcohol abuse
Attorney	The articles and bylaws are up to date and include necessary antitakeover protections
CFO	Waivers of debt/preferred stock covenant violations are in place
CEO or COO	Industry and market information has been downloaded off the Internet or sourced elsewhere to support the business plan
CEO or CMO and CTO	Marketing materials show only products or services now being sold; the web site is updated and error-free
Patent attorney	Patents, trademarks and trade names are assigned to the company; filings with the Patent and Trademark Office are made; licenses are in effect; royalties are up to date
CEO	Disputes with suppliers or customers are settled where possible
CFO and attorneys	Financing files include all agreements and schedules
Attorneys	Equity financing files include subscription agreements, private placement memorandums, and federal and state notices and filings
COO and CFO	All sales, tax or other licenses from government agencies are up to date, and all fees paid
CFO	Leases and insurance policies are updated; all rents and premiums are paid
COO or CFO	Binders for new insurance policies are in place
CFO and attorneys	For real estate you own, the title work is complete, taxes are paid, environmental surveys are done, and abatement work completed and certified by licensed contractors

TABLE 9-1
Continued

Who's Responsible	Corporate Cleanup Description
Attorneys and officers	Each officer, director, and principal stockholder has filled out a background questionnaire
Attorneys and officers	Employment and indemnification agreements are signed and up to date; option grants and stockholder/board approvals of option and benefit plans are done
Board members and attorneys	Independent board members approved dealings between the company and its officers or directors
Attorneys and board members	The company has audit, compensation, and nominating committees that comply with exchange listing requirements (or will before IPO)
Attorneys and officers	The company's files contain all press releases, other public material, and reports to the board and stockholders
Attorneys and board members	Minutes or consents are signed and cover all transactions/issues outside the usual course of business

- A *stockholder rights plan*, for public companies, that lets each stockholder buy more shares at a token price if the company gets a hostile buyout offer.

UNDERSTANDING ANTIDILUTION CLAUSES

As you recall, antidilution clauses are designed to keep an investor's ownership constant even if the company sells new convertible debt or equity. Stockholder agreements usually have antidilution protection—either ownership maintenance or price antidilution. *Ownership maintenance antidilution clauses* are similar to rights of first refusal. These let an investor buy into later financings to keep its percentage ownership in the company unchanged. Ownership maintenance rights don't apply to all financings, but investors usually want coverage for equity or convertible debt sales. Ownership maintenance protection typically lasts several years or until there is a liquidity event like an IPO or sale. Ownership maintenance clauses normally *allow* an investor to invest more capital, rather than *making* it invest. So, if the investor believes the next round is overpriced, the investor can pass on that round. Some ownership maintenance clauses say that if an investor passes on one round, it forfeits antidilution protection in all rounds that follow. This is a great clause to use if you intend to raise funds in multiple rounds and the investor wants antidilution rights. Both ownership maintenance and price antidilution clauses apply to mergers, stock dividends, stock splits, and similar standard events.

Price antidilution clauses are more common than ownership maintenance rights, particularly in venture and private equity investments. The main difference between ownership maintenance and price antidilution is that with price antidilution, *the investor gets stock for free* if you sell equity or convertibles to a new investor at a price below that paid by the old investor. The free stock is added to the stock bought by the old investor until its effective price per share equals what the new investor paid. Let's look at an example. Your company sells stock to an initial investor, referred to as the Primary Investor, at $5 per share and later sells stock to another investor for $3.50 per share. The price antidilution clause entitles the Primary Investor to get more shares until the Primary Investor's effective price goes down to $3.50 per share. The Primary Investor's new stock has no separate price but is considered "paid for" when the Primary Investor paid $5 per share for the original stock. As a result, *the company issues new stock and gets no more capital from the investor with price antidilution protection.* Because different price antidilution language can cause investors to get varying share amounts, you must clearly understand how price antidilution works if the Primary Investor asks for this protection.

If a venture or private equity group is the Primary Investor and bought convertible preferred stock in your company, a price antidilution clause will reset the preferred stock's conversion price. This conversion price reset automatically takes place on new sales of

- Preferred stock at a price per share below the Primary Investor's
- Preferred stock with a lower conversion price to common stock than the Primary Investor 's conversion price

- Common stock at a price below the Primary Investor's conversion price
- Convertible debt or warrants with conversion or exercise prices below the Primary Investor's conversion price

After the price has reset, the Primary Investor can convert its preferred stock to common stock at the new, lower conversion price. Consider a price antidilution clause's impact on the Primary Investor (a private equity group) and the other stockholders of a small business in Table 9-2; assume that the Primary Investor has full price antidilution protection.

In this example, assume that the new buyers made a $1.25 million bridge investment, getting 500,000 shares at $2.50 per share. When the bridge financing closes, the Primary Investor's preferred stock conversion price automatically resets to $2.50 per share. Now the Primary Investor will get 3.5 million shares, rather than 2.5 million shares, when its preferred stock converts. The 1,000,000 shares at the bottom of Table 9-2 represent the new equity the Primary Investor will get from the price antidilution protection. After the preferred stock converts, the total outstanding shares increase to 10,750,000 shares, so the founders' ownership falls to 46.5% instead

TABLE 9-2
Price Antidilution Clause Impact

Stockholder & Interest	Number of Shares	Share Price
Founders common stock	5,000,000	$0.50
Non-founder management common stock	1,000,000	$1.25
Common stock owned by angels	750,000	$1.75
Primary Investor (private equity group) preferred stock convertible into common stock on 1:1 basis	2,500,000	$3.50
Common stock sold to new buyers	500,000	$2.50
Primary Investor antidilution common stock	**1,000,000**	**$0.00**

of staying over 50%. You and the other founders not only lose voting control but also the bridge financing's effective cost is more than triple what you expected!

Table 9-2 shows that price antidilution clauses can be very damaging to you and your stockholders. Venture firms and private equity groups often say they won't negotiate on antidilution, but don't take this at face value. If your business has other potential investors or a particularly attractive business, you can sometimes negotiate limits on price antidilution.

Strategies to Deal with Antidilution

You can modify price antidilution language in several ways to make it better than the illustration in Table 9-2. Here are some strategies to use when your investor insists on price antidilution protection.

■ **Negotiate time limits on price antidilution protection.** If your business will need more capital soon, ask that the price antidilution clause kick in after six months or a year. This protects the investor from longer term dilution without limiting your short-term capital raising. Because a price antidilution clause can discourage other potential investors from investing in your business, ask the Primary Investor to limit price antidilution protection to three or four years. In this conversation, focus on the huge negative impact that funding shortfalls will have on the investor's stock value and the business's success. Point out that overly aggressive antidilution clauses merely invite later investors to insist that price antidilution protection be waived. This is especially true if the Primary Investor has no further funding commitments and the business desperately needs capital. Argue that some reasonable limits on price antidilution can play an important role in closing future financings.

■ **Give** *ownership percentage* **protection if sales are made at a price below the Primary Investor's.** This is technically not price antidilution. Rather, the Primary Investor is given the shares needed to keep its ownership percentage identical to that before the financing. This is different from ownership maintenance because

- The investor doesn't buy the shares
- The new investors' price is not the issue

Let's use the Primary Investor in Table 9-2 to see how it works. Remember that the 500,000-share sale to new buyers increased the total shares outstanding to 9.75 million before any antidilution shares go out. Since the Primary Investor owned 27.03% of the shares before the 500,000-share sale, ownership percentage protection gives the Primary Investor 135,000 new shares to keep its ownership at 27.03%. As a result, the company keeps 865,000 shares by giving ownership percentage protection instead of full price antidilution, a much better situation for you and the other stockholders. Argue that if dilution rather than getting the best price is the Primary Investor's main concern, you have dealt with that issue by protecting its percentage interest. Not coincidentally, you'll avoid the big negative impact of a full price antidilution clause.

■ **Propose proportional price protection that goes up as the new equity's price goes down.** In other words, if a later equity sale is priced above 80% of the Primary Investor's price, there is no antidilution protection. If the later sale is between 70 and 80% of the Primary Investor's price, the Primary Investor gets 50% antidilution coverage. If the later sale is less than 70% of the Primary Investor's price, there is full antidilution coverage. This proportional protection gives you real incentives to get the highest possible value in later rounds and to fight for that last 1%. Investors should appreciate that proportional protection makes you their ally in keeping dilution down.

■ **Price antidilution protection is not needed if the Primary Investor's valuation is right.** Although the "just say no" strategy is a nonstarter with institutional investors, try to focus attention on the Primary Investor's valuation efforts. The Primary Investor worked hard to value your business, and price antidilution seems like admitting in advance that the valuation is wrong and that's why it needs this clause. If your business needs more capital that comes in at a lower value than the Primary Investor's, the falling value might indicate changing industry or market conditions. The Primary Investor's knee jerk response will be to blame management (remember the banker's old saying about "it's the jockey, not the horse"), whether or not other factors affected the bottom line. The Primary Investor will argue that price antidilution simply "shares the pain" of a lower value among you and the other stockholders. In the last analysis, full price antidilution protection doesn't so much spread the pain but rather penalizes everyone *except* the Primary Investor.

Real World Example

A semiconductor business that successfully raised substantial private capital from U.S. investors was negotiating a $5 million to $10 million injection from an offshore investor. The investor insisted that it get antidilution protection with the investment. The company knew that it would need more funding, so giving full price antidilution protection could really hurt its other stockholders. After long and stressful negotiations, the company persuaded the investor to take only ownership percentage protection. The antidilution protection in the final agreement was *even better for the business* because the antidilution clause had exceptions built in that let the business issue

- Options up to an agreed-upon cap
- Shares for acquisitions
- "Equity kickers" to banks/financial institutions that funded company debt
- Shares to strategic partners
- Shares when warrants are exercised by officers and early investors

These carve-outs gave the business more financing options and the officers/early stockholders a chance to get more ownership, both great results. For this company, sticking to its position and having a compelling business plan gave it leverage to negotiate fair antidilution protection and still close the financing.

EMPLOYMENT AGREEMENT ISSUES

Employment issues come up late in most financings because employment agreements are often treated as a "detail" handled right before closing. The term sheet usually says that key officers will sign employment agreements with terms acceptable to the company, the investor, and the officers. Even designating key officers is sometimes a touchy subject if you intend to hire new officers after the closing. Differences among the officers' employment agreements also trigger disagreements with the investor or between the officers. Let's consider some typical employment agreement issues.

Termination, Severance, and Buybacks

Negotiating termination and severance clauses in your employment agreement really highlights the potential loss of control after a financing. If the business's financial results are below par or the board decides it wants a change, you and the other officers can quickly find yourselves out of work. Since there is no such thing as "guaranteed" employment, your employment agreement needs to protect you from unfair termination and give you a safety net until you find another job. Here are some key points on termination, severance, and buybacks.

▬ **Cause can be anything from failure to meet projections to a felony conviction.** Pay close attention to how the employment agreement defines termination "for cause." If the board can define *cause* or you can be terminated for "action construed by the board to be adverse to the company" (another real life example!), you can be in a dangerous spot. Here is a good rule to follow: the more specifically *cause* is defined, the less likely you'll be terminated for cause. If cause means the business hasn't made its projections, the agreement should say that the financial goals must be reasonable and agreed to *in advance* by you and the board in writing. This will stop the board from using trumped-up financial benchmarks to terminate you after the fact. *The cause definition is critical because most employment agreements give minimal or no severance/benefits to an officer terminated for cause.* Conversely, an officer terminated without cause usually gets generous severance, continuing benefits, and a longer time to exercise stock options. If *cause* is not carefully defined in your employment agreement, you could quickly end up with no job, a lower net worth, and in an expensive legal battle with the company. Being slightly paranoid when negotiating your employment agreement is a good idea!

▬ **Look for notice and opportunity to cure for termination "without cause."** Most often, a termination without cause is due to personal differences with board members or a more senior officer. Most officers are keenly aware of these relationships and are not surprised if poor relations cause their dismissal. However, there are times when an officer isn't aware of issues that, in the board's opinion, support termination without cause. If the employment agreement says the company will

- Tell the officer facts that support termination without cause
- Give the officer an opportunity to "cure" any problems

the officer can better defend against arbitrary termination. Unfortunately, even when notice and opportunity to cure is given, it doesn't do much good if the board is determined to make a change. In these circumstances, the officer's severance should take into account

- The time needed to find a similar job
- The fact that the termination was without cause

In most instances, a senior officer gets one year's severance, although periods as short as 6 months or as long as 18 months are sometimes used.

■■■ **The type of termination decides if an officer's shares are bought back and at what price.** Most employment or stockholders' agreements say the business has an absolute right to buy back stock owned by an officer terminated for cause. These agreements often set a buyback price substantially below fair market value if the officer is terminated for cause. Conversely, an officer terminated without cause usually keeps most of his/her shares and sometimes has the right to put shares to the company. In these situations, the price is often a multiple of EBITDA or equal to the last price paid by an outside investor. No matter the formula, the price will be considerably higher than the price paid to an officer terminated for cause. If an ex-officer needs cash, he or she is often forced to sell stock to the company or other stockholders if the company is private. Again, the price is usually higher if the officer is terminated without cause and the buyback is in writing. You are wise to focus on termination language in your employment agreement and how this relates to any buyback in the stockholders' agreement. Remember that the agreement's language can give or take away negotiating leverage to/from you or the company. If you get as much leverage as you can now, it can save you money later.

Your personal wish list should include a buyback that pays the stock's market value on the termination date. Most agreements give the business and the ex-officer some time to agree on market value, or both the business and the ex-officer appoint an appraiser if no agreement is reached. If the parties can't agree on an appraiser, then each appoints one appraiser, and the two appraisers jointly appoint a third appraiser. The appraisers use several methods to set market value unless one method is given in the stockholders' agreement. If your agreement uses a process like this, you stand a good chance of getting fair value in your buyback.

If the business can't buy back your stock for cash or the stockholders' agreement lets the company give you a note, get collateral from the company or personal guarantees from other officers. The stockholders' agreement should require the business to secure the note with the stock being repurchased and other collateral. If the business has free and clear assets or the other founders are wealthy, put additional collateral on your wish list for buyback language. If you leave the company, additional collateral can be a great bargaining chip to use or trade for something else you need.

Noncompete/Related Obligations

▬ **Noncompete and confidentiality clauses are weapons in the wrong hands.** Many entrepreneurs are used to having rank-and-file employees sign confidentiality and/or noncompete agreements. As a small business founder or senior officer, you probably weren't asked to sign noncompete and confidentiality agreements. Sophisticated investors will want all senior officers to sign noncompetes and confidentiality agreements before closing. Although a few states like California almost never enforce noncompetes, other states will if the noncompete has reasonable territorial and time limits. Rather than gamble with litigation, focus on negotiating limits on the time and territory for the noncompete. *Pay particular attention to noncompetes that go beyond termination or the term covered by your employment agreement, as this language is what usually gets ex-officers in trouble with old employers.* Try to have the noncompete waived if the company

- Fails to get more funding
- Doesn't buy back your stock if it's obligated to do so
- Doesn't pay your severance on time
- Cuts off your benefits before an agreed time period has elapsed

Also, make sure that the agreement says the business waives a noncompete if you're terminated without cause. This gives you some leverage if you are terminated without cause and need to negotiate a buyback or longer severance. Alternatively, you have the option to start competing with the company right away if that's what you choose or negotiations for a buyback don't succeed.

▬ **Confidentiality and nonsolicitation clauses are more dangerous than a noncompete.** The Uniform Trade Secrets Act, or UTSA, protects companies from ex-officers using trade secrets learned during employment. Many states use the UTSA or similar laws to protect employers from unfair competition. Courts are more likely to enforce confidentiality clauses than noncompetes, particularly if the company shows that the officer is using trade secrets to compete. Your employment agreement should state that your preexisting knowledge is not a trade secret, which the UTSA and most state laws will not. Also, some courts look at nonsolicitation agreements more favorably than noncompetes. Nonsolicitation agreements say that the officer won't solicit the company's officers, employees, customers, or suppliers for some time after termination (usually one or two years). When negotiating this language, keep the nonsolicitation term short and include exceptions for general help wanted ads not targeted directly at your old firm's employees, customers, and so on.

Most outside investors insist that their employment agreement form be used for the business's founders and officers. Assume that these forms will be in the company's favor, particularly on issues like competition and confidentiality. It's easy to think that because you founded or have been with the business since its early days, you will be there for many years. However, keep in mind that changes in board members, shifting alliances, and changes in stockholdings can transform "your business" into someone else's.

Miscellaneous Employment Provisions

■ **Negotiate for an evergreen employment agreement.** An "evergreen" clause automatically adds a year to your employment agreement for each year you finish. This is a great clause from your perspective because the time remaining on your employment agreement often dictates your severance if you are terminated without cause.

■ **Have your individual attorney get state-of-the-art indemnities and expense reimbursements.** Indemnity clauses can be written in many ways but, in their best form, will make the business indemnify and hold you harmless to the greatest extent the law allows. You can also sign a separate indemnification agreement with the business that has more indemnities than does the law. Although no indemnity can protect you from personal wrongdoing, indemnities are powerful defenses to claims you are personally responsible for corporate actions. Expense reimbursement clauses are also critical if, for example, you are forced to litigate your employment agreement with the company. Favorable reimbursement clauses will reimburse legal fees as they are charged, rather than after the fact. This is extremely important if the company is holding back your severance during the suit and you are cash-strapped until the dispute is settled or you get another job. Ask your individual counsel to review these parts of the employment agreement so that you're well protected.

▬ Watch for clauses that allow the company to move you without consent. If the company moves its headquarters and you don't want to work in the new offices, the company could terminate you for cause because you "refuse" to work. Try to add language that says if the company asks you (without your consent) to move more than 100 miles from the existing headquarters, this is a termination without cause *by the company*. This language can really give you a negotiating edge because

- The company won't have cause for termination
- You will get severance/benefits for being terminated without cause if you are forced out

This will also stop the board from using a relocation to force your resignation and avoid paying you severance/benefits on termination.

Real World Example

An executive was negotiating his employment agreement with several outside directors of a public company. The agreement was originally used for another officer years earlier. The old form said the company could not relocate the executive or "substantially change his working facilities, duties and benefits" without his consent. The outside directors wondered if this provision was needed in the new agreement. The executive felt it was, telling the directors he was worried about the old "officer in a closet" trick. He described this as a situation where an officer is given a new, closet-sized office at the back of the plant after a change in control. If this trick forces the officer's resignation and avoids a termination without cause, the company pays less severance and doesn't pay a "golden parachute." Once the board members understood the officer wasn't concerned about his situation *today* but was trying to anticipate future possibilities, they said the language could stay in the agreement.

STOCKHOLDER AGREEMENTS

Most institutional investors want a private company's officers, directors, and major shareholders to sign a stockholder agreement with the investor before closing. As described previously, these agreements typically cover how a departing officer's stock is handled. Stockholder agreements also deal with related issues like

- Stock option vesting and exercise
- Stock sales/transfers by officers and large investors
- Rights to buy new equity

Here are some common issues in stockholder agreements.

OWNERSHIP/TRANSFER OF STOCK AND OPTIONS

▬ Transfer restrictions applied to nonparties. Stockholder agreements typically say you cannot sell your stock to anyone unless you first offer the stock to others who signed the stockholder agreement. The agreement should have exceptions for

- Estate planning
- Legal transfers (e.g., divorce or death)
- Discretionary sales (on a one-time basis) for 10% or less of an officer's shares

If you sell shares to a nonparty, advise the buyer that he or she must sign the stockholder agreement for the sale to be valid in the company's eyes. This usually won't be an issue since the stock certificate should have a legend on it that says the same thing.

Real World Example

An investor agreed that a business's officers and directors could sell less than 10% of their stock in private sales. But, the investor insisted that it receive a five-year voting proxy covering any stock sold in discretionary sales. The proxy was canceled if the company had an IPO or was sold within five years. The officers and directors did not appreciate how this clause could come back to haunt them—if each person sold 10% of their shares, the investor would vote over 50% of the outstanding stock. This result was avoidable had the stockholder agreement limited officers' and directors' combined sales to less than a "change in control" amount. However, even a clause like this could cause an unexpected result if a "stampede" to sell began before the limit took effect. A better alternative would have been to cap the shares covered by the proxy. If the investor were using the proxy to gain control through "the back door," this would be obvious when it refused to agree to a cap on the shares covered by the proxy.

▬ **Negotiate favorable option language for officers terminated without cause.** An officer dismissed without cause should get accelerated option vesting and maybe a "cashless" exercise right. In a cashless exercise, the exercise price is subtracted from the stock's fair market value, and the officer gets a net cash payment for the difference. Early and operating stage businesses avoid giving cashless exercise rights since cash is scarce, but many later-stage businesses will give these rights. The officer dismissed without cause should also be allowed to exercise vested options for a longer time and perhaps have a right to put some or all of the option shares to the business at fair market value.

Caution. If the stockholder agreement does not cover these topics, you might later discover that the option plan

* Allows the compensation committee of the board to accelerate vesting at its sole discretion
* Gives 90 days to exercise options after termination
* Says the option holder must pay the exercise price in cash or stock (no cashless exercise)
* Doesn't cover company buybacks of option shares

Because of the disadvantages of standard plan language, be sure that these issues are covered fully in the stockholder agreement. Remember you could find your option compensation at the mercy of an unfriendly board if there is a change in control.

▬ **Buying stock from a stockholder, departing officer, or estate of a deceased stockholder.** Most stockholder agreements let the signers buy a pro rata share of stock owned by a selling stockholder, departing officer, or estate. Sometimes the agreement says that the stock can be bought at a preset value and sometimes a right of first refusal to match a third-party offer. Either way, this right can be positive or negative depending on the company's ownership. For example, if an investor owns 30% of the business and a departing officer owns 15%, the investor's right to buy its pro rata share of the officer's stock is not very important. Conversely, if the investor owns 40% of the business and the departing officer owns 30%, the investor will get voting control if it exercises its rights. Try to cap any pro rata rights if the selling shareholder, departing officer, or estate sales can cause a change in control. If the investor objects to a cap, you and the other officers can give each other a right of first refusal so that you'll keep voting control if one of you departs or dies. The investor can object, but a possible change in control is a powerful reason to stick to your guns on this issue.

■■■ **Look for both tag-along and drag-along rights in the stockholder agreement.** As discussed earlier, tag-along rights let

- An investor tag-along in a sale by officers
- Officers tag-along in a sale by the investor

in a private stock sale (i.e., not on a public market). Drag-along rights are the reverse, allowing management to drag-along the investor if you and the other officers sell some stock privately or sell the business. Drag-along rights aren't usually mutual (given to an investor) unless an investor has a large ownership stake. Drag-along rights stop the investor from blocking a proposed sale or increasing its control if several officers sell stock. Equally important, tag-along rights give you and the other officers the chance to participate in a sale set up by the investor. Because institutions have excellent investor contacts and can usually find a coinvestor if they want to, tag-along rights can be very rewarding. Keep in mind that you don't have to tag-along but can sell your pro rata share at your option. So, if the institution sells shares at a lower price than you'll accept, you aren't forced to tag-along. Most officers are glad to make tag-along rights mutual because it is more likely that the investor has sale contacts than the officers.

■■■ **You must get some minimum value to drag-along an investor in a sale.** Most stockholder agreements say that you can drag-along an outside investor in a private sale only if it's over a minimum price. The minimum is usually the outside investor's cash invested plus some return. This language is fair because the investor's capital played a big role in growing the business and the investor shouldn't be forced to take a loss if it doesn't want to sell. Try to include a clause that allows exercise of the drag-along rights if more than 66 or 75% of the outside investors vote for a sale. Getting unanimous votes is hard and can be impossible if your investor relations aren't up to par. If you have multiple investors and can't get a unanimous vote, a majority vote clause could be critical to closing a private sale where you drag-along the outside investors.

▬ **Watch out for preemptive rights that can force a change in control.** The stockholder agreement gives its signers preemptive rights to buy new stock from the company on a pro rata basis. Some stockholder agreements say if a stockholder doesn't exercise its preemptive rights, they will pass to the other stockholders pro rata. This is dangerous because many officers don't have cash to buy stock that gets more expensive in each round. However, an investor with deep pockets can exercise its preemptive rights and others it "inherits" from officers that don't exercise. Multiple exercises of an investor's preemptive rights can

- Force wealthy officers to buy in later rounds to keep up with the investor's ownership
- Cause a change in control if the officers can't afford to exercise preemptive rights

The solution is to cancel preemptive rights that aren't exercised or to cap their exercise by a single stockholder at 120% of its present ownership.

Registration Rights
Registration rights are in stockholder agreements or in a separate registration rights agreement. As previously discussed, these rights allow an investor to register and sell its shares in the public market after an IPO. These rights are usually exercisable six months or a year after the IPO and until:

- All the registered stock is sold
- The investor's stock can be sold under Rule 144
- They expire in one or two years

▬ **Beware unlimited registration rights and cash penalty clauses.** We previously covered the different registration rights that a company can give to an investor including full demand rights, short form demand rights, and piggyback rights. If an investor gets unlimited demand rights and several piggyback rights, you can pay hefty costs to register the investor's stock. The investor will argue that short form registrations are bargains due to their length and piggybacks are low cost since the company's registering other shares. Though true, these arguments don't deal with how long you must keep each registration statement "current and effective" with the SEC. If the agreement says the time is 90 days or more, you'll pay sizeable legal and accounting fees to update the filing. Consult with your attorney and accountant to get some idea of the fees charged for this work. Remind the investor when negotiating registration rights that it's both preparation and update costs that you're concerned about.

Some stockholder agreements say the company pays the investor a cash penalty if the registration isn't done in 90 or 120 days after the investor's request. This can be very costly if unexpected delays at the SEC, accounting issues, or management changes take place while you're in registration. If the investor won't drop the cash penalty, get plenty of time to finish each registration (e.g., 90 days for a short form and maybe 150 days for a full registration). The best argument against the cash penalty is that you can't control the SEC's review time or comments and can only use your best efforts to register the shares quickly.

▄▄ **Don't give demand rights for a year after the IPO and give piggyback instead of demand rights.** If an investor demands its stock be registered in the first year after the IPO, your business will pay substantial legal, accounting, printing, and other costs that only benefit the investor. This is because

- Demand registration costs are almost always paid by the business
- The business can't use a short form to register the investor's stock for a year after the IPO

If you think of an early demand registration like an IPO, you can imagine the work that registering the investor's shares could involve. You'll be paying a lot more to register stock anytime you can't use a short form registration, although having your IPO prospectus handy will reduce the prep time. Remember that piggyback rights are far less expensive than demand rights because you are already registering stock for the company or other stockholders. Once an institution has gotten its invested capital back, ask to limit further registrations so you can control these expenses. Alternatively, ask the investor to pay part of later registration costs.

■ **Drop most favored nation clauses giving automatic upgrades in registration rights.** Experienced institutional investors sometimes use a "most favored nation" (MFN) clause to improve their registration rights. The MFN clause says that if the business gives new investors better registration rights than those in the stockholder agreement, the existing investor's rights are upgraded to whatever the new investors get. In a sense, this language resembles a price antidilution clause: today's investor benefits from more favorable terms negotiated by tomorrow's investors. MFN language can come back to haunt you, so be strong on this point!

■ **Make sure the investor signs a lock-up identical to yours.** Don't easily agree to register an investor's stock in the IPO because of regulatory concerns and how the market perceives this registration. An investor's early exit can raise issues about "investment intent" and questions about why it's selling in the IPO. If the lock-up is reasonable, many IPO investors will wonder why an investor can't wait to get out and wants to sell in the IPO. Because investment bankers and large investors often have cozy relationships, the bankers might give big investors a shorter lock-up than other stockholders. If a large block of stock is sold right before you and the other officers can sell, your stock price could be driven down and scare off buyers just when you want to sell some stock. If the stockholder agreement says you and the investor are locked up for the same time, the investor's negotiation (or a banker's gift) of a shorter lock-up will work to your advantage too. Try to add equal-lock-up language to the stockholder agreement if it isn't there.

BOARD MEMBERSHIP AND VOTING RIGHTS

Venture and private equity firms usually get board representation and sometimes get a rachet clause that lets them add directors if the business doesn't meet preset financial goals. Angel investors and mezzanine lenders are typically allowed to observe board meetings, but the investment agreement rarely lets them appoint board members. In stockholder votes, venture and private equity firms vote their preferred stock on an *as-converted basis*, meaning the preferred stock votes with common stockholders as if the preferred had already converted. Institutional investors treat these voting rights and the preferred stock's rank as sacred. As you will recall, rank is a preferred stockholder's right to get its investment plus a return before other stockholders when the business is liquidated or sold. This means common stockholders get liquidation or sale profits only *after* the preferred holders take their share.

▬ **Don't waste your energy on nonnegotiable issues; turn the tables and invest on the same terms.** When you buy preferred stock, you and the other officers can get the same benefits the institution enjoys like interest or dividends, preferred capital return, and approval rights. If you can't buy preferred stock with cash, consider buying it for services. Because the preferred stock's value is taxable income, be cautious about buying too many shares for services. Buy a smaller amount and ask your accountant or tax advisor if agreeing to transfer restrictions on the preferred stock can reduce its tax value.

▬ **Consider voting rights carefully.** Here's an example. The stockholder agreement says an investor can nominate three board members. Some years later, two retirements reduce the board from seven to five members. If the investor's directors stay on, the investor will control the business unless you and the other stockholders can elect new directors. The stockholder agreement must be clear about what happens in this and similar situations to avoid an unintentional or carefully planned change of control. Pay close attention to proportional board clauses and make sure they work when the board size is reduced, not just increased.

Stockholder and loan agreements usually say the company must get at least 51% of the investors or lenders to approve

- Deals that affect major assets or collateral
- Changes in articles, bylaws, or preferred stock preferences that affect the investor or lender
- Option or warrant grants to employees over set limits
- Company dealings with an officer or director that aren't approved by independent directors
- Changes in control
- Mergers, buybacks, or capital structure changes
- Dividend payments or distributions

These clauses are referred to as negative or restrictive covenants in loan agreements. Negative covenants restrict or take away the company's freedom to do these transactions without the investor or lender's consent. Chapter 7 discusses negative covenants in greater detail, particularly those that affect you in less obvious ways.

▬ **Since most negative covenants are nonnegotiable, focus on votes needed for approval.** If the investor or bank syndicate asks that 75% of the stockholders or lenders approve these transactions, try to get $66\frac{2}{3}$ or 51% if possible. If this isn't accepted, ask the investor or lender to keep the issues they believe are most important at the higher approval rate and use a lower approval rate for all others. Also, ask that some negative covenants expire when part of the loan is repaid or when some of the preferred stock is redeemed or converted.

Miscellaneous Provisions in the Stockholder Agreement

■■■ **Plan ahead—get audited financial statements.** Nearly all investors insist that the company get its financial statements audited before closing. Occasionally, early-stage companies with limited operations are allowed to deliver audited statements starting *after* the closing. Because many banks want a small business to get audited financials as a condition to receiving or renewing a revolver, plan ahead and get an audit before this becomes an issue.

■■■ **Consider a PIK payable in new preferred stock or notes to conserve cash.** Using PIK securities to pay a current return is a great way to retain cash and yet be responsive to what investors want, particularly early on. If the preferred stock is convertible and dilution is a concern, suggest that the business be given the option to pay interest in cash or in a promissory note that converts to stock if the business can't pay cash interest. This way, if your cash flow is great, you can use excess cash to pay interest and avoid potential dilution in your ownership.

■■■ **Look out for investor expenses you have to pay.** Most investors make the company pay the investor's out-of-pocket costs, including legal and accounting fees. Try to negotiate a cap on the fees above which the investor will pay its expenses. Some investors will let your attorney put together the first version of the investment documents to save on fees, while other investors insist that their attorneys write the first version. If cost is a big concern, ask that your attorney write the first version starting from a form the investor used in a recent financing. This takes away the investor's argument that the new form will need lots of changes and cost more in the long run.

CHAPTER PERSPECTIVE

It is inevitable that one or several of the deal breakers we've reviewed will come up as you go from a term sheet to final agreements. Because due diligence impacts value and gives investors early clues about your management skills, focus on putting together complete and up-to-date diligence materials. This will speed up diligence, avoid surprises, and add to your credibility. When you get the first versions of employment and stockholder agreements, look for the issues we've discussed. Success here is limiting the impact of these issues on you, other officers, and the stockholders. You now understand the inner workings of

- Antidilution protection
- Employment and post-employment duties
- Stock ownership, buyback, and transfers
- Registration and voting rights

If investors use employment and stockholder agreements to make new demands or expand their rights, you'll know what to expect and how to respond.

Recognizing and Dealing with Legal and Accounting Obstacles

CHAPTER

10

INTRODUCTION AND MAIN POINTS

Equity financings during the corporate life cycle will either be a sale of registered free-trading stock or restricted stock. Free-trading stock is included on a registration statement filed with the SEC. Restricted stock has to be sold in an exempt transaction. Private placement exemptions that let you sell restricted stock under Rule 504, 505, or 506 of the federal securities laws are used for most private financings. If your business doesn't comply with an exemption, the SEC can sue you and your business and get injunctions, fines, or bars that prevent you from serving as an officer or director of a public company. This means that you need to comply strictly with exemptions and registration requirements when you do an equity financing. After studying this chapter, you will

▬ Know the disclosure documents used in different equity financing transactions

▬ Understand the financial statements that your business has to give investors

▬ Learn how to avoid common disclosure pitfalls and what your options are if your business didn't meet disclosure requirements in prior offerings

HOW PRIOR NONCOMPLIANCE COMES TO LIGHT

As your business grows and does more sophisticated financings, you'll start to run into investors and bankers that are very knowledgeable about your industry, market, and business. This knowledge comes from their research and involvement in other financings in your industry. If you engage a banker or get an investor interested in financing your business, you'll find out that their due diligence will quickly expose most noncompliance with registration requirements or exemptions. Like the failure to disclose exceptions, noncompliance with the securities laws can kill a financing and make you disclose publicly and to the SEC what's happened.

You might be tempted to stretch accounting and legal advice about an exemption's terms when your business is smaller and needs a quick capital injection. Keep in mind, though, that failure to comply with an exemption can later cost you a lot more than money.

DISCLOSURE DOCUMENTS

Table 10-1 lists different financings for your business and the disclosure documents used in each financing.

Here are a few points to consider as you study Table 10-1:

▬ Loan agreements for smaller credit facilities with banks rarely have a separate disclosure schedule. Larger credit facilities include exhibits to the loan agreement. These exhibits will usually include

- The promissory note
- Compliance certificates saying the business has complied with debt service coverage ratios, interest coverage ratios, flow of fund coverage ratios, minimum tangible and/or book net worth, debt to tangible and/or book net worth, EBITDA, capital expenditure amounts, and other financial ratios
- Security agreements
- Financing statements
- UCC-1's
- Existing liens
- Allowed debt other than this facility
- Guarantees
- A capitalization chart
- Lists of subsidiaries*
- Lists of collateral locations*
- Lists of officers
- Locations where you do business*
- Lists of patents and trademarks*

The points marked by an asterisk are disclosures from the business to the bank, focused on the collateral for the loan and its location.

▬ Early-stage angel investors sometimes offer to invest by just signing an agreement to buy stock, called a *subscription agreement*, that contains little or no disclosure. Even an abbreviated term sheet is preferable to no disclosure at all. The term sheet should note that you offered the investor access to all documents the business had and that you and the other officers offered to answer any questions from the investor. Even when you don't have much to disclose, the securities laws still apply.

TABLE 10-1

Disclosure Documents Used in Financings

Type of Disclosure Document	Bank or Mezzanine Loan	Type of Financing				
		Private Equity		Retail private placement	Public Equity	
		Angels	VC's and private equity groups		Small Business	Over $25 million in revenue or public float
Schedules or exhibits to purchase or loan agreement	X	X	X			
Term sheet (abbreviated private placement memo)		X		X		
Private placement memorandum		X		X		
SB-2 registration statement					X	
S-1 registration statement						X

Real World Advice

I've often told clients a simple story to help them understand how our securities laws work. If I put together a private placement memorandum that fully disclosed that I was going to raise $1 million, go to Las Vegas, and put all the money on red at the roulette wheel, and that is what I did, I will have complied with the securities laws. Our securities laws don't require that the offering be a good one, only that I fully disclose how the funding will be used. Now assume that I went to Las Vegas and only put $500,000 down on red at the roulette wheel and put the other $500,000 in my pocket. Now I've violated the antifraud rule, which says that I must give full, complete, and accurate disclosure to investors about how their funds will be used. Here's one more twist: if I said that I was only going to put $500,000 on red and that I was going to put the other $500,000 in my pocket, I would have complied with my disclosure obligation. In other words, if investors were willing to pay me that much to gamble away half their money, and that's what I did, I wouldn't have violated our securities laws.

▬ For placements to a few sophisticated and accredited individual investors who can look out for their own interests, consider using an abbreviated private placement memorandum, sometimes referred to as a term sheet. This is not the same as the term sheet that comes from venture or private equity investors, but it is a short version of a private placement memorandum. This term sheet will usually include

- A section that discusses the investment terms and summarizes the business
- A complete risk factors section that outlines the business risks and the risks of buying restricted stock in the placement
- A dilution section that focuses on ownership percentages of current stockholders and new investors

- A brief discussion of operations, competition, and business strategy
- Biographies for the officers and directors
- A description of the stock being sold and whether any compensation is going to investment bankers
- Historical financials

Real World Advice and Caution

A common issue that businesses face in raising money through term sheets and private placement memorandums is this: should we give potential investors our projections? Legal counsel will tell you that projections should not be given to investors. This is sound legal advice because if the business doesn't make its projected numbers but gave out its projections, the business and the officers will later get sued based on the failure to make the numbers. But many early-stage businesses find this advice hard to follow. If the investors don't know what management thinks it can achieve using this capital, the investor won't know what the bottom line looks like and what returns he or she can get.

You're caught on the horns of a dilemma: if you give projections to the investor, you might be liable for failing to achieve the projections. But if you don't, the investor might not have enough information to make an investment. Most businesses solve this situation by taking the practical, but more risky, approach. The projections are given out, but they come with several disclaimers worded in the strongest possible terms. Some management teams have even included a risk factor in the disclosure that warns investors not to rely on the projections when they make their investment decision.

If you find yourself in this situation, consider discounting your projections by some percentage before furnishing them to potential investors. Building in a safety net might give you some protection from later claims that you failed to make the numbers.

WHAT EXEMPTION DO WE RELY ON?

A business that's doing a retail private placement needs to find an exemption to make offers and sales of its stock to potential investors. The exemption's terms dictate (1) what the private placement memorandum must include and (2) which investors are able to invest. A business usually relies on one of these exemptions for private stock sales:

- Section 4(2)
- Rule 504 by Regulation D
- Rule 505 by Regulation D
- Rule 506 by Regulation D

Let's briefly discuss each exemption.

Section 4(2).

■ Section 4(2) says that a business can offer and sell stock or debt securities that don't "involve any public offering." This exemption is sometimes called the *nonpublic offering exemption.*

■ The SEC has said that this exemption is meant to be used when you sell notes or debentures to banks, sell equity or debt to institutional investors, and in sales to a few "closely related" persons.

Rule 504.

■ Rule 504 lets a business offer and sell stock to as many people as it wants if the business doesn't raise more than $1 million.

■ Rule 504 lets stock sales made six months before or after the placement not count toward the $1 million limit as long as there are no sales in the six-month period.

■ Rule 504 says the business won't make any general solicitation or use advertising unless the offering is registered in a state or unless sales are made only to accredited investors in states that allow general solicitation or advertising.

■ Rule 504 doesn't call for any specific disclosure to be given to investors. But, remember my story about Las Vegas: the antifraud rules still apply.

Rule 505. Rule 505 says a business can raise up to $5 million if

■ It doesn't sell stock during the same six months before and after the placement as is described in Rule 504

■ No more than 35 purchasers buy in the placement, except that accredited investors don't count toward this limit

■ The business uses no general solicitation or advertising

▬ Sales are made to nonaccredited investors so that the business must give ALL investors the disclosure and financial statements equal to what the investor would get in a public offering.

What is an accredited investor? An accredited investor is

- A bank, brokerage firm, business development company, investment company, or employee benefit plan or trust with assets exceeding $5 million
- A person with a net worth over $1 million or a combined net worth with his or her spouse over $1 million
- A person with individual income over $200,000 in each of the last two years, or joint income with spouse over $300,000 for the most recent two years, and who reasonably expects to reach that income level in the current year
- Any entity that has accredited owners

Rule 506.

▬ Rule 506 is similar to Rule 505, but it has no upper limit on the amount being raised.

▬ Rule 506 says that nonaccredited investors must be sophisticated in financial or business matters so that they can evaluate the investment's merits and risks. Nonaccredited investors should use a purchaser representative that is sophisticated.

WHAT SPECIFIC DISCLOSURE MUST I INCLUDE IN MY PRIVATE PLACEMENT MEMO?

For a private offering exempt under Rule 505 or 506, you need to include

▬ The same information you would give investors in a public offering form that your business could use

▬ Financial statements

- For offerings up to $2 million, a current audited balance sheet
- For offerings up to $7.5 million, audited operating statements for two years and one year's balance sheet, and unaudited interim financials
- For offerings over $7.5 million, audited operating statements for three years and two years' balance sheets, and unaudited interim financials

All this information must be given to the investor a reasonable time before the sale.

Real World Advice

The SEC says that if the business makes sales *only to accredited investors*, the business doesn't have to give investors ANY of the information we've already discussed. Again, remember my Las Vegas story—if you don't give any information to investors, how can you ever prove that you gave them full disclosure? You shouldn't rely on this loophole unless you are dealing with very savvy investors and you don't mind putting your net worth at risk by having these folks come in as investors without any disclosure!

TYPICAL COMPLIANCE VIOLATIONS IN PRIVATE OFFERINGS

The most common compliance violations in private offerings happen in three categories: first, giving inadequate disclosure to investors; second, making sales to nonaccredited investors in "accredited investor only" offerings; and third, making sales that violate state blue sky laws. This isn't an exclusive list, but it has the most common issues that come up when a sophisticated investor, investment banker, or regulator looks closely at the financings you've already done.

Inadequate disclosure. This issue is specific to each business, but you can avoid many problems caused by inadequate disclosure by using qualified attorneys and accountants to help you put together your disclosure. This process is time consuming and more expensive than doing it yourself, but it will help you avoid obvious pitfalls. For example, if you use short form disclosure like a term sheet, your professionals need to give you guidance on meeting disclosure rules. Also, where private offerings are reviewed by state regulators, called *merit review states*, the professionals can help guide you through the state regulatory maze.

The SEC does not review or approve private placement memorandums. Sometimes, though, the SEC will ask for a copy of a memorandum you previously used when you file with them for your IPO. If you give the SEC well-prepared disclosure documents from your private placement, you'll reinforce positive perceptions about your business and its disclosure practices. This is another good reason to use professionals when you go out for equity financing.

Sales to nonaccredited investors in "accredited investor only" offerings.

As we have already seen, you don't have to give investors any information if you sell to accredited investors only. The problem is that businesses doing private offerings often aren't paying close attention to whom they sell. When the business sells stock to nonaccredited investors, the business must have given the disclosure, or it no longer has the ability to rely on Rule 505 or 506. If you're selling stock in an "accredited investor only" placement, you have to review the subscription agreements signed by the investors and be sure each one is accredited. If you don't, you're the one who will lose when someone later tells you that your private offering violated the securities laws.

The SEC does not make you get a personal financial statement from each investor who claims to be accredited. If the investor fills out a subscription agreement and claims to be accredited, the business only needs to have a "good faith belief" that this is accurate.

Real World Example

I was called in by an audit committee to investigate allegations that a business had violated Rule 505 when it sold stock. The business had raised $3 million in a private placement in an "accredited investor only" offering. When I looked at some subscription agreements, the "accredited investor" box had been checked by someone, but the handwriting was different from the people who signed the subscription agreements. When I looked at the investors' occupations, they turned out to be schoolteachers, retired state employees, and travel agents. Even though these investors could have been accredited if they met the $1 million net worth requirement, it seemed obvious that several must have inherited large family fortunes or won the lottery to be accredited. Once I looked further and was able to confirm that these investors weren't accredited, I was able to report back to the audit committee that the rumors about the business having violated the exemption were true.

Sales that violate state blue sky laws. Unlike the SEC, which says your business has to file a notice form about the placement within 15 days *after* your first sale, state securities laws often require filings *before* sales are made. In some states, a late filing can make an exemption unavailable—meaning that you violated the state's securities laws when you made an offer or sale. Exemptions like Rules 504, 505, and 506 didn't do away with state securities laws, so compliance with a federal exemption doesn't help you in many states. Some state exemptions say that offers and sales in that state and any other state can't be made to more than 10 or 15 investors. Even though you might wonder about one state's ability to regulate what you do in another, this explains why you must be careful about state exemptions when you're doing a private placement.

WHAT DO WE DO ABOUT A COMPLIANCE VIOLATION NOW?

Most statutes of limitation on securities actions run for one year from the date the investor knew or should have known of the violation. If the business informs its stockholders and they don't take any legal action, the stockholders will probably be barred from suing over a previous compliance violation. If the business sold stock to a single investor in a state that violated a state blue sky law, another stockholder in a different state could buy the investor's shares. The transfer wouldn't cure the original violation, but the disclosure would look better.

Here are some other alternatives if you find out your business has a compliance issue from an old offering:

▄▄ *Private rescission offer.* A private rescission offer is a private offering to old investors that tells them about the compliance violation and offers to refund their investment, with interest. State law says a rescission offer must remain open for 30, 60, or 90 days after investors get the new disclosure. Private rescission offers, just like a private placement where you raise money, must also be exempt under Rule 504, Rule 505, Rule 506, or Section 4(2). A private rescission offer usually requires you to put together a full private placement memorandum that focuses on the violation and the investors' rights to rescind. The memorandum also must update disclosure about the business to reflect changes since the original offering.

▄▄ *Registered rescission offer.* If a business has raised money in several private placements and each offering had compliance violations, the business might have rescission liability from several placements. An exemption might not be available to the business that would let it make a rescission offer to all the investors. In that case, the business might register the stock with the SEC and the states that would be offered to investors that didn't want their money back. Registered rescission offers are expensive and time consuming and get much unwanted regulatory attention.

■ *Disclosure of rescission liability.* A business that goes this route must disclose its prior compliance violation and its contingent liability to old investors. This is a real demonstration that "disclosure cures all." The business is disclosing to today's investors a compliance violation that could expose the business to claims from its old investors.

WHY WOULD A BUSINESS JUST DISCLOSE A RESCISSION LIABILITY?

You might choose to simply disclose a potential rescission claim by your old investors for several reasons. The business's cash may not be sufficient to pay back investors that want to rescind. The SEC has said that if you can't fund a rescission offer for all investors, you can't make the offer only to some.

A rescission offer, particularly a registered rescission offer, can take a long time to get through the SEC and state reviews. Because a business can't register stock for an IPO or anther offering while the registered rescission offer is pending, the business might not be able to raise capital for some time. This is why disclosure can be a better choice if you find yourself in this spot.

CHAPTER PERSPECTIVE

Businesses can use different disclosure documents to give investors information when equity is being raised. From a simple subscription agreement to a purchase agreement or private placement memorandum, you can tailor your disclosure to fit investor needs and legal requirements. You'll need to carefully consider and consult professionals about what disclosure is required, what filings need to be done, and whether to include projections in your materials. For private financings, you need to know what exemption you'll rely on, what information and financial statements must be given to investors, any purchaser and dollar limitations, when you might need to raise more capital, and how state blue sky laws can affect the placement. Compliance with federal and state securities laws is critical when your business goes out for private funds. All too often these violations come to light at a later, inopportune time that will put you in a difficult position. Whether you choose to make disclosure or do a rescission offer, the cost and time that's consumed by a compliance violation is something to avoid. Rather than playing Russian roulette with securities regulators and your future financings, plan to avoid compliance violations, give investors comprehensive disclosure, and follow exemption requirements to the letter. It'll save you money, time, and stress, and let you focus on what you do best—managing and growing your business.

Post-Closing Matters: Communications, Covenants, and Costs

CHAPTER 11

INTRODUCTION AND MAIN POINTS

Once your business is funded, you'll need to focus on managing your relationship with the investor or lender. Your business will have new reporting requirements and should keep the investor or lender fully informed about positive or negative developments. You'll also want to lay the groundwork for the next financing, through this investor or lender or new ones. If you manage both your business and your investor or lender relationships well, getting more funding becomes much easier. Keep in mind that potential investors doing due diligence usually want to talk with your existing investors, and earlier investors' perceptions are important to new ones. Like other growing businesses, your business will have its ups and downs. But how you respond to these challenges and how you handle your financing relationships directly impacts your business's ultimate success or failure. After studying this chapter, you will

■■■ Know basic reporting requirements in covenants and law that apply to your business after a financing

■■■ Understand how you can use low-cost investor relations ideas to keep investors and lenders informed and build relationships with them

■■■ Appreciate how handling negative developments in a straightforward and timely way can create positive impressions about your business

THE COMPANY'S REPORTING REQUIREMENTS

Most purchase agreements for private equity and debt have affirmative reporting covenants covering

- Monthly, quarterly, and audited annual financial statements
- Management letters from outside auditors and reports on internal controls and accounting policies
- Compliance during each reporting period with financial ratios

- Defaults, nonpayments, suits, loss of licenses or insurance, and other events that might hurt your business
- Reports to stockholders and those filed with the SEC, IRS, and other agencies
- Changes or additions to pension plans or notices from tax authorities about pension plans
- Changes in location, property, assets, key members of management, or unusual events
- Updated or changed projections

Reporting covenants are much fewer for equity financings where the investor has a seat on the board. Since the board knows about events like those above, equity investors will often eliminate many reporting covenants or waive them as long as they're represented on the board.

Large revolvers have reporting requirements like those described in Chapter 7. The business also has to give monthly collateral reports that include accounts receivable aging, inventory certification, and eligible borrowing calculations. Bankers usually require that the business hire outside firms to do collateral audits at least annually, and more often if industry conditions warrant. Smaller revolvers will have more limited reporting requirements that focus on compliance with financial ratios, collateral certifications, and getting financial statements.

PUBLIC COMPANY REPORTING REQUIREMENTS

Public companies must file reports with the SEC under the Securities Exchange Act of 1934. These reports are available on-line at www.sec.gov. These reports include

- Quarterly reports on Form 10-Q or 10-QSB
- Annual reports on Form 10-K or 10-KSB
- Proxy statements and "glossy" annual reports to stockholders
- Current events on Form 8-K
- Changes in stock ownership of officers, directors, and 5% or more stockholders under Form 4 and Schedule 13D and notices filed under Rule 144 when they sell restricted stock in the market

The Sarbanes-Oxley Act of 2002 has added many new reporting requirements for public companies and their officers and directors. Each public company must have an audit committee, a financial expert on the audit committee (or disclose why it does not), financial and disclosure certifications by the chief executive officer and chief financial officer, expanded duties for board members and committees, and faster disclosure of current events. The SEC is also working more closely with the NYSE, AMEX, and Nasdaq to strengthen corporate governance and reporting requirements.

Timely financial reporting under the Securities Exchange Act is crucial to a business's credibility in the financial markets. For private businesses, an occasional request for more time to finish an audit or report won't usually be denied. But if the business starts to report late consistently, most financing sources will start to monitor the business more closely.

INVESTOR RELATIONS IS IMPORTANT FOR PRIVATE COMPANIES

Most people think of investor relations as what a public relations firm does. These firms help public companies write and send out press releases or press kits and help put together roadshows for investors, investment bankers, and industry conferences. Investor relations can also include more generalized efforts to build a favorable public image for the business, its brand, and its products. Even though a private business might use a public relations firm for more general purposes, it's rare to see private companies that give much more than lip service to investor relations until after a public offering. This is usually because investor relations firms are expensive and a private business doesn't focus on managing its investor relations like a public business.

In the early and operating stages of the corporate life cycle, you and the other officers probably handled most investor relations. This doesn't have to end, but once you've completed more or bigger financings, you should give some thought to how you can improve investor relations without spending a fortune. Put another way, look at the financing as starting, not ending, the need for investor relations.

Here are some low-cost suggestions for good investor relations practices that private companies might consider:

- Send monthly or quarterly updates to all investors by e-mail
- Send press releases announcing new products, customers, additions to the management team, and similar events to investors by e-mail
- Give investors overviews of industry developments in monthly or quarterly e-newsletters
- Hold open houses and invite investor principals and associates
- Offer web casts or videoconferencing question-and-answer updates (this is excellent practice for when you are public)

- Forward copies of news, magazine, and trade articles about your business to investors
- Get customer testimonials and approvals to use them in e-newsletters

DEALING WITH THE INEVITABLE: NEGATIVE FACTS

At some point in your business's life, there'll come a time when you lose an important customer contract, fall behind a competitor, lose a needed supplier, or announce a key manager's resignation. It's natural to feel caught between the desire to prevent damage to the business by limiting what you say, and the knowledge that investors surprised with negative news might feel blind-sided. As we covered in our discussion of due diligence in Chapter 9, you should avoid surprises because presenting an investor with information "after the fact" can undermine faith and trust in your team. Having an open door for your investors and lenders will demonstrate that your team welcomes input from stockholders and operates in an open communications environment. Operating in this way is good practice for what you'll encounter when your business becomes a public company.

Dealing with lenders is different from dealing with equity investors. Lenders don't have an ownership interest in the business and aren't entitled to get reports or information that would automatically go to equity investors. Sometimes losing a key customer or competitive developments won't trigger any covenant reporting requirement. You should think further about these issues before making a decision based only on what's in writing, however. Like the equity investor, bankers hate surprises. If you know that business is probably going to get tougher later in the year and you're likely to be out of covenant compliance, opening communications with the lender earlier can help soften the blow. This also gives you time to try to renegotiate the covenant or to get a waiver. If neither is possible, by starting early you'll have given yourself time to look for mezzanine funding, equity, or a new lender.

For public companies, prompt disclosure of negative developments is both required and good business. Managers that learn negative facts and fail to make a public release can expose the business to liability for civil or monetary penalties, insider trading claims, class action lawsuits, individual lawsuits, whistle-blower lawsuits, and even criminal penalties.

CHAPTER PERSPECTIVE

Investors and lenders that finance your business should be treated with respect and given timely and complete reports called for by affirmative covenants. It's good practice and good business to keep your investors and lenders informed about your business as events occur. You can use several low-cost investor relations initiatives to manage your investor and lender relationships. Not only are your existing investors and lenders good future funding sources, but they can also serve as excellent references for future investors. Negative developments in your business will occur and can hurt investor and lender relations if they're not handled correctly. Remember to avoid surprising your financing partners and to give them enough data that they'll know you are making an effort to keep them informed. Whether your business is public or private, effective investor relations means that you don't forget about your financing partners when the closing dinner is over. If you work and manage your investor relations, it will give you a great return on your investment.

Exit Strategies and Maximizing Your Stockholders' Value

INTRODUCTION AND MAIN POINTS

As your business reaches maturity, you'll start to turn your attention to getting liquidity, refinancing debt that's due, or redeeming preferred stock. If the balance sheet is relatively clean, you might consider a leveraged recap to keep control of your business and to get some liquidity. Other liquidity alternatives like a sale, public offering, or merger should also be explored. This chapter discusses the positives and negatives of different liquidity plans and suggests strategies for maximizing value. After studying this chapter, you will

▬ Understand options for refinancing debt and redeeming preferred stock

▬ Know the most important positive and negative factors affecting your liquidity options

▬ Learn strategies to get your stockholders better returns when a liquidity event happens

The liquidity and refinancing options discussed in this chapter exclude negative outcomes like bankruptcy, distress sales, or liquidation. These situations are usually driven by lenders and preferred stockholders that have collateral priority or liquidation preferences. More often than not, companies that survive bankruptcy and are not liquidated will end up in the lenders' or preferred stockholders' control. Now let's look at the positive outcomes your business can achieve in the liquidity stage.

LIQUIDITY OPTIONS FOR REFINANCING

If your business needs capital to redeem preferred stock or retire sub debt, it's in a different position than a business that needs only stockholder liquidity. Assume for a moment that your business is private and you're going to need to redeem preferred stock in three annual $2 million installments. If you do an IPO or sell the business, you'll have the funding to redeem the preferred stock, but you're not sure if that's the right course of action. In this situation, you'd need to consider

- IPO market conditions in your industry and overall
- Values in the private and public markets based on recent offerings or sales
- Likely buyers for the business, their potential interest, and their ability to pay the right price
- Changes in economic conditions or industry-specific factors affecting your business's value now or in the near future
- Refinancing availability and cost, both in dollars and equity give-up
- The time needed to conduct an IPO, sale, or refinancing
- Your stockholders' liquidity needs, the chances of extending the redemption date if alternative financing isn't available, and the extension's cost
- Penalties that increase the cost of not redeeming preferred stock
- Whether cash flow from the business is enough to pay all or part of the redemption

The last factor is clearly the most important. If your business has enough cash flow to redeem the preferred stock, you'll probably have several other attractive refinancing options. If cash flow is better used in your business and is not abundant, you'll need to consider other refinancing options.

One way to begin this analysis is to decide which options aren't available so that you can narrow the possibilities to a targeted list with good chances of success. If you have a distribution business, for example, you'll know that few distributors get an IPO done unless they're quite large. If your business has patented or licensed products that are selling well and carry nice margins, an IPO might be best if the "window" is open. Even if the window is open, other factors like the management team's age, the need to attract highly qualified employees, or competitors' values in the public market can affect your decision. For example, a management team looking to retire is more likely to sell than do an IPO, while a younger team might want to take the business public and grow by acquiring other companies using stock.

After narrowing your options, you'll need to compare the cost of capital for different financing options. To do so, you should put together a business plan and get it to some equity investors and mezzanine lenders to see what interest they have and on what terms. If business has slowed, you'll likely have few financing or refinancing options. If sales and income are up, you could get more offers than you can use. You should allow more time to explore financing alternatives or to solicit investment proposals if sales or income have been weak. The business with strong results needs to consider low-cost capital like bank term debt, securitizations, and rated debt to replace higher cost financing.

LIQUIDITY OPTIONS WITHOUT REFINANCING

A business that doesn't need to refinance other obligations can sell the business for cash, merge into a larger public organization, or do an IPO. Each of these has positive and negative factors.

Sale of the Business for Cash

▬ If liquidity is king, this option is superior to all others.

▬ A private business sold for cash, except in unusual circumstances, will sell for a lower price than a public company in the same industry. As already discussed, private companies change hands at multiples of three to five times EBITDA. A public company sells for prices based on trading multiples of nine to 12 times EBITDA or higher multiples of earnings. Although sale prices are business and industry specific, the general rule is that the private company will sell for a lower cash price than a public company.

▬ A cash sale lets the stockholders diversify their net worth among different assets, as opposed to holding a large stock position in a bigger public company or holding restricted stock after an IPO.

▬ The indemnities and purchase price holdbacks are usually greater in an all-cash sale.

▬ Tax consequences are usually immediate for cash sales, as opposed to tax deferral in a tax-free merger or exchange. Using installment sale tax treatment can help if your business qualifies, but many businesses won't qualify.

▬ If the founders or management stay to get purchase price holdbacks or to receive an earn-out, working for the buyer's management can be hard. Also, selling management might not get the resources needed to achieve targeted results, souring relations with the buyer.

Merger into a Larger Public Company

Public companies are bought by other public companies in stock or cash transactions. Unlike buying a private company, the public company's management team can't get an earn-out because any future payments belong to all stockholders. This is why golden parachutes and severance packages are used to reward public companies' management teams when one public company is bought by another. Values in public/public acquisitions are fairly straightforward because each party's investment bankers must give a fairness opinion, and the purchase price is usually above the prevailing market prices. Here are a few other points to consider about a merger.

■ The buyer can pay a premium to the business's stockholders based on the differences in trading multiples for the two businesses. For example, if the target (smaller) business is trading at a multiple of 10 times EBITDA but the buyer is trading at a 13 times multiple, the buyer can pay a premium of 11.5 times and still add to its earnings per share. Investment bankers refer to this as an *accretive acquisition* because the buyer is paying a lower multiple than what its stock is trading at. The target company get its greatest value in a stock transaction with a buyer that has stock trading at above-average multiples.

■ If the buyer's prospects improve via the acquisition or if industry conditions are getting better, holding stock in the buyer can be as good as or better than holding stock in your business.

■ In a tax-free merger, the tax consequences are deferred, sometimes indefinitely. Tax regulations often prohibit management stockholders from selling stock for a year or more, meaning liquidity isn't immediate. If tax regulations let you use hedging strategies without the sale losing its tax-free status, you still might succeed in getting some liquidity and diversifying into different assets.

■ Loss of control and lack of input into the buyer's operations can frustrate you and other key managers and make you think that you're at the mercy of events outside your control. This is difficult to accept for key managers who have had long-term relationships with your business.

■ If your business is public, the time needed to finish a merger between two public companies, and the expense, is considerable. Regulatory complications including antitrust reviews, regulatory filing reviews, and international regulatory approvals can delay the merger, sometimes indefinitely.

Initial Public Offering

■ The IPO sets a public value for the business without management losing control.

■ Offering proceeds can be used to grow the business, increasing its value without debt financing's interest cost or a private equity financing's ownership give-up.

■ Stock sales in the offering itself, sales using the overallotment option, debt repayment, sales under Rule 144, hedging strategies, and participation in exchange funds can generate liquidity for stockholders. Liquidity offered by these options can increase if the business successfully executes its strategic plan.

▰ There are no immediate tax consequences from an increase in value; favorable tax treatment likely for management's incentive stock options; or possible Subchapter S distributions of accumulated and undistributed earnings at IPO.

▰ Stock options can be used to recruit and keep key employees, reward management, offset some of the IPO dilution, and get more liquidity.

▰ Accountability and disclosure are, or can be perceived as, negative issues affecting you and the other key managers.

▰ Pressure to grow earnings each quarter can be a distraction from the business's long-term focus and success.

▰ A higher profile is associated with being public, often leading to class action lawsuits, insider trading accusations, and SEC penalties; these are issues that don't affect you if the business is private.

▰ Public reporting expense is considerable.

▰ Liquidity for you and the other managers is reduced by stock sale limits, illiquid markets, pressure from investment bankers not to sell, or the market perception that insider sales mean that business will decline.

LEVERAGED RECAPITALIZATION

The leveraged recap transaction is used in a refinancing or where liquidity is the primary goal. In a refinancing, the leveraged recap uses mezzanine debt or preferred stock to retire existing debt, with a small portion going to redeem some shares held by founders or management. This lets the management team keep control and get some liquidity, a nice combination. Where a refinancing isn't needed, proceeds from the leveraged recap are used for growth or to fund acquisitions and for liquidity for you and other key managers. The leveraged recap

- Is typically faster than an IPO
- Doesn't involve public disclosure and earnings pressure facing a public company
- Doesn't cause a loss of control like a sale or merger into a larger business
- Lets the business expand or refinance debt and generate some liquidity for you and other managers, at a cost comparable to traditional private equity financings

The flexibility offered by a leveraged recap comes at a price. Many leveraged recap financing sources have targeted returns far higher than traditional lending sources. Also, leveraged recap financing sources often want board representation and some involvement in day-to-day management; they also want management to have employment, noncompete, and stock escrow agreements. These agreements are structured to penalize key managers if they resign or are terminated before the "leveraged" part of the recap is repaid. If the business doesn't meet its financial goals, management is forced to forfeit stock ownership and the leveraged recap investor usually takes control.

MAXIMIZING VALUE—A FEW SUGGESTIONS

To maximize your business's value, the board of directors should put together a sale plan to accomplish this objective. Here are a few suggestions:

▬ If the business has maxed out its lower cost debt financing, and a window for an IPO opens, the IPO can increase permanent capital, retire some debt, and offer some stockholder liquidity. If the business is already public, it can get more growth capital using a Private Investment in a Public Entity or PIPE. A PIPE is simply a private investment made by an institution in an already public company. Because the PIPE is priced at some discount from the stock's trading price, it causes less ownership dilution than institutional financing will for a private business.

▬ If more capital isn't needed and management wants to set the stage for a high sale price, you'll want to increase the bottom line before getting an investment banker to find a good merger partner. To do so, the business might increase its capital expenditures or start more marketing programs to increase productivity and sales in the following two years. Late in the two-year period, you can retain an investment banker to assemble the "pitch book" and start the sale process. The goal is for the sale to close as the business's sales and bottom line peak.

▬ Numerous companies have "shopped" themselves to strategic or financial buyers when they're private and failed to find a buyer at the right price. In these circumstances, a few enterprising firms have used an IPO filing as leverage to encourage a buyer to make an offer before the IPO closes. In other words, because the IPO filing is public and there's often publicity about the offering in financial and industry media, the business counts on the offering coming to the buyer's attention. If the buyer knows that completing the IPO will only make the business more expensive to buy and the management team was willing to sell, the buyer with genuine interest might increase its offer before the IPO's completed. This situation is good for the business because the IPO filing places a value on the business that the buyer must meet or come close to if the buyout offer will succeed. If the buyer fails to materialize, the business can always elect to proceed with the IPO and revisit the sale process later.

Real World Example

An investment banker introduced me several years ago to one of the founders of a large sporting goods business. The founder had retired some years before when the business was sold for about $200 million to a large conglomerate with several holdings in the sporting goods industry. When I asked, he told me the story of how the business was sold. The business had been growing by leaps and bounds, and it had held discussions with several potential buyers while it was private. No one had offered what the founders were looking for, so for two or three years they built the business and continued to gain market share. They then decided to do an IPO and actually filed with the SEC to do the offering. Two weeks later, one of the potential buyers they had previously talked to came to see the founders and told them it would pay $200 million in cash for the business. This price was very close to what the investment bankers had set as the pre-money value of the business before the IPO, and almost $60 million above the buyer's last offer. The founders were obviously pleased that the filing had finally prompted a full price offer and accepted it. The investment bankers were disappointed, but did get paid an advisory fee for helping the business close the sale. This was a real life example of how an IPO filing helped maximize a sale price!

■ When preparing the business for sale or merger into a larger company, founders and management must remember that strategic and financial buyers have somewhat different goals. Public strategic buyers look for acquisitions with superior growth rates or earnings that add to earnings per share and tell a compelling story to the investment community. If the business has enjoyed superior growth at the expense of earnings, your management team needs to explain the reasons behind these results so the buyer's management can address this issue with its bankers and analysts. If a strategic buyer has a high growth history and is concerned about keeping this growth rate up, the strategic buyer will often pay a premium even for businesses with lower earnings or relatively small sales. You can see why the buyer's own growth targets can force it to pay more even if traditional multiples might justify a smaller price.

■ A financial buyer is more concerned with how operations can be streamlined in the short term to increase cash earnings and accelerate repayment of debt taken on in the acquisition. As a general rule, financial buyers pay less than strategic buyers. Public strategic buyers are more inclined to buy a business for stock than cash and will pay more in stock value for the business. This lets the public company conserve its cash; however, it exposes you to the risks we've already discussed about taking stock.

CHAPTER PERSPECTIVE

The operating-stage or mature business, whether private or public, should have strategic plans for refinancing debt and debt-equivalent preferred stock well before the due date. Planning ahead for refinancing and liquidity options involves developing feasible alternatives and then narrowing your options. Ultimately you'll select a primary plan, with a suitable backup, to best meet your stockholders' goals. Careful consideration should be given to liquidity transactions that will maximize value, defer taxes, minimize any loss of control, and cut off any continuing liability resulting from indemnities and purchase price holdbacks. If you need liquidity, look at an IPO, sale, or merger, and then plan ahead for how you can get top dollar for your stockholders.

Appendix

SAMPLE TERM SHEETS, LETTERS OF INTENT, AND ENGAGEMENT LETTERS

The samples in this appendix do not constitute legal advice but are only guides to the issues (and paperwork) you'll run into during a financing. Federal securities laws apply to the sales of equity and debt securities and the disclosure you must give investors and lenders. State laws concerning securities, business opportunities, franchises, and disclosure also apply to financings. You should definitely consult a lawyer about these laws and your disclosure obligations before preparing or signing financing documents.

Samples included:

SAMPLE TERM SHEET FOR PREFERRED STOCK PURCHASE
BY VENTURE OR PRIVATE EQUITY INVESTOR

CONFIDENTIAL TERM SHEET

Date

Company, a Delaware corporation (the "Company"), has developed a potentially revolutionary technology. The Company believes that this technology greatly improves the performance of _____.

I. Securities Being Offered by Company (the "Company")

Minimum Number of Shares Offered: 2,000,000 Shares ($4,000,000)

Maximum Number of Shares Offered: 2,500,000 Shares ($5,000,000)

Minimum Subscription: 500,000 Shares ($1,000,000)

Price: U.S.$2.00 per Share

Use of Proceeds: Working capital

Pro Forma Ownership: Giving effect to the offering, the fully diluted ownership of the Company on an as-converted basis will be as follows:

	Minimum Offering (as converted)	Maximum Offering (as converted)
	Common Stock Outstanding	
Preferred Stock Purchasers	2,000,000	2,500,000
Common Stockholders	6,000,000	6,000,000
Total	8,000,000	8,500,000

The above excludes reserved and granted options.

II. Terms of the Preferred Stock

Conversion Rights: Optional Conversion: Each share of Preferred Stock is convertible at any time at the option of the holder into one share of Common Stock.

Mandatory Conversion: The Preferred Stock will automatically convert into Common Stock upon closing of a Qualified Public Offering. A Qualified Public Offering is an underwritten public offering of the Company's Common Stock at an offering price equal to at least $10.00 per share and generating total proceeds before expenses to the Company of at least $20,000,000.

Conversion Price: $5.00 per share, subject to standard pro rata anti-dilution adjustments for stock dividends, stock splits and similar transactions affecting the Common Stock.

Liquidation Preference:

Upon any liquidation, dissolution or winding up of the Company, each holder of Preferred Stock shall be entitled to receive, prior to any distribution with respect to the Company's Common Stock, an amount in cash equal to the greater of (i) $2.00 per share, plus any declared and unpaid dividends thereon (the "Liquidation Value"); or (ii) the amount such holder would have received in such liquidation as a holder of Common Stock on an "as-converted" basis.

Voting Rights:

In addition to those voting rights provided by law, the Preferred Stock shall vote with the Common Stock on an as-converted basis on all matters submitted for stockholder approval. See also IV. hereof.

Dividend Rights:

The Preferred Stock will not be entitled to a stated rate of dividends but rather will participate in all dividends paid on pari passu or junior securities on an as-converted basis.

Preemptive Rights:

The holders of Preferred Stock, on a pro rata basis, will have the right to purchase any future offerings of equity securities by the Company in an amount equal to the percentage ownership of the holders in the Company calculated on an as-converted basis, subject to customary exceptions including, but not limited to, issuances to strategic partners. If any holder of Preferred Stock declines to participate in such offering (i) no anti-dilution adjustment for issuances of Common Stock at less than the Conversion Price then in effect shall be available to such declining holder with respect to such offering, and (ii) the other holders of Preferred Stock shall be entitled to purchase the declining holder's portion of such offering.

Redemption Rights:

The Company will be obligated to redeem one-third of the Preferred Stock on each of the eighth, ninth, and tenth anniversaries of the date of original issue at a redemption price equal to the then-current Liquidation Value.

Registration Rights:

At any time following the Company's initial public offering, the holders of 40% or more of the Registrable Securities (as defined below) may require the Company to register on one occasion only the Registrable Securities under the Securities Act of 1933, as amended (the "Securities Act").

Expenses:

The expenses of such registration (including the fees and expenses of one counsel to the holders of Registrable Securities but excluding underwriting discounts and commissions) shall be borne by the Company.

Registrable Securities: Common Stock issued or issuable upon conversion of the Preferred Stock, provided that any such Common Stock shall cease to be Registrable Securities following a transfer registered under the Securities Act or in an open-market transaction under Rule 144.

III. Transfer Restrictions

Right of First Refusal: Transfers of the Preferred Stock shall be subject to a right of first refusal in favor of the Company, subject to customary exceptions for transfers to affiliates or transfers for estate planning purposes.

Tag-Along Rights: The holders of Preferred Stock shall have the right to participate on a pro rata basis in any sale or transfer by any holder of 10% or more of the Company's Common Stock, with the exception of a Qualified Public Offering or any exercise of the Company's repurchase right.

Drag-Along Rights: If the holders of a majority of the outstanding voting capital stock (voting together as one class on an as-converted basis) approve a Sale of the Company (an "Approved Sale"), each stockholder shall vote for, consent to and raise no objections against such Approved Sale. "Sale of the Company" shall be defined as any transaction or series of transactions pursuant to which any person(s) or entity(ies) in the aggregate acquires (i) capital stock of the Company possessing the voting power to elect a majority of the Company's board of directors (whether by merger, consolidation, reorganization, combination, sale or transfer of the Company's capital stock, shareholder or voting agreement, proxy, power of attorney or otherwise), or (ii) all or substantially all of the Company's assets determined on a consolidated basis.

IV. Covenants

Information Rights: Board Representation: The holders of Preferred Stock shall have the right to elect one member of the Company's board of directors. The reasonable travel expenses of such Investor Director incurred in attending board meetings shall be reimbursed by the Company.

Advisory Board: The Company shall establish an Advisory Board made up of industry experts and strategic partners. The Advisory Board shall meet at least four times per year in accordance with a schedule to be agreed upon, and the reasonable travel expenses of each member incurred in attending such meetings shall be reimbursed by the Company. Each member shall also be compensated with stock options according to a policy to be established by the Board of Directors of the Company.

Financial Information: Each holder of Preferred Stock shall be entitled to receive audited annual and unaudited quarterly financial statements. In addition, each holder of 5% or more of the outstanding Preferred Stock shall receive (i) an operating budget and updated strategic plan prior to the commencement of each fiscal year of the Company, and (ii) periodic reports on the Company's progress with respect to milestones set forth in the strategic plan.

Inspection Rights: Each holder of 5% or more of the outstanding Preferred Stock shall have reasonable access, on a minimum of 20 days' prior written notice, to the Company's books and records, properties and personnel.

Operational Information: Each holder of 5% or more of the outstanding Preferred Stock shall be entitled to receive a brief written monthly operational status report and to participate quarterly in a brief (not more than one hour) conference call reviewing the operational progress of the Company.

Affirmative Covenants: Customary in transactions of this type, including maintenance of corporate existence, compliance with laws, payment of taxes and other obligations, etc.

Negative Covenants: Customary in transactions of this type, including prohibition of the following without the consent of the holders of a majority of the outstanding shares of Preferred Stock:

(i)   to create, issue or authorize the issuance of any additional Preferred Stock or any other capital stock of the Company that is senior to or pari passu with the Preferred Stock;

(ii) to amend the Company's Certificate of Incorporation or by-laws in a manner that adversely affects the holders of Preferred Stock;

(iii) the issuance of incentive stock (through options, restricted stock or otherwise) in excess of 20% of the Company's fully diluted common equity; and

(iv) transactions with affiliates, not approved by a majority of the Company's disinterested directors.

V.   Miscellaneous

Documentation: The purchase and sale of the Preferred Stock will be effected pursuant to definitive Purchase Agreements and related documentation containing the terms set forth herein as well as representations and warranties, closing conditions and other provisions customary in transactions of this type.

Company Management: All key employees must be engaged as full-time employees of the Company, with no other known or anticipated employment obligations.

Expenses: The Company shall reimburse all out-of-pocket expenses of the purchaser (including fees and expenses of one law firm representing the purchaser up to a maximum of $_____) incurred in connection with the transactions contemplated hereby, including negotiation of this term sheet and the definitive purchase documentation.

**Sunset
Provision:** Upon the consummation of a Qualified Public Offering, the preemptive rights, transfer restrictions and information rights described above shall expire automatically.

**SEC
Compliance:** At such time as the Company becomes subject to the reporting requirements of the Securities Exchange Act of 1934, as amended (the "Exchange Act"), the Company will use its reasonable efforts to timely file all required reports under the Exchange Act in order to enable the Investors to utilize Rule 144 in connection with transfers of the Preferred Stock (as converted). At such time as any Preferred Stock (as converted) is eligible for transfer under Rule 144(k), the Company will instruct the transfer agent to remove any restrictive legend from the certificates evidencing such capital stock upon request.

Philosophy: It is important that the management and investors of the Company share a common philosophy that the purpose of the Company is to maximize long-term shareholder (both internal and external) value. Value being defined as the appropriately discounted present value of cash the Company can generate or otherwise return to shareholders over the Company's life, whether from operations, a sale of the Company, or an IPO.

This non-binding Term Sheet is intended to facilitate the resolution of investment terms between Purchasers and the Company with respect to an equity investment by Purchasers in the Company. Due diligence by Purchasers is underway and is not yet complete. Nothing contained herein shall be binding upon either party, except and until such time that Purchasers are satisfied, in their sole discretion, with the results of due diligence, and a mutually acceptable definitive agreement is executed between the parties. However, the parties recognize their mutual obligation to negotiate and proceed in good faith toward a mutually acceptable definitive agreement to be executed by the parties.

Investment in the Shares offered hereby is highly speculative. Prospective investors should retain their own professional advisors to review and evaluate the economic, tax and other consequences of investment in a private offering and are not to construe the contents of this Term Sheet, or any other information furnished by the Company, as legal or tax advice.

PURCHASER: **COMPANY:**

_____   _____

SAMPLE TERM SHEET FOR SENIOR SUBORDINATED DEBT
SUBMITTED BY INSTITUTIONAL INVESTOR

Company:	Your Business (the "Company").
Type of Security:	Senior Subordinated Debt ("Subordinated Debt").
Issue Size:	$12 million.
Use of Proceeds:	To fund $10 million in capital expenditures and to fund $2 million in anticipated working capital requirements associated with introduction of new products.
Interest on Subordinated Debt:	14% per annum, payable quarterly.
Maturity of Subordinated Debt:	Earlier of (i) five years from closing or (ii) Liquidity Event (as defined below).
Warrants:	Detachable warrants ("Warrants"), representing the right to purchase shares of the common stock of the Company equal to 20% of the total outstanding when exercised. The exercise price for the warrants will be $.01 each.
Exercise Period of Warrant:	Earlier of (i) five years from closing or (ii) Liquidity Event (as defined below).
Liquidation Preference:	Preference to common stock on liquidation plus an amount equal to the deemed value of the Warrants on an as-converted basis.
Registration Rights:	Unlimited piggy-back registration rights on registrations by the Company and other holders, covered by standard underwriter's cutback. Three demand registration rights at the Company's expense.
Board Representation:	One member or observer, at investor's option.
Anti-Dilution Language:	Protection for issuances of shares of stock at a price less than that equal to the price paid in the most recent sale by the Company, common stock splits, dividends and combinations. No options, warrants or rights will be sold by the Company above 8% of the shares outstanding at closing, and all options, warrants or rights sold will have an exercise price equal to or greater than the last sale price of the common stock.

Redemption Option:

The Company must redeem the Subordinated Debt at par plus accrued interest at any time upon the earlier of a follow-on offering or after five years from closing. For each quarter that the Subordinated Debt remains unpaid after five years, the investor's Warrant will entitle the investor to buy an additional 2% ownership in the Company; that is, if the Subordinated Debt is not repaid before one quarter passes after the five years, the investor's Warrant will purchase 22% of the total outstanding shares; if two quarters pass after the five years, the Warrant will purchase 24% of the total outstanding shares. The total exercise price of the Warrants will not increase if the Subordinated Debt is not repaid in the initial five years and the Warrants will then buy a greater percentage of the Company.

Restrictive Covenants:

The Company may not, without the consent of the Subordinated Debt, so long as at least 50% of Subordinated Debt remains outstanding, (i) enter into a transaction that results in a change of control in which the Subordinated Debt is not paid in full; (ii) materially change the nature of the Company's business; (iii) liquidate or sell the Company or sell its assets in a transaction in which the Subordinated Debt is not paid in full; (iv) amend its articles of incorporation or bylaws in a manner that would negatively affect the holder of the Subordinated Debt; (v) redeem or pay any dividend or distribution on its common stock or make any payment to management on termination of employment unless previously approved by investor; (vi) issue new subordinated debt that is senior to the Subordinated Debt; or (vii) engage in any transactions with officers, directors or principal stockholders except if approved by independent members of the board of directors.

Reporting Requirements:

The Company shall give the investor the same standard financial reports that the Company gives to its senior lender, so long as at least 50% of the Subordinated Debt remains outstanding. The Company's financial statements will be audited by a firm acceptable to investor.

Drag-Along Rights:

If the Board and the holders of a majority of the shares of common stock (voting as a single class) outstanding approve a sale of the Company (an "Approved Sale"), each holder of Subordinated Debt and Warrants shall take all needed or desirable actions in connection with the consummation of the Approved Sale as requested by the Board, a majority of the Company's stockholders or the Company. This obligation is subject to (i) each holder of Subordinated Debt and Common Stock receiving the same form of payment and the same amount per share or per note; (ii) if any stockholders get a choice as to the form and amount of payment, each stockholder getting the same option; and (iii) each option or warrant holder getting an opportunity to either (A) exercise the options or warrants before the Approved Sale and participate in such sale as stockholders, or (B) receive in exchange for such options or warrants payment equal to (1) the same payment per share received by stockholders less the exercise price of the options or warrants, multiplied by (2) the number of shares that the options or warrants would buy when exercised.

Transfer Restriction:	The Company will have a right of first refusal to any proposed sales, transfers, or another dispositions by the holder of the Subordinated Debt. No transfers will be made to competitors of the Company.
Tag-Along Rights:	Except for public sales and other limited exceptions, a Warrant holder can exercise the Warrant and participate in any sale of shares of common stock by selling stockholders up to its *pro rata* part of the securities to be sold, on the same terms and conditions given to other stockholders.
Pre-Emptive Rights:	Until an IPO or an Approved Sale, each Warrant holder has the right to purchase on a *pro rata* basis (based on the number of shares of common stock held by the Warrant holder on a fully-diluted and "as if exercised" basis) any securities the Company may sell in the future.
Expenses:	The Company will pay at closing the expenses of the holder of Subordinated Debt for legal fees and out-of-pocket due diligence expenses. Such fees and expenses will not exceed $150,000. The Company shall pay a deposit of $50,000 on execution of this term sheet. The deposit will be credited against the total fees and expenses at closing.
Voting Rights:	The Warrant holders will vote on an "as if exercised" basis on each item that stockholders of the Company vote on.
SEC Compliance:	The Company will comply with the reporting requirements imposed on it by the Securities Exchange Act of 1934 after its IPO occurs.

SENIOR CREDIT FACILITY PRELIMINARY TERM SHEET

Borrower

Borrower: Borrower

Agent: Bank

Lenders: Bank and all other syndicate participants

Purpose: To finance (i) the acquisition of _____, (ii) working capital requirements, and (iii) general corporate purposes.

Type and Amount of Senior Facility: **Term Loan:** $_____ million term loan, subject to reduction as set forth below.

Revolving Credit Facility: $_____ million revolving credit facility, including a sublimit for Letters of Credit, if necessary.

Closing Date: The date of the initial borrowing under the Senior Facility.

Final Drawing Date: The one-year anniversary of the Closing Date.

Final Maturity: **Term Loan:** Five years from the Final Drawing Date.

Revolving Credit Facility: Five years from the Closing Date.

Amortization: **Term Loan:** The Term Loan will be amortized in quarterly installments beginning on the Final Drawing Date and ending on the Final Maturity Date, as follows:

Year	% of Total
1	10.0%
2	15.0%
3	20.0%
4	25.0%
5	30.0%

Revolving Credit Facility: The Revolving Credit loans shall be paid in full at maturity.

Availability:	**Term Loan:** A single drawing of up to $_____ million (the "Initial Term Amount") may be made at the Closing Date to finance the acquisition of _____ and to pay related fees and expenses. The amount of Term Loan unutilized on the Closing Date (the "Escrowed Term Amount") shall be funded in escrow. The Borrower shall have the ability to draw upon the Escrowed Term Amount on the Closing Date and periodically thereafter up to but excluding the Final Drawing Date, provided that the Borrower has met certain thresholds (to be determined) pertaining to its financial performance. Further, it is contemplated that funding of the Escrowed Term Amount may be allowed pursuant to either a secondary offering of common stock or the call of certain issued and outstanding warrants. Lenders' commitments under the Term Loan shall automatically be reduced on the Final Drawing Date by the unutilized portion of the Escrowed Term Amount on such date.

Revolving Credit Facility: Assuming full utilization of the Term Loans and subject to availability under the Borrowing Base, a drawing of up to $_____ million may be made on the Closing Date to finance working capital and to pay related fees and expenses, and additional drawings may be made at any time from the Closing Date to, but excluding, the Final Maturity of the Revolving Credit Facility for working capital and general corporate purposes.

Borrowing Base:	The sum of ___% of Eligible Accounts Receivable (to be defined) and ___% of Eligible Inventory (to be defined).
Interest:	At the Borrower's option, Base Rate loans and loans made at the London Interbank Offered Rate (LIBOR) will be available as follows:

Base Rate Option: Interest shall be at the Base Rate of the Agent plus the appropriate interest margin, calculated on the basis of the actual number of days elapsed in a year of 365 days, payable quarterly in arrears. The Base Rate is defined as the higher of the Federal Funds Rate as published by the Federal Reserve Bank of New York plus ½ of 1%, or the prime commercial lending rate of the Agent as announced from time to time at its head office. Base Rate drawings shall be made available on the same-day basis if requested prior to 10:00 a.m. New York time and shall be in minimum amounts of $_____ and incremental multiples of $_____.

LIBOR Option: Interest shall be determined for periods ("Interest Periods") of one, two, three, or six months (as selected by the Borrower) and shall be at an annual rate equal to the LIBOR for the corresponding deposits of U.S. Dollars plus the appropriate interest margin. LIBOR will be determined by the Reference Lenders at the beginning of each Interest Period. Interest will be paid at the end of each Interest Period or quarterly, whichever is earlier, and will be calculated on the basis of a 360-day year and actual number of days elapsed. LIBOR drawings shall require three business days' prior notice and shall be in minimum amounts of $_____ and incremental multiples of $_____.

	Base Rate Loans	LIBOR Loans
Interest Margin: The applicable interest margins shall be as follows:		
Term Loan	2.00%	3.50%
Revolving Credit Loans	1.50%	3.00%

Default Interest: ___% per annum in excess of the rate otherwise applicable upon the occurrence and during the continuance of any payment default and after the lapse of any applicable grace periods, payable upon demand.

Commitment Fees: Commitment Fees of ½ of 1% per annum on the unused commitments under the Senior Facility shall be payable to the Agent, for the account of the Lenders, from and after the Closing Date. Accrued commitment fees will be payable quarterly in arrears (calculated on a 360-day year basis).

Mandatory Payments: 100% of the net proceeds (to be defined) received from (i) the sale or disposition of all or any part of the assets of the Borrower or any of its subsidiaries (other than sales of inventory in the ordinary course of business), (ii) the incurrence of any indebtedness for borrowed money or the issuance of debt or equity Securities by the Borrower after the Closing Date, (iii) at the Agent's discretion, insurance recoveries other than recoveries of less than a threshold amount to be determined that are promptly applied toward repair or replacement of the damaged property. In addition, whether 90 days after the end of each fiscal year of the Borrower, a mandatory prepayment equal to 75% of Excess Cash Flow (to be defined) for such fiscal year shall be required. Mandatory prepayments shall be applied without penalty or premium (except for LIBOR breakage costs, if any) to Term Loan installments in inverse order of maturity, and thereafter to reduce outstanding loans under the Revolving Credit Facility.

Voluntary Prepayments: Permitted in whole or in part with prior notice but without premium or penalty, subject to minimum prepayments of $_____ or integral multiples of $_____ in excess of $_____. LIBOR loans may only be prepaid on the last day of the applicable Interest Period. Voluntary prepayments shall be applied without penalty or premium (except for LIBOR breakage costs, if any) to Term Loan installments in inverse order of maturity, and thereafter to reduce outstanding loans under the Revolving Credit Facility.

Security: The Senior Facility will be secured by perfected first-priority security interest in favor of the Lenders in all accounts receivable, inventory, property, plant and equipment, intangibles, contract rights, and other personal, intellectual, and real property of the Borrower and its subsidiaries, if any.

Conditions Precedent: Conditions precedent to the initial borrowing under the Senior Facility will include those customary for the Agent and which are appropriate to this transaction.

Covenants: Covenants for the Senior Facility will include those customary for the Agent and that are appropriate to this transaction.

Events of Default: Will include those customary for the Agent and that are appropriate to this transaction.

Fees and Expenses: Borrower is responsible for all reasonable counsel's fees and expenses regardless of whether a definitive loan agreement is executed or the transaction is closed, as well as expenses for collateral audits.

Indemnification: As agreed between the parties in separate Indemnification Agreement.

Assignments and Participations: Each Lender may assign all or a portion of its loans and commitments under the Senior Facility (which shall not have to be pro rata among the Senior Facility) or sell participation therein to another person or persons subject to limitation, if any, established by the Agent.

Governing Law: The law of the State of _____.

APPENDIX

SAMPLE LETTER OF INTENT FOR IPO [LONG FORM]

Date

Company
Address

      Re: Letter of Intent

Dear _____ :

      Discussions have taken place during the past several weeks between the representatives of the undersigned and Company (the "Company") regarding a proposed public offering ("Public Offering") of securities of the Company. Based upon such discussions, the Company and the undersigned have agreed to enter into this letter of intent.

      In the course of such discussions, you have provided or will provide the undersigned with certain information regarding the Company, including but not limited to, recent unaudited financial statements that you and the Company represent as fairly reflecting the financial condition of the Company and the results of its operations for the periods mentioned therein, and financial projections as prepared by the Company's management, and various industry and other information.

      After review of the material submitted, your representations, and other investigations, the undersigned is pleased to submit for your approval a program for the financing of the Company by means of a Public Offering. The Public Offering will be arranged by the undersigned as the managing underwriter on a "firm commitment" basis in accordance with the terms and conditions set forth below.

      1.   Public Offering. Underwriter would be willing to act as the representative of the underwriters (the "Representative"), acting on a firm commitment basis, and as managing underwriter in the Public Offering by the Company of 1,000,000 shares of common stock ("Shares") at an offering price to be determined by the Company and the Representative immediately prior to the date a registration statement with respect to the Shares is declared effective by the Securities and Exchange Commission (the "Effective Date"). The Company and the Representative expect that the offering will be priced between $8.00 and $9.00 per share, but in no event to be more than $9.00 per share.

      2.   Over-allotment Option. In order to cover over-allotments, if any, the Company shall grant the Representative an option to purchase from it all or part of an additional number of Shares equal to 15% of the number of Shares sold in the underwriting (the "Over-Allotment Shares") at a price per Share equal to the price per Share to be paid by the Representative for the Shares. The option shall be exercisable, in whole or in part, from time to time during the 45 day period commencing with the Effective Date, at the sole discretion of the Representative.

      3.   Syndicate Formation. In connection with the Public Offering, we shall have the right to form a syndicate of co-underwriters and selected dealers who will assist us in the Public Offering. Any firm with whom we associate will be a member in good standing of the National Association of Securities Dealers, Inc. ("NASD"). The Representative shall have the sole right to determine whether one or more co-underwriters shall assist in underwriting the Public Offering and the identity of such co-underwriter or co-underwriters, although the Company may assist in the identification of such potential co-underwriters.

4. Registration Statement.

a. The Company shall file with the Securities and Exchange Commission (the "Commission"), a registration statement on Form S-1, or, as the case may be, Form SB-2, (the "Registration Statement") in conformity with the Securities Act of 1933, as amended (the "1933 Act"), covering the Public Offering of the Shares and the Over-allotment Shares. Further, the Registration Statement shall cover a sufficient number of Representative's Warrants (defined below) which may be issued by the Company to us or our assigns.

b. Neither the offer nor sale of the Shares or the Over-allotment Shares pursuant to the Registration Statement nor any of the Representative's Warrants shall be subject to any preemptive right, however characterized or described. It is our understanding and agreement with the Company that prior to the filing of the Registration Statement, the Company will have an authorized capitalization of approximately 100,000,000 shares of Common Stock and approximately 15,000,000 shares of Preferred Stock. Approximately 5,000,000 shares of Common Stock will be outstanding, and approximately $500,000 in liquidation value of Redeemable Convertible Preferred Stock will be outstanding. Notwithstanding anything contained herein to the contrary, in the prospectus portion of the Registration Statement ("Prospectus") there may be disclosed an equity incentive stock option plan covering approximately 500,000 shares. No securities other than the outstanding preferred stock described above or that is issued in conjunction with acquisitions or that are exercisable for or convertible into shares of the Company's common stock shall be outstanding prior to the Effective Date.

c. After approval by us and our counsel of the final draft of the Registration Statement, the Company shall file the Registration Statement with the Commission as soon as practicable. The Registration Statement shall include appropriate consolidated financial statements audited by an independent certified public accountant, which accountant shall give an opinion in the final Registration Statement, and which accountant shall issue appropriate "cold comfort" letters on the Effective Date and the closing date of the Public Offering ("Closing Date") to within three business days of such dates. Thereafter, the Company shall utilize its best efforts and due diligence to cause the Registration Statement to be declared effective by the Commission so that the Public Offering may commence; provided, however, effectiveness shall not be allowed to occur without our prior written consent. The proceeds to be realized by the Company shall be used as set forth in the Registration Statement and shall not be used to repay debt to officers, directors, stockholders, derivative security holders, or affiliates of the Company without the Representative's written consent.

5. Authorized Capital. The Company shall represent and warrant to us, in an Underwriting Agreement to be furnished by us in customary form and content, that the Company has sufficient authorized securities to be offered and sold as contemplated hereby, and to provide for the Representative's Warrants and the securities underlying such Representative's Warrants.

6.   Representative's Share Purchase Warrants. At the Closing of the Public Offering, the Company will sell to the Representative for a total purchase price of $100, warrants (the "Representative's Warrants") entitling the Representative or its assigns to purchase one share of the Company's common stock for each 10 Shares sold in the Public Offering (excluding the Over-allotment Shares). The Representative's Warrants shall be exercisable commencing one year from the Effective Date and shall expire five years from the Effective Date. The Representative's Warrants will contain the maximum antidilution provisions as permitted by the NASD and may provide for the cashless exercise of such Representative's Warrants utilizing securities of the Company (which may include the implicit value of the Representative's Warrants being surrendered). The exercise price of the Representative's Warrants shall be an amount equal to 120% of the offering price of the Shares sold in the Public Offering. The Company shall set aside and at all times have available a sufficient number of securities to be issued upon exercise of the Representative's Warrants. The Representative's Warrants and underlying securities will not be transferable to anyone for a period of one year after the Effective Date of the Company's Registration Statement, except to officers of the Representative, co-underwriters, selling group members, and their officers or partners. Thereafter, the Representative's Warrants and underlying securities will be transferable provided such transfer is in accordance with the provisions of the 1933 Act.

The Company will agree that, upon written request of the then holder(s) of at least a majority of the Representative's Warrants and the securities underlying the Representative's Warrants which were originally issued to the Representative or to its assigns, made at any time within the period commencing one year from the Effective Date and ending five years after the Effective Date, the Company will file, at its sole expense, no more than once, a registration statement or post-effective amendment under the 1933 Act registering the securities underlying the Representative's Warrants. The Company agrees to use its best efforts to cause the registration statement or post-effective amendment to become effective. The holders of the Representative's Warrants may demand registration without exercising the Representative's Warrants and, in fact, are never required to exercise same. The Registration Statement will include the securities underlying the Representative's Warrants.

The Company understands and will agree that if, at any time within the period commencing on the Effective Date and ending seven years after the Effective Date, it should file a registration statement with the Commission pursuant to the 1933 Act, regardless of whether some of the holders of the Representative's Warrants and underlying securities shall have theretofore availed themselves of the right above provided, the Company, at its own expense, will offer on two occasions to said holders the opportunity to register the securities underlying the Representative's Warrants. This paragraph is not applicable to a registration statement filed by the Company with the Commission on Form S-8 or any other inappropriate form of registration statement or offering statement.

In addition to the rights above provided, the Company will cooperate with the then holders of the Representative's Warrants and underlying securities in preparing and signing a registration statement, on two occasions only, in addition to the registration statements discussed above, required in order to sell or transfer the securities underlying the Representative's Warrants and will supply all information required therefor, but such additional registration statements shall be at the then holders' cost and expense unless the Company elects to register additional shares of the Company's Common Stock in which case the cost and expense of such registration statements will be prorated between the Company and the holders of the Representative's Warrants and underlying securities according to the aggregate sales prices of the securities being issued.

7. <u>Additional Commission Filings</u>. Prior to the Effective Date, the Company shall have properly and timely filed with the Commission a registration statement on Form 8-A to register its securities under the Securities Exchange Act of 1934, as amended (the "1934 Act"). The Company shall for a period of five years after the Effective Date promptly furnish us with copies of all material filed with the Commission pursuant to the 1934 Act or otherwise furnished to stockholders of the Company.

8. <u>Nasdaq Listing</u>. The Company shall at its cost and expense take all necessary and appropriate action so that the Shares, to the extent eligible, are listed for trading on the Nasdaq National Market or, as the case may be, the Nasdaq SmallCap Market, on the Effective Date, and that the securities remain listed for at least 10 years thereafter provided that the Company otherwise complies with the prevailing requirements of Nasdaq. In addition, if at the time of the Public Offering the Shares are not eligible for listing on the Nasdaq National Market, the Company shall, at such time as the Company qualifies for listing its securities on the Nasdaq National Market, take all steps necessary to have the Shares listed on the Nasdaq National Market.

9. <u>Report Listing</u>. The Company shall, on or about the Effective Date, apply for listing in Standard and Poor's Corporation Records and shall use its best efforts to have the Company listed in such reports for a period of not less than 10 years from the Closing Date. The Company will request accelerated treatment in the Daily News Supplement of Standard and Poor's Corporation Records.

10. <u>Due Diligence</u>.

a. The Company shall supply and deliver to us and our counsel at their respective offices, all information reasonably required to enable us to make such investigation of the Company and its business prospects as we or our counsel shall desire and shall make available to us at our offices such person(s) as we shall deem reasonably necessary and appropriate in order to verify or substantiate any such information supplied. We shall have the right to review any materials prepared in connection with the offering of securities of the Company conducted prior to the Public Offering for compliance with applicable federal and state securities laws.

b. For a period of five years after the Closing, the Company shall furnish unaudited quarterly financial statements including both a balance sheet and statement of income to us on a timely basis in addition to any other reports that may be issued. The Company shall cause its Board of Directors to meet, at least quarterly, upon proper notice. The Representative shall receive notice of any regular or special meetings of the Company's Board of Directors concurrently with the sending of such notice to the Company's directors and shall have the right to have a representative attend such meeting as an observer, as described below.

11. Blue Sky and Other Costs. The Company shall be responsible for and shall bear all expenses directly and necessarily incurred in connection with the proposed financing, including: (i) the preparation, printing, and filing of the offering documents and amendments thereto, including the Commission, NASD, Nasdaq filing and/or application fees, and preliminary and final Prospectuses and the printing of the underwriting agreement, the agreement among underwriters and the selected dealers' agreement, preliminary and final "Blue Sky" memorandums, and the material to be circulated to the Underwriters by us and other incidental material; (ii) the issuance and delivery of certificates representing the Shares, including original issue and transfer taxes, if any; (iii) the qualifications of the Shares under state securities or Blue Sky laws, including reasonable fees of counsel to the Representative, who shall be retained by the Company at its expense to prepare and file all such qualifications and who shall prepare a preliminary and final blue sky survey; (iv) the fees and disbursements of counsel for the Company and the accountants for the Company; and (v) any other costs of qualifying the Shares, to the extent eligible, for listing on the Nasdaq SmallCap Market or the Nasdaq National Market.

12. Signing of Underwriting Agreement. Within 24 hours of the Effective Date of the Registration Statement, we shall enter into an underwriting agreement with the Company ("Underwriting Agreement"), which Underwriting Agreement shall by its terms become effective on the Effective Date and shall contain terms and conditions usually and customarily found in instruments of like nature and containing among other things, the usual market-out conditions, calamity clauses, and cross-indemnity provisions against liabilities, including liabilities under the 1933 Act. A form of such Underwriting Agreement shall be furnished to the Company by us. In addition, the Underwriting Agreement shall provide that the Closing of the proposed Public Offering shall occur on the third business day subsequent to the Effective Date, unless the Registration Statement is declared effective by the Commission after 4:30 p.m. Eastern time, in which event the Underwriting Agreement shall provide that the Closing of the Public Offering shall occur on the fourth business day after the Effective Date. The Company shall utilize its best efforts to obtain an effective date for the Registration Statement, as amended, on or before_____.

13. Underwriting Compensation.

a. The Underwriting Agreement shall provide that the several Underwriters shall be entitled to an underwriting discount of 10% (or such lesser discount as shall be approved by the NASD) from the total Public Offering price, such that the Underwriters may purchase the Shares and Over-allotment Shares, if any, from the Company at 10% less (or such lesser discount as shall be approved by the NASD) than the Public Offering price fixed by the final Prospectus.

b. The Underwriting Agreement shall provide that, upon the successful completion of the Public Offering, we, as Representative, shall be reimbursed on a non-accountable basis for our expenses in a sum equal to 3% of the total Public Offering price of the Shares (including the Over-allotment Shares). The Company agrees to deliver to the Representative, upon execution of this letter of intent and contemporaneously with the filing of the Registration Statement, advances of $_____ each, to be considered advances upon the nonaccountable expense allowance. The Representative shall return to the Company any unaccounted portion of the amounts advanced to it in the event the offering is not consummated. Likewise, if the Public Offering is not consummated, the Representative will be reimbursed only for its actual accountable out-of-pocket expenses. Any expense incurred by the Representative shall be deemed to be reasonable and unobjectionable upon a reasonable showing by the Representative that such expenses were incurred, directly or indirectly, in connection with the proposed and/or relationship of the parties hereto, as described herein.

c.   If, after executing this letter of intent and prior to the execution of the Underwriting Agreement, the Company elects not to expeditiously proceed with the Public Offering even though the Representative is ready, willing, and able to proceed with the Public Offering within the price range set forth herein, then the Company agrees that it will not sell any of its capital stock to the public through another underwriter for a period of at least 12 months from the date hereof. If after executing this letter of intent and prior to consummation of the Public Offering, the Company is acquired, merges, sells all or substantially all of its assets, or otherwise effects a corporate reorganization with any other entity and, as a result, the Public Offering is abandoned by the Company, then the Company shall pay the Representative a financial advisory fee of $_____ which the Company and the Representative agree is fair compensation to the Representative. The Representative shall act as the Company's investment banker in connection with any such acquisition and render such services as are customary in connection therewith in consideration for this fee. Any fee payable with respect to a fairness opinion shall be in addition to the advisory fee discussed above.

d.   If the Public Offering is not consummated, the Representative shall return to the Company such portion of the amounts advanced to it pursuant to paragraph 13(b) above that is not accounted for by the Representative, so that the Representative will be reimbursed only for its actual accountable out-of-pocket expenses, including its legal fees and disbursements, calculated as provided in paragraph 13(b) above.

e.   If the Public Offering is not consummated because the Representative determines, in its sole judgment, that market conditions are unsuitable for such an offering or if information comes to the Representative's attention relating to the Company, its management or its position in the industry that could, in the Representative's sole judgment, preclude a successful offering of the Shares to the public, then the maximum amount to which the Representative shall be entitled shall be the reimbursement of its out-of-pocket expenses which shall be deducted from the advances against the nonaccountable expense allowance. If the Company elects not to proceed expeditiously with the Public Offering for reasons other than that set forth in paragraph 13(c) above, or if the conditions, representations, warranties, and covenants of the Company are not materially correct and cannot be complied with, then the Company shall (1) reimburse the Representative in full for its out-of-pocket expenses including its legal fees and disbursements, but not to exceed an aggregate of $_____ in excess of the advances paid by the Company to the Representative pursuant to paragraph 13(b) hereof, (2) pay all Blue Sky filing fees and expenses, including Blue Sky legal fees of the Representative's counsel retained by the Company for such purpose, and (3) indemnify and hold harmless the Representative for any expenses incurred by the Company in connection with the Public Offering including, but not limited to, printing expenses and the Company's accounting and legal fees.

14. Other Agreements.

     a.   The Representative shall have the right to designate an observer to meetings of the Company's Board of Directors, which right shall begin at the Effective Date and survive for a period of five years from the Effective Date. If designated, such observer shall attend meetings of the Board of Directors and receive reimbursement for all reasonable costs and expenses incurred in attending such meetings, including but not limited to, food, lodging, and transportation, together with such other cash fee or other cash compensation as is paid by the Company to members of the Board of Directors (but excluding options or other non-cash consideration). Moreover, to the extent permitted by law, the Company will agree to indemnify the Representative and its observer in relation to the observer's activities as observer. In the event the Company maintains a liability insurance policy affording coverage for the acts of its officers and/or directors, it will agree, to the extent permitted under such policy, to include each of the Representative and its observer as an insured under such policy. The observer, whether the Representative or its designee, shall receive cash compensation equal to the highest cash compensation received by any independent member of the Board of Directors of the Company.

     b.   The Company shall engage the services of a reputable public relations firm that is reasonably acceptable to the Representative, as of the Effective Date and for a minimum period of 12 months thereafter, for the purpose of facilitating appropriate dissemination of information by the Company to its stockholders, the media, and the public securities markets.

     c.   The Company shall use a financial printer acceptable to the underwriter.

15. Conflict of Law. If any provision of this letter of intent conflicts with any rule or regulation under the 1933 Act, or the state securities Blue Sky laws or the jurisdictions in which the Public Offering is to be qualified, the NASD, Nasdaq, or any other state or federal authority possessing jurisdiction over the Pubic Offering, the Company shall meet with us and together we shall use our best efforts in good faith to review the terms of the Public Offering so as to comply with any such rule or regulation.

16. Restriction on Securities.

     a.   All officers, directors, and stockholders of the Company prior to the Effective Date (including holders of derivative securities) shall agree not to sell, transfer, pledge, or convey any capital stock or securities that are issuable upon exercise or conversion of the derivative securities, by registration or otherwise, for a period of nine months from the Effective Date without the prior written consent of the Representative (which consent will not be unreasonably withheld), or for any greater period required by any state in which the offering of the Shares is to be registered; except that, subject to compliance with applicable securities laws, any such officer, director, or stockholder may transfer his or her stock in a private transaction, provided that any such transferee shall agree, as a condition to such transfer, to be bound by the restrictions set forth herein and further provided that the transferor, except in the case of the transferor's death, shall continue to be deemed the beneficial owner of such Shares in accordance with Regulation 13d-(3) of the 1934 Act. The Company shall also cause its officers, directors, and employees that may rely on Rule 701 to make sales of common stock after completion of the Public Offering to enter into lock-up agreements for a period of nine months. Such officers, directors and stockholders shall agree to enter into a lock up agreement in standard form, to the placing of a related restrictive legend on the certificates representing their shares and to the Representative holding such securities in an account designated by the Representative. The nine-month lock-up shall also apply to the registration of shares underlying stock options using Form S-8.

b. The Company and all officers, directors, and holders of 5% or more of the Common Stock of the Company will further agree not to sell, transfer, hypothecate, or convey any capital stock or derivative securities of the Company through a "Regulation S" transaction for a minimum period of three years from the Effective Date without the prior written consent of the Representative. In addition, the Company will agree not to sell, transfer, hypothecate, or convey any capital stock or derivative securities of the Company for a minimum period of 12 months from the Effective Date without the prior written consent of the Representative, which consent will not be withheld unreasonably, except the Company may issue its common stock on the exercise of stock options and may issue common stock or preferred stock for use in acquisitions.

17. Finders. The Company and we represent that no person has acted as a finder in connection with the transactions contemplated herein, and each will agree to indemnify the other with respect to any claim or finder's fee in connection with the Public Offering.

18. Further Representations of the Company.

a. The Company shall employ the services of an auditing firm acceptable to the Representative in connection with the preparation of the financial statements required to be included in the Registration Statement and shall continue to appoint such auditors or such other auditors as are reasonably acceptable to the Representative for a period of five years following the Effective Date of the Registration Statement.

b. Prior to the Effective Date, the Company will enter into employment agreements with its key management employees with the terms thereof including the term and the compensation of each person subject to the reasonable approval of the Representative. The compensation payable to such persons shall be acceptable to the Representative so long as such compensation is within industry standards.

c. The Company shall bear the cost of preparing and delivering to the Representative and its counsel four leather bound volumes containing copies of all documents and appropriate correspondence filed with or received from the Commission, Nasdaq and the NASD, and all closing documents.

d. The Company will for a period of five years:

(i) Furnish to the Representative and to the Company's stockholders annual audited financial statements.

(ii) Distribute an annual report meeting the requirements of Rule 14a-3 under the 1934 Act to all stockholders setting forth clearly the financial position of the Company.

(iii) Designate an Audit Committee and a Compensation Committee (the members of which shall be subject to our reasonable approval), which will generally supervise the financial affairs and executive compensation of the Company, respectively. The Audit Committee shall be comprised of members that meet the listing standards of the Nasdaq Stock Market, Inc., and will comply with its obligations as outlined in 1934 Act Release No. 34-42266.

(iv)   At its expense, cause its regularly engaged independent certified public accountants to review (but not audit) the Company's financial statements for each of the first three fiscal quarters prior to the announcement of quarterly financial information, the filing of the Company's quarterly reports and the mailing of quarterly financial information to security holders, all in accordance with the obligations imposed upon such accountants by 1934 Act Release No. 34-42266.

e.   The Company will cause its transfer agent to furnish to the Representative a duplicate copy of the daily transfer sheets prepared by the transfer agent during the six-month period commencing on the Effective Date and, for a period of four and one-half years thereafter, the Representative shall have the right to request duplicate copies of such transfer sheets and/or a duplicate copy of a list of stockholders, in its sole discretion and at the Company's expense.

f.   Our obligation under the underwriting agreement shall be subject to, among other things, there being, in our opinion: (i) no material adverse change in the conditions or obligations of the Company or its present or proposed business and affairs; or (ii) no market conditions that might render the offer and sale of the Shares herein contemplated inadvisable. Further, our obligations shall be subject to the Company's successful listing of its securities on the Nasdaq SmallCap Market or the Nasdaq National Market.

g.   This letter is not, and your acceptance hereof does not, constitute a prior agreement to consummate the financing outlined above. Such binding agreement shall be contained only in the Underwriting Agreement or an agreement to enter into an Underwriting Agreement.

h.   The Company agrees that in the event the Committee on Corporate Financing of the NASD shall determine that any Company stock or stock options issued to, or financial consulting or other agreements of the Company with, any person or persons who are unaffiliated with the Representative are nevertheless considered underwriting compensation, the Company will take such action as the NASD may require to prevent such stock options or agreements from having any adverse effect on the Representative's allowable compensation. In the event that the NASD still deems the Representative's compensation to be unacceptable, the Representative shall, in its sole discretion, make such further adjustments to the form of its compensation as it deems necessary to obtain NASD clearance, so long as such compensation adjustments do not increase the amount of total compensation provided for in this letter of intent.

i.   Certificates for the securities offered first shall be submitted to the Representative for approval prior to printing. The Company shall, as promptly as possible after filing the Registration Statement with the Commission, have the Shares eligible for closing through Depository Trust Company.

19.   Aftermarket Support. As a matter of policy, the Representative sponsors its underwriting clients with aftermarket activities to ensure that its customers, other members of the investing public, and the various segments of the financial community will be kept abreast of developments relating to the Company and its industry. The Representative intends to make a market in the Company's securities after the Public Offering and will use its best efforts to interest other investment banking firms and research analysts in following the Company. The Company shall assist the Representative in its aftermarket support activities by being available to hold periodic updates with the Representative, market makers, analysts, and their representatives.

20. <u>Performance Escrow</u>. The majority shareholder of the Company's common stock outstanding prior to the Public Offering will place in an escrow account an aggregate of 600,000 shares of common stock at or prior to the Effective Date. Such shares of common stock shall be subject to release from escrow upon: (i) the Company achieving revenues exceeding $100.0 million *and* EBITDA exceeding $10.0 million in fiscal year 2004; or (ii) the Company achieving revenues exceeding $250.0 million and EBITDA exceeding $25.0 million in fiscal year 2005. In the event the Company fails to meet the criteria set forth above in fiscal 2004 or fiscal 2005, the escrowed shares of Common Stock shall be released at the earlier of: (i) seven years from the Effective Date, or (ii) consummation of a merger, acquisition or exchange in which the Company is not the surviving entity or in which the majority shareholder of the Company owns less than 50% of the outstanding capital stock of the surviving entity following such transactions or the sale of all or substantially all of the assets of the Company that is approved by a majority of the holders of the outstanding shares, excluding the shares held in the escrow account.

21. <u>Letter of Intent</u>.

a. Notwithstanding anything contained herein to the contrary, it is expressly understood that this document is a letter of intent and that no liability or obligation of any nature whatsoever is intended to be created between any of the parties hereto, except for the liability for expenses provided for in Paragraphs 11 and 13. This letter does not and is not intended to constitute a binding agreement to consummate the Public Offering outlined herein, nor an agreement to enter into the Underwriting Agreement. The parties propose to proceed promptly and in good faith to conclude arrangements with respect to the proposed Public Offering, and any legal obligations between the parties shall be only as set forth in the Underwriting Agreement.

b. This letter of intent shall be construed under the Laws of the State of _____. The Representative and the Company agree that any controversy arising out of or relating to this letter of intent or proposed Public Offering shall be arbitrated under binding arbitration in _____ in accordance with the rules then in effect of the NASD.

This letter of intent may be signed in counterparts, but all such counterpart signatures shall be considered as a single document.

c. If a party signs this letter of intent and transmits an electronic facsimile of the signature page to the other party, the party who receives the facsimile transmission may rely upon the electronic facsimile as a signed original of this letter of intent. By acceptance hereof, the Company agrees not to "shop" this letter of intent with other investment bankers. This letter of intent shall be effective only if executed by the parties on or prior to the close of business on _____.

If the foregoing is agreeable to you, kindly execute a duplicat copy of this letter of intent and deliver it to the undersigned at the address set forth on the first page hereof.

UNDERWRITER

By: _____

The terms of this letter of intent have been accepted and agreed to as of the date first above written.

COMPANY

By: _____

SAMPLE LETTER OF INTENT FOR FOLLOW-ON OFFERING

Date

Company
Address

Gentlemen:

This is to record the mutual intention of Company (the "Company") and Underwriters (the "Underwriters") to undertake a public offering of 2.6 million shares of Common Stock (the "Common Stock").

      1.   Subject to the satisfactory completion of our normal due diligence analysis, market conditions at the time of such offering and execution and delivery of the definitive underwriting agreement referred to below, it is our intention to purchase 2.6 million shares of Common Stock from the Company and to resell such securities to the public in an offering (the "Offering") to be registered with the Securities and Exchange Commission (the "SEC") on Form SB-2 under the Securities Act of 1933. The Company will also grant the Underwriters a 30-day over-allotment option to purchase up to an additional 390,000 shares of the Common Stock.

      2.   In consideration of our effort to market the Common Stock, the Company will proceed to prepare and to file a registration statement with the SEC. The registration statement, all amendments thereto and all related finings with the SEC shall be subject to approval by us and our counsel before the filing is made.

      3.   The Company will pay all expenses normally related to an underwriting, including, but not limited to, the fees and expenses of its counsel, printing, accounting, postage, SEC and NASD filing fees, state fees and the portion of the fees and expenses of our counsel which relate to the obtaining of Blue Sky qualifications in various states. In addition, the Company will pay all out-of-pocket travel expenses of its officers relating to the roadshow. The Underwriters will pay for the expenses, including meeting room, food and beverage charges, of holding information meetings with respect to the Offering for institutional and retail investors. In addition, the Underwriters will be responsible for their own expenses (including the fees and the expenses of their counsel) and will pay the expenses of running the customary advertisements in various publications following the Offering. Notwithstanding the foregoing, the Company shall reimburse the Underwriters on demand for all their out-of-pocket expenses, including, without limitation, the fees and disbursements of their counsel, in the event that the Underwriters discover during due diligence an issue concerning the Company or its business, financial condition, results of operations or prospects which the Underwriters reasonably determine could have a material adverse effect on the marketing of the Offering and end their involvement in the Offering, or if the Company, for whatever reason, decides not to pursue, abandons or otherwise fails to proceed with the Offering or decides to terminate the involvement of the Underwriters in the offering.

      4.   The exact terms of the underwriting will be set forth in an underwriting agreement to be entered into by the Underwriters and the Company. The public offering price per share of the Common Stock will be determined immediately prior to commencement of the Offering, and such price shall be agreed to by the Underwriters and the Company after full consideration of market conditions existing at that time. The underwriting spread is expected to be 7.0% of the public Offering price and will be determined at the time of final pricing. The underwriting agreement between us will contain customary reciprocal indemnification provisions.

5.   The Underwriters will not be bound to receive and pay for, and the Company will not be bound to issue and sell, the Common Stock until Blue Sky qualifications have been assured in a reasonable number of states to our mutual satisfaction, and a final underwriting agreement satisfactory to each of us is executed.

6.   This letter of intent is submitted by us as a statement of mutual intention and creates no binding obligation of any kind on the Company or us other than as set forth in the last sentence of the fourth paragraph of this letter. The document which defines the formal commitment is the underwriting agreement which, subject to the conditions described herein, would be created by the Company and the Underwriters immediately prior to the commencement of the Offering. We look forward to working with you and your associates on the proposed Offering.

If the foregoing is in accordance with your understanding of the intentions of the parties, please note your approval on this letter and return it to us.

Sincerely,

AGREED:
This _____ day of _____, 200_.

UNDERWRITERS

COMPANY

By: _____
Its: _____

By: _____
Its: _____

SAMPLE INVESTMENT BANKING ENGAGEMENT LETTER FOR INSTITUTIONAL PLACEMENT

Date

Company
Address

Gentlemen:

This letter will confirm the terms and conditions of the engagement of the Advisor (the "Advisor"), by Company (the "Company") to act as the exclusive financial advisor to the Company in connection with the exploration of one or more private equity or debt offerings ("Financing Transactions"). The Advisor's services in connection with the Financing Transactions are hereinafter referred to as the "Engagement." The decision to complete a Financing Transaction will be at the sole discretion of the Company.

1.   As the Company's exclusive financial advisor, the Advisor will immediately assist the Company, on a best efforts basis, in completing a private debt or equity offering, the success and completion of each of which would be subject to, among other things, the performance of the Company. The Advisor shall provide financial advisory services, including, but not limited to, the following:

(a)   assisting the Company and/or its consultants in developing a financial model based upon management's operating assumptions that will incorporate various capital structures and market assumptions to allow management to understand the potential impact of its various financing strategies;

(b)   assisting the Company and its board of directors in developing and executing a financing strategy;

(c)   assisting the Company in its presentations to potential lenders and purchasers of the Company's securities;

(d)   assisting the Company in executing the Financing Transactions; and

(e)   advising the Company's management and board of directors on matters related to the Financing Transactions.

2.   In performing its services hereunder, the Advisor shall familiarize itself with and consider, among other things, the history and nature of the business of the Company; the condition and prospects of the Company's industry; the operations, financial results, conditions, properties, and prospects of the Company; and such other factors as the Advisor deems relevant. The Advisor shall be entitled to rely entirely, without independent investigation, on publicly available information and such other information as may be supplied by the Company. The Company shall be solely responsible for the legal sufficiency, accuracy, and completeness of any information memorandum or other disclosure document as well as for the Company's compliance with all applicable laws and regulations relating to the Financing Transactions. For the sake of clarity, the scope of our engagement shall not include giving tax, legal, regulatory, accountancy, or other specialist or technical advice from other sources.

3.   The Company acknowledges that the availability of the Advisor to perform its services is in large part dependent on the Company furnishing the Advisor with information regarding the Company in a timely fashion. The Company agrees to promptly furnish the Advisor with all financial and other information regarding the Company and its business and financial prospects, insofar as such information is available to it, that the Advisor may reasonably request, and to provide to the Advisor reasonable access to the Company's officers, directors, employees, accountants, legal counsel, and other advisors.

4.   The Company hereby represents and warrants that all information furnished to the Advisor by the Company shall be complete and correct in all material respects when furnished and shall not contain any untrue statements of a material fact or omit to state a material fact necessary in order to make the statements therein not misleading in the light of the circumstances under which such statements were made.

5.   The Advisor agrees to keep all information it receives from the Company, its employees, and its affiliates confidential, except to the extent such information (a) is or becomes generally available to the public (other than as a result of a disclosure by the Advisor), (b) was available to the Advisor on a nonconfidential basis from a person other than the Company who, to the knowledge of the Advisor, is not bound by a confidentiality agreement with the Company or is otherwise prohibited from transferring such information to the Advisor, (c) was disclosed pursuant to the Company's permission, (d) the Advisor is required by law, regulation, legal process or regulatory authority to disclose after reasonable notice to the Company, or (e) is required by the Advisor to enforce its rights under this letter. The obligations of the Advisor under the preceding sentence shall survive the consummation of any Financing Transaction and the termination of the Engagement.

6.   For its services in connection with the Engagement, the Company shall pay to the Advisor a non-refundable retainer fee ("Retainer Fee") and a contingent fee, as set forth below (the "Contingent Fee"). The Retainer Fee in the amount of $_____ shall be due and payable upon the signing of this Agreement. The Contingent Fee shall be contingent upon the closing of a Financing Transaction and shall be payable on the date of such closing.

7.   In the event debt or equity capital is raised by the Advisor on behalf of the Company, the Company shall pay the Advisor the Contingent Fee on closing and funding of each Financing Transaction described below in an amount equal to the following:

(a)   _____ percent (____%) of the gross proceeds raised in the private placement of equity or debt, which is convertible into equity, so long as such proceeds were raised from investors introduced by the Advisor.

(b)   _____ percent (____%) of the gross proceeds raised in the private placement of debt, which is subordinated to the Company's primary credit facility, whether such proceeds were raised from investors introduced by the Advisor or otherwise.

(c)   Should the Company terminate this engagement:

(i)   once the Advisor has entered the private market and delivered the Memorandum to potential institutional investors, but before institutional investors have submitted written proposals, the Company shall pay the Advisor a cash fee equal to $_____;

(ii)   *after* institutional investors have submitted written proposals on terms and conditions substantially similar to those contained in the Memorandum, but prior to the Company accepting proposals, the Company will pay the Advisor a cash fee of $_____; or

(iii)   *after* the Advisor has arranged for a commitment for the Financing, which has been accepted in writing by the Company, the Company will pay the Advisor a cash fee equal to one-half of the Contingent Fee.

Company closes any Financing Transaction within 12 months from and after the termination of the Engagement from a party introduced by the Advisor or to whom the Advisor provided the Memorandum on behalf of the Company during the term of the Engagement.

8. In addition to the foregoing fees, the Company shall reimburse the Advisor promptly, on a monthly basis, for all the accountable out-of-pocket expenses (including reasonable legal fees and expenses) incurred by the Advisor in connection with the Engagement, regardless of whether a Financing Transaction is consummated.

9. In addition, if the Advisor places the private equity/debt contemplated herein, the Company shall grant to the Advisor the right of first refusal to serve as a comanaging underwriter of any future public or private offering of common stock or debt, at fees, and upon terms, customary and consistent with industry practice that would be agreed between the Company and the Advisor in good faith. The Company acknowledges that this Agreement is neither an expressed nor an implied commitment by the Advisor to act in any capacity in any such transaction or to purchase or place any securities in connection therewith, which commitment shall only be set forth in a separate underwriting, placement agency, or other applicable type of agreement.

10. Whether or not a Financing Transaction is effected, the Company and its affiliates, successors, and assigns will jointly and severally indemnify and hold harmless the Advisor and its officers, directors, employees, attorneys, consultants, agents, servants, parents, affiliates, successors and assigns, jointly and severally (hereinafter collectively "Indemnitee"), from and against any and all losses, claims, damages, liabilities, awards, costs, and expenses, including but not limited to reasonable attorneys' fees to which Indemnitee may become subject by virtue of, in connection with, resulting from, or arising out of the Engagement (hereinafter collectively "Claim" or "Claims"). Claims shall include reasonable legal and other expenses, including the cost of any investigation and preparation, incurred by Indemnitee in connection with any pending or threatened Claim by any person or entity, whether or not it results in a loss, damages, liability, or award. Indemnitee shall be indemnified and held harmless by the Company for any and all Claims whether they arise under contract, foreign, federal, state or local law or ordinance, common law or otherwise.

11. Notwithstanding anything above to the contrary: (1) the Advisor shall promptly notify the Company after any Claim is asserted, and the Company shall have the right, upon notification to the Advisor within 10 days thereafter, to assume the defense of such Claim or action and to appoint counsel reasonably satisfactory to Indemnitee to conduct such defense, provided that all expenses and costs related thereto shall be borne by the Company; and (2) the Company shall not be liable for any Claim to the extent that a court having jurisdiction shall have determined by a final, nonappealable judgment that such Claim resulted from an Indemnitee's gross negligence or willful misconduct.

The foregoing indemnification commitment of the Company will survive any termination of the authorization provided by this letter.

The Company agrees to promptly notify the Advisor of any assertion against the Advisor, the Company, or any other person of any Claim or the commencement of any action or proceeding relating to the services comprising the Engagement.

12. The Company agrees that the Advisor has the right to place advertisements in financial and other newspapers and journals at the Advisor's own expense describing its services to the Company in connection with the Engagement provided that the Advisor will submit a copy of any such advertisement to the Company for its prior approval, which approval shall not be unreasonably withheld or delayed.

13.   Either the Company or the Advisor may terminate the Engagement (except as provided above with respect to any earned Retainer Fee, Contingent Fee, reimbursement of expenses and indemnification) at any time, with or without cause, effective upon the other party's receipt of written notice to that effect.

14.   This Agreement shall be governed by and construed in accordance with the laws of

_____.

If the foregoing correctly sets forth our agreement, we would appreciate your signing both enclosed copies of this letter in the space provided below and returning one of them to us. In the event that we do not receive a copy of this letter evidencing your acceptance and agreement within 10 days of the date hereof, the terms of this letter shall be null and void and of no further force and effect.

Very truly yours,

ADVISOR

Accepted and Agreed:

COMPANY   **ADVISOR**

By: _____   By: _____
Title: _____   Title: _____

SAMPLE INVESTMENT BANKING ENGAGEMENT LETTER FOR SALE OF BUSINESS

Date

Company
Address

Ladies and Gentlemen:

This letter confirms our understanding of the basis upon which Investment Banking Firm ("Investment Banker") is being engaged to provide investment banking advice and services to Business (the "Company") in connection with the proposed sale of the stock or assets of Company.

1. We understand that the directors of the Company will entertain proposals for the possible sale of substantially all of the assets or all of the stock of the Company (the "Transaction"). Investment Banker will serve, as your sole and exclusive financial advisor in connection with a potential acquisition of the Company by the purchasers listed in Exhibit A, to perform the following functions:

    a. Prepare a summary description of the Company to be provided to potential buyers along with certain financial information to assist them in evaluating their interest in an acquisition of the Company. Such a document will be utilized in discussions with prospective purchasers, and its form and contents will be reviewed and approved by the Company. The Company recognizes and confirms that (i) Investment Banker will be using and relying on information and data furnished to Investment Banker by the Company and (ii) Investment Banker does not assume responsibility for the accuracy or completeness of that information and data. Investment Banker will not undertake to independently verify such information and data and will not make an appraisal of any of the assets of the Company.

    b. Advise the Company on structural and valuation issues pertaining to the Transaction.

    c. Assist the Company in negotiations with potential buyers, and consult with and assist counsel and independent accountants in structuring and carrying through to settlement any agreement that may be reached.

2. In consideration of our services as the Company's financial advisor as described in Section 1 of this letter, the Company agrees to pay Investment Banker the following fees and expenses:

    a. Contingent upon the closing of the Transaction, the Company will pay Investment Banker at the closing a cash fee (the "Success Fee") equal to 0.86% of the purchase price consideration up to $22 per share and 3% of purchase price consideration in excess of $22 per share.

    b. The Company will pay Investment Banker a fee of $125,000 for rendering a fairness opinion in connection with the subject transaction.

The Fairness Opinion Fee of $100,000 and any separate confirmation or reaffirmation of the Fairness Opinion will be deducted against the Success Fee at closing.

For the purpose of this Section 2, purchase price consideration shall include the face value of any cash payments made to the Company's shareholders or the Company, the fair market value of any securities issued in exchange for the Company's securities, the face value of any debt assumed by the purchaser, the present value of any noncompete agreements, and the fair market value of any assets or securities of the Company retained by the shareholders. The purchase price consideration will not include the Company's profit-sharing plan, cash within the business, or real estate. In the event an agreement for acquisition of the Company calls for contingent or other payments over time, Investment Banker shall receive its payment at the time the Company is paid.

In addition to the fees described above, and whether or not any proposed transaction is consummated, the Company will pay all of Investment Banker's reasonable expenses in carrying out its duties under this engagement not to exceed $50,000 without the prior consent of the Company.

In order to coordinate our efforts during the term of our engagement hereunder, the Company will not initiate any discussions with the potential purchasers on Exhibit A relating to the Transaction without first notifying Investment Banker. This Agreement is exclusive only with respect to the potential purchasers on Exhibit A but shall be non-exclusive with respect to any other potential purchasers.

Investment Banker agrees to not release any confidential information to any third party without an executed confidentiality agreement in hand.

3.   In consideration of our services as the Company's financial advisor under this letter, the Company agrees to indemnify and hold harmless Investment Banker and each of its directors, officers, agents, employees, and controlling persons (within the meaning of the Securities Act of 1933, as amended) against any losses, claims, damages, or liabilities (or actions or proceedings in respect thereof) related to or arising out of our engagement, and will reimburse Investment Banker and each other person indemnified hereunder (each, an "Indemnified Party") for all legal and other expenses reasonably incurred in connection with investigating or defending any such loss, claim, damage, liability, action, or proceeding whether or not in connection with pending or threatened litigation in which an Indemnified Party is a party; provided, however, that the Company will not be liable in any such case (except cases arising out of the use of information provided by the Company) for losses, claims, damages, liabilities, or expenses that a court of competent jurisdiction shall have found in a final judgment to have arisen solely from the gross negligence or willful misconduct of Investment Banker or the party claiming a right to indemnification. The provisions of this Section 3 shall survive the termination of Investment Banker's engagement under this letter and shall be binding upon any successors or assigns of the Company.

Our nonexclusive engagement will expire one year from the date hereof and shall renew automatically on a month-to-month basis thereafter unless either party has given 30 days written notice to the other that it desires to terminate this engagement; provided, however, that in any such event the Company shall be responsible for the reimbursement of expenses referred to in Section 2 incurred through the date of termination and the payment of the fees as set forth in Section 2 for a Transaction with a party identified on Exhibit A with whom Investment Banker or the Company has had contact during the term of the engagement that is concluded within one year of the date of such termination.

If the foregoing letter is in accordance with your understanding of the terms of our engagement, please sign and return to us the enclosed duplicate hereof. This letter will be null and void if not executed within one week of the date first written above.

Very truly yours,

INVESTMENT BANKER

By: _____

Accepted and Agreed as of _____, 200_:

COMPANY

By: _____
   Chief Executive Officer
   and Chairman of the Board

Glossary

accredited investor (1) A person with a net worth of over $1 million or a joint net worth with his or her spouse of over $1 million. (2) A person with income of over $200,000 in each of the last two years, or joint income with a spouse of over $300,000 for the most recent two years, and who expects to earn that income in the current year. (3) Any entity in which all of the equity owners are accredited. (4) A bank, brokerage firm, business development company, investment company, or employee benefit plan or trust with assets exceeding $5 million.

aftermarket the trading market for a business's stock after it completes a public offering. The price in the aftermarket means the prevailing market price of the stock.

all or none a type of private placement (or a rare public offering) that requires the company or its investment banker to raise a minimum dollar amount or all of the collected funds are returned to potential investors.

AMEX the American Stock Exchange.

angel or angel investor usually a high net worth individual who invests in early-stage businesses looking for high rates of return and who is willing to assume high investment risk. An angel usually knows something about your industry or business and may have been in management or on the board of a company like yours. Angels often want to be mentors to your management team or serve as board members.

antidilution rights protect an investor from having its ownership percentage in your company reduced if you later sell more debt or equity securities. These rights come in three forms: *standard, price*, and *ownership maintenance antidilution*.

articles/certificate of incorporation governing documents filed with the secretary of state in the state of incorporation to create the corporation that will conduct your business. They typically cover who is initially appointed to the board of directors, the authorized common and/or preferred stock that the company can sell, indemnification rights, and corporate governance procedures considered too important to leave in the bylaws.

as converted or as if converted refer to rights of preferred stockholders or warrant holders to vote at stockholder meetings or receive dividends as if the holder had already converted its preferred stock to common stock or had already exercised its warrants.

best efforts offering usually a retail or institutional private placement being sold by an investment banker that agrees to use its best efforts to sell the placement. The investment banker doesn't put any of its capital at risk and doesn't guarantee or underwrite the placement. Occasionally refers to a best efforts public offering. There are two types of best efforts offerings, the *all-or-none* and the *mini-maxi*.

blank series preferred stock authorized preferred stock that the board can set the terms for when it decides to sell preferred stock. It is sometimes sold to friendly stockholders as an antitakeover defense.

blue sky laws state securities laws in the United States. These laws were adopted in response to the stock market bubble of the late 1920s, when various promoters were found to have sold pieces of "blue sky" to the public.

blue sky qualifications requirements a business must meet, or be exempt from, in order to sell securities under state securities laws or *blue sky laws*.

bylaws a governing document for your business that covers the duties of officers and directors, corporate governance, stockholder matters, stock certificates and transfers, dividends, and indemnity of officers and directors, among other things.

CFO chief financial officer.

charter documents the articles or certificate of incorporation and the bylaws of your company.

classified board of directors a board that can divide itself into three or more classes, with each class having a three-year term. Also known as a "staggered" board, this anti-takeover measure is used to prevent the entire board from being replaced at one time.

cold comfort letter a letter of assurance that's delivered by the business's outside audit firm to the investment banker at the closing of a public offering. The letter describes the procedures used by the auditor to confirm numbers throughout the prospectus.

comanager an investment banking firm that together with one or more other investment banking firms jointly act as the lead investment bankers for a public offering.

common stock an equity ownership interest in a corporation that entitles the holder to share in the earnings of the business when a dividend is declared by the board.

convertible debt debt that can be converted into common stock or preferred stock.

corporate cleanup the process of reviewing, revising, and updating your business's operating, financial, and legal documents to help speed up due diligence by investors and investment bankers.

corporate governance the set of controls and principles that guide the activities of your business, like requirements for independent board members on the audit committee, board approval of expenditures over preset limits, approval of independent board members for related party dealings, and codes of ethics or corporate policies.

covenants promises to investors or lenders to take action (affirmative covenants) or refrain from taking action (negative covenants) in the future.

credit enhancement a guarantee, insurance policy, or rating from a rating agency that makes a debt instrument more attractive to lenders or investors and as a result lowers your business's interest costs.

cumulative dividends dividends that accumulate from year to year even if the business doesn't have the funds to pay the dividend; the dividend must be paid once funds are available.

demand registration rights rights that an institutional investor can exercise to force the business to register the investor's stock in a separate filing with the SEC, usually at the company's expense.

drafting conference a meeting of the business principals, investment bankers, and their counsel to review and revise the prospectus to be used in a public offering before it is filed with the SEC. Investment banking counsel also use drafting conferences to ask management questions about the business and to uncover inconsistencies with, or to add to, due diligence.

drag-along rights rights that let a business drag-along a venture firm or other institutional investor in a sale or partial sale of shares by the company, its management team, or its large stockholders.

due diligence a complete review and investigation of your business and its industry, financial performance and projections, operations, management team, and current financing structure.

EBITDA earnings before interest, taxes, depreciation, and amortization.

EBITDAC earnings before interest, taxes, depreciation, amortization, and stock or option compensation expense.

effective date the day when the SEC declares a public offering "effective," meaning that the offering can now be sold. For IPOs, trading usually starts on or within 24 hours of the effective date.

equity ownership, or the right to get ownership, in your business with a right to share in earnings. Equity includes common stock, preferred stock, and hybrids like warrants, options, and PIK securities.

equity claw-backs rights given to you and other officers to earn out or buy more stock if your business meets revenue, EBITDA, net income or other benchmarks.

fairness opinion an opinion given by investment bankers when a public company is being acquired or going private, that says that the price being paid is fair to the target company's stockholders.

financial buyers institutional investors that purchase companies for investment purposes.

firm commitment offering a public offering underwritten by an investment banker that obligates the banker to commit its capital to complete the offering three days after the effective date.

follow-on public offering another public offering by a business that's already completed its IPO. Follow-on offerings typically raise money for the business, for selling stockholders, or both.

forfeiture escrow an escrow account set up at a bank or stock transfer agent that holds part of management's stock. If the business meets it projections for the escrow period, the stock goes back to management; if not, the stock is canceled.

hard money lenders sources of funds that are the "last resort" for businesses needing loans because these lenders charge high up-front fees and exorbitant interest rates, ask for personal guarantees or home mortgages as collateral, and won't hesitate to liquidate a business that can't make its payments.

incentive stock options options granted to officers or employees that qualify for favorable tax treatment under the Internal Revenue Code.

indemnities and indemnification rights given under law or contract that make the business pay damages or expenses awarded against the business's officers and directors except if they engage in gross negligence, willful misconduct, or intentional wrongdoing.

institutional investor company-sponsored capital pools, insurance companies, money management firms, mutual funds, pension funds, private equity groups, and venture capital firms.

institutional private placement a private offering of equity or debt to one or a small number of institutional investors.

investment banker a firm that raises private or public equity or debt for businesses from retail and/or institutional investors. Many investment bankers have retail and institutional trading operations through which they trade equity and debt securities.

IPO the initial offering of a business's stock for sale to the public.

lead investment banker an investment banker that has its name above and to the left of the names of all other investment bankers on the front cover of a prospectus. The lead investment banker invites other firms to become underwriters and syndicate members.

lead manager or lead underwriter other names for the lead investment banker.

lease a contract that gives a business the right to use property or assets for a scheduled stream of payments due over the lease's term.

liquidating distribution a distribution of assets, cash, or securities to stockholders when a business is sold or is shut down.

liquidation preferences preferred stockholders' rights to make claims against a business's assets in a bankruptcy or when a liquidating distribution occurs; these are honored ahead of the common stockholders.

lock-up agreement an agreement by which you and the other officers, directors, and stockholders agree not to sell stock for a specific period of time after an IPO.

metrics investment banker speak for operating data commonly used in your industry to measure how the business is performing.

mezzanine debt an intermediate layer of capital that usually consists of a combination of debt and equity.

mini-maxi a type of private placement that can close if the company collects the minimum proceeds but that lets the company or its investment banker continue selling until the maximum is reached or the offering period ends.

NASD regulating body that oversees compensation paid to investment bankers for underwriting or participating in public offerings.

Nasdaq an automated quotation service on which equity and debt securities trade. Nasdaq operates the Nasdaq National Market and Nasdaq SmallCap Market.

negative covenants promises that a business makes to investors or lenders that it will not take specific actions in the future.

non-accountable expense allowance fee paid to a lead underwriter of a retail public offering to cover the banker's expenses for due diligence, legal counsel, mailing, telephone, and travel. It usually ranges from 3 to 1% of offering proceeds, depending on the offering's size.

NYSE the New York Stock Exchange.

one-on-one a roadshow presentation by a business's management team that is made directly to an institutional investor—that is, one on one.

options rights to buy a set number of shares from the business for a fixed price. An option is usually exercisable for a period of 1 to 10 years and can be either a nonqualified or incentive stock option.

overallotment option an option given to the lead investment banker in a public offering that lets the investment banker buy, at its sole discretion, more stock from the business at the IPO price for up to 45 days after the offering. The maximum number of shares that the NASD lets the banker buy when exercising this option is 15% of the shares sold in the offering.

ownership maintenance antidilution rights contract rights that let an investor buy into later rounds of financing to keep its percentage ownership in the company unchanged, but at the same prices charged other investors in the later rounds.

participating preferred stock shares in the earnings of the business on the same basis as common stock. Most preferred stock is non-participating, meaning dividends are paid at a fixed rate regardless of earnings or dividends paid on common stock.

piggyback registration rights rights that let selling shareholders "piggyback" and have their stock registered on a filing made by the business with the SEC to register stock for sale primarily by the business.

PIK securities payment-in-kind securities that pay dividends or interest to investors in the form of more stock or promissory notes, as opposed to cash.

PIPE Private Investment in a Public Entity.

pitch book a book put together by an investment banker to (1) present your business to potential financing sources or buyout groups or

(2) give you information about the investment banking firm, its prior financings, and its personnel.

post-money value the value of your business after an investor has put its capital in. Post-money value equals the pre-money value plus the amount of the financing.

preemptive rights statutory rights to purchase additional stock to let stockholders maintain their percentage ownership. These rights are functionally equal to ownership maintenance antidilution rights, except that those rights are contractual.

preferred stock stock that has "preference" over, or ranks above, common stock, usually in dividend rights and distributions on liquidation.

pre-money value the value of your business before an investor's capital comes in.

price antidilution rights antidilution rights that give an institutional investor more stock (at no cost) if the company sells convertible debt or equity in a later round priced below the investor's conversion price.

private equity groups usually hedge funds or other pools of private capital that are funded by pension funds, money management firms, other institutions, and select high net worth investors.

private offering, private placement, or placement terms that are used interchangeably to describe stock that is sold privately to institutions and/or retail investors and not in a public offering.

ratchet clauses contract clauses that reduce an institutional investor's preferred stock conversion price, and so increase its ownership percentage, if the business doesn't meet preset revenue, EBITDA, net income, or other financial targets.

redemption rights rights that are typically part of preferred stock rights and require the business to repurchase the preferred stock at preset times. If the business can't do so, then the preferred stock conversion price goes down, and the investor may get a redemption premium (a penalty payment).

registration rights rights given to investors that allow them to register the stock they buy, making the stock freely tradable, or sellable in the public market.

representations and warranties historical statements of fact or promises that a condition exists.

representative another term used in public offerings to refer to the lead investment banker. That is, this firm "represents" the other underwriters and syndicate members in negotiating offering terms with the business.

retail investors individual investors, not institutional investors.

retail private placement a private sale of stock or debt to retail investors.

retail public offering almost always a firm commitment offering that is sold primarily to individual investors by investment bankers.

revolvers revolving credit lines typically secured by a first-priority claim on inventory, accounts receivable, or both.

roadshow a series of in-person management presentations to potential institutional investors, underwriters, and syndicate members in financial centers and large cities while a public or private offering is pending. A roadshow usually has a slideshow or video presentation, management reviews of operational and financial issues, and a question-and-answer session. Roadshows are now being videotaped and put on the Internet by larger companies to reduce the two- to four-week time needed to do a typical roadshow.

Rule 144 an SEC rule that lets officers, directors, and other holders of restricted stock sell shares into the market without being registered, up to volume limits and subject to other conditions.

SEC the U.S. Securities and Exchange Commission, which regulates the sale and trading of equity and debt in the United States.

securitization a type of off-balance-sheet financing where the business transfers loans or receivables to a subsidiary that issues trust certificates to institutional purchasers. The trust certificates give the institutions the cash flows from the loans or receivables in exchange for their making a cash payment to the subsidiary that represents the discounted present value of the cash flows.

self underwriting usually a private placement or the occasional public offering that is sold by a business's officers and directors, rather than by an investment banker.

selling shareholders shareholders of a business who can, or have rights to, sell stock at the time of an IPO or a follow-on offering.

senior debt debt that includes long-term revolvers or credit lines with first-priority liens on inventory and receivables.

standard antidilution rights antidilution rights that let a preferred stockholder or warrant holder keep the same percentage ownership in the business if there is a common stock split or stock dividend.

strategic buyers potential buyers of your business that operate in your industry or in a related one, and may include suppliers, customers or product integrators.

strategic partner companies in your industry or in a related one that have a "strategic" reason to finance your business, like getting access to your technology, entering a new market, or getting a competitive advantage.

subordinated debt or sub debt debt that has a second priority or lower claim on the business's assets; it is typically more expensive than senior debt. Sub debt can take various forms like term debt, mezzanine debt, or convertible debt.

syndicate member an investment banking firm that participates in selling a public offering.

tag-along rights rights that allow an institutional investor to sell a pro rata portion of its ownership in the business to an outside party if the management team agrees to sell part of its shares to the outside party.

term debt debt that has scheduled payments of principal and interest over the period of the loan or that may have a balloon payment at maturity. Term debt is usually used for working capital, to finance a plant expansion, or to buy another business.

underwriter an investment banking firm that leads or participates in underwriting a public offering and that puts its capital at risk when the offering becomes effective.

underwriter's cutback the right of the lead underwriter in a public offering to reduce the number of shares that are sold by selling stockholders in an IPO or follow-on offering.

underwriter's warrant usually a five-year warrant sold for a token amount to the lead underwriter of a retail public offering representing the right to buy 10% of the shares sold in a firm commitment public offering for 120% of the public offering price.

underwriting discount the commission paid to an investment banker for selling equity or debt in public offerings.

valuation the process of determining a company's value to investors or buyers. There are several well-accepted valuation methods, including multiples of earnings, sales or EBITDA, discounted cash flow, and trading prices of comparable public companies.

warrant type of equity that lets an investor buy shares of common or preferred stock from a company for a set price during a period of time known as the exercise period. A warrant functions just like an option to allow an investor or lender to purchase stock from your company.

Index

More selected BARRON'S titles:

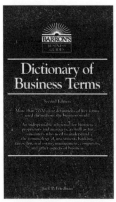
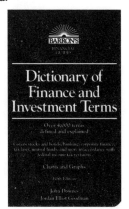

About the Author

Robert W. Walter is a graduate of the Duke University School of Law and Colorado State University and has counseled entrepreneurs and small businesses for over 20 years. He has represented private and public companies in a variety of equity and debt financings, as well as investment banking firms active in underwriting public offerings and private placements. He has written numerous books and continuing education courses on small business finance and business ethics for financial managers. He has also been an instructor for securities, financing, and ethics courses offered by the American Institute of Certified Public Accountants throughout the United States and internationally since 1998. In 2003, he joined Holland & Hart LLP, the largest law firm in Colorado with almost 300 attorneys and offices in six states, where he continues to represent entrepreneurs and small businesses in financing, merger and acquisition, and change of control transactions. Mr. Walter is a member of Mensa and Beta Gamma Sigma, is admitted to practice before federal and state courts in Colorado, and is admitted to practice before the Tenth Circuit Court of Appeals and the United States Supreme Court. In late 2003, Mr. Walter was admitted to membership in the National Speakers Association, the leading national organization for experts who speak professionally. Comments or questions about this book may be directed to the author at rwalter@hollandhart.com.